CW00553488

Where Did
it all go
Wrong?

Where Did it all go Wrong?

The Story of Football in the West Midlands

John Samuels

BREWIN BOOKS

First published by
Brewin Books Ltd, 56 Alcester Road,
Studley, Warwickshire B80 7LG in 2019
www.brewinbooks.com

© John Samuels 2019

All rights reserved.

ISBN: 978-1-85858-582-6

The moral right of the author has been asserted.

A Cataloguing in Publication Record
for this title is available from the British Library.

Typeset in Haarlemmer MT Std.
Printed in Great Britain by
Hobbs The Printers Ltd.

CONTENTS

INTRODUCTION

At the time this book was being planned and up to the time just before its completion, it was thought necessary to include a chapter examining whether or not sport really mattered. With the interest and excitement surrounding the England team's performance in the World Cup in Moscow in 2018 the answer to the question became obvious. For a few days the England team's performance and the behaviour of the manager and players gave pleasure to many people. Over 26 million watched the semi-final match on TV with many more watching in pubs and on giant screens. It demonstrated that sport did matter.

Modest success in sport allowed people to feel good and helped restore self-respect. It offered hope for the future. The performance was of course over hyped by the media, the team's results exceeded all reasonable expectations but did not reach the level that much of the nation was being led to believe was possible. The team, with the manager, re-connected with the public. The team were young and there was promise for the future. In 2020 the final match of the UEFA Championship would take place in London. So the game would return to the country that developed the modern rules and there was hope that the England team would be in that final. The 2018 World Cup showed that sport did matter to many people.

Would the renewed interest and support for the England team benefit the West Midlands clubs? Unfortunately the answer is likely to be 'no' the success could well bypass the region. None of the squad of 23 played for West Midlands clubs (two in fact did play for an East Midland club). It had been a number of years since the West Midland clubs produced players for the national team;

one that they had produced was Gareth Southgate. What had the local football fans to look forward to?

Nothing is certain. Football never stands still. This book was completed in July 2018. During that month two new shareholders appeared on the scene at Aston Villa. They made the usual promises. The 2017/18 season began with only one of the top football clubs in the West Midlands in the Premier League. Three were in the Championship. The 2018/19 season also begins with only one club in the top tier and with three in the second tier. No overall improvement, but there had been a change. WBA were no longer a Premier League club, they had been replaced at the top level by their near neighbours and bitter rivals Wolverhampton Wanderers. Aston Villa had narrowly failed to gain promotion.

There had been plenty of drama for the fans of the West Midlands clubs to enjoy during the last few months of the 2017/18 season. Three of the clubs were engaged in relegation battles, and three fighting for promotion. Unfortunately in terms of football overall in England the outcome of these final matches were of minor importance. None of the teams were really involved in the major events. What was happening in the West Midlands was a sideshow.

WBA, having been bottom of the league for most of the season, improved under a new manager and were only relegated in the last week of the season. They had been in the Premier League for eight years and appeared to have settled comfortably at that level. Something had clearly gone wrong. Wolves were runaway winners of the Championship. Aston Villa finished in fourth place in the Championship, not good enough to obtain automatic promotion but good enough to qualify for a place in the play-off matches. Unfortunately they lost in the final. Hardly anybody involved in football likes play-off games; the result of a single match can depend on chance, on good luck or bad luck.

Birmingham City were again involved in an end of season fight against relegation. As in 2016/17 and 2013/14 they only escaped relegation on the last day of the season. They finished the 2017/18 season in 19th place (out of 24 clubs). In the third tier, Walsall also had a fight against relegation also finishing in 19th place out of 24. In the fourth tier Coventry finished the season in sixth place and so qualified to take part in the play-off games. They were successful and were promoted to League One (the third tier) for the 2018/19 season.

An interesting season for locals but a disappointing one, except for Wolverhampton and Coventry. The teams were hardly setting the world alight and they were not adding to the reputation of the region.

What of the future? It was well known that failure by Villa to obtain promotion would mean that they would face financial problems in the 2018/19 season but it came as a surprise to many when it was revealed that the club was having cash flow problems in 2017/18. They were having difficulty in paying players wages, they were late in paying a tax bill, and they were struggling to pay instalments on transfer fees. There was talk of the club moving into administration which would have led at best to a point's deduction; there was even talk that the club might need to be wound up, to be liquidated. Tony Xia, the owner, had gambled on Villa being promoted. He should have looked at what had happened to other clubs who had gambled, an extreme example being Glasgow Rangers. Villa needed cash quickly, the club sold the naming rights to its training complex to Dr Xia's company "Recon". The owner fell out with the chief executive who was at first suspended then dismissed. There was talk of the owner selling the club but being a Chinese businessman he did not wish to lose face; he did not wish to sell at a loss. He was seeking to sell a percentage of the shares he held in the business and for the new shareholders to invest in the region of £40 million in the club. This, it was hoped, would help with the cash flow problems of 2017/18 and help them to satisfy the Financial Fair Play requirements for 2018/19. What a mess. The Blues were not in a much better financial position.

What would happen in 2018/19? That would depend on decisions being made many thousands of miles away – in Boardrooms in China. The big four local clubs were all owned by

Chinese investors. How much would the owners decide to invest in the clubs? What decisions would they make on the appointment of managers, of coaches and of executives? To be fair to the 2018 owners there had been much wrong with the local clubs before they came on the scene.

This is a football book, but one with a difference. It is concerned with the history of the football clubs from the Birmingham region, but it is more concerned with the governance side of the clubs, with the ownership, and with the managers than with the individual players (the so called legends). There are three questions that the book seeks to answer; one, why have the local clubs failed, two, would success in football have benefited Birmingham and the region, and three, will results be better in the future? In the following chapters an attempt is made to answer these questions by considering the history of the local clubs and of the region and by analysing the situation at the end of the 2017/18 season. The conclusion reached regarding where the clubs have gone wrong is that it is the result of poor leadership, poor governance and a poor image. These are problems that have troubled the West Midlands region, not just in football.

The region was strong in football before the Football League was formed. Indeed it was William McGregor who was chairman of Aston Villa at the time, who was the driving force behind the formation of the League in 1888. Six of the 12 founder member clubs came from the Midlands. From that time until the beginning of the First World War Aston Villa were the most successful team in the country, (a global name?) Since that time the local clubs have had only modest success. To be fair, Villa were European Champions in 1982 (one of only 5 English clubs to have achieved this). They have also been Division One champions seven times, won the FA Cup seven times, and the League Cup five times. For a time in the 1950s, the Wolves were the best team in the country, they were Division One champions on three occasions. For a time in the late 1950s and early 1960s the Albion were thought by many to be the most exciting team in the country. But apart from these few good times the local clubs have been disappointing and have underperformed compared with clubs from other regions.

Over the period from the 1950s through the 1990s of the clubs who finished in either first, second or third place in the top division (Division One/Premier League), 8 were from the North West region of the country, 5 clubs were from the North East, 6 from London and 3 from the West Midlands. Not a conspicuous record for the local clubs.[1] But what about the future, perhaps things will get better?

The Owners

Money is now by far the most important factor in determining the success of a football club. The owner is now the most important person at the club. Those who provide money, or those who speak for the providers of the money, whether or not they are the sole owner, the majority shareholder or a fund manager are the most important people at the club. The Chairman may or may not be the provider of funds. The governance of football clubs has changed. Many years ago, Bill Shankly, the manager who built Liverpool up to be the top team in Europe expressed the view that there was a Holy Trinity in football "the players, the management and the supporters. The directors do not come into it they are only there to sign cheques".[2] Under Shankly's leadership Liverpool were Division One champions three times, FA Cup winners twice and UEFA Cup winners once. But Shankly died in 1981, and much has changed since. The average length of time a manager was left in charge of a club in the 1970s was 3 years 5 months. The power is now with the owners. Managers are bought and sold like players. The average length of time a manager has been left in charge of a club over the period from the 2010 to the present is 1 year 3 months. The Holy Trinity is now; the players, the media and the owners. The supporters, wherever they are in the world, are customers and the media, as a result of changes in technology have a huge product to exploit.

The motives for owning a club vary. There are owners who see the acquisition of a football club as a political move, an exercise in soft power. There are those who see it as a means of self-promotion, an ego trip. There are those who see it as a financial investment, as a means of making money. There are, or perhaps more accurately there were, those who saw it as a way to support a local community, to be identified with a region. There are now only two or possibly three of the Premier League clubs whose owners come into this later category. There are, in contrast, twelve of the Premier League clubs owned by foreigners, and nearly half of the Championship clubs. England has the highest concentration of foreign ownership in any of the major European countries. The Birmingham region has the highest concentration of any region.

We do not know very much about the current owners of the West Midlands clubs, about their wealth or about their motives. It is doubtful whether the owners of the local clubs are involved simply for the pleasure of owning a football club or even to give them local prestige. We do know that China has a long term plan to become a global power in football. The fans of football clubs hope that the owner of their club will be both wise and wealthy. Unfortunately such owners seem to be few and far between these days. We have wealthy owners, with Sheikh Mansour, the major shareholder at Manchester City said to be worth well over £20 billion, and Roman Abramovich at Chelsea said to be worth close to £10 billion. What of the local clubs? The owners of the Wolves are said to be worth in excess of £5 billion, of the Albion £2.8 billion, of Tony Xia £1.2 billion and of the Blues, (whoever they might be) probably less than £0.5 billion.[3] With such inequality no wonder results vary so much.

However good or bad the present owners are of the Greater Birmingham clubs they cannot be blamed for the relatively poor performance over the last 30 years or so. In later chapters we will assess the performance of the local clubs owners and managers.

The title Manager and the title Head Coach will at times in the book be used interchangeably. Some clubs use the one term, some the other. In fact the term manager is probably now a misnomer. Once managers such as Ferguson and Shankly were in charge of almost everything to do with the football side of the business. Now it is frequently a team of executives, each with a grand sounding title who collectively make the decisions. But it is nevertheless the so called manager who appears before the TV cameras to explain what is going on at the club, who gives the press material to write about, it is the manager who is the face of the club, it is the manager who is first to be sacked when things go wrong. It is, however, now the owners who have the major influence on the fortunes of a club, they hire and fire the managers, they are responsible for the financial state of the club. The size of a club's wage bill now explains somewhere in the region of 80% of the league position of a club at the end of a season. The wage bill is a fairly accurate predictor of a club's final league position.[4] In any one season the prediction might not be perfect, but it is a very good predictor of the average league position of a club over a period of time. There can on rare occasions be a season like 2015/16 where a smaller club, Leicester City won the Premier League, even though their wage bill was only the 14th highest.

A club can perform better or worse in a season than expected because of factors such as good luck or bad luck, an injury to a key player, a player having an exceptional season or the impact of an exceptionally good manager. But even this very good manager needs the financial backing to continue to deliver above average performance. Over time it is how much a club spends on wages that determines its position in the league. The better players can command higher wages and the better players are more likely to achieve success for the club. Money is a necessary requirement for continuing success. The close correlation between success and wage and salary spending applies not only to football in Europe but also to the major US sports. The relationship is stronger in the Premier League than in the Championship.

This statistical relationship between wages and success is recognized by those running clubs. In November 2017 at the time when West Bromwich Albion were sacking their manager, Tony Pulis, the Director of Football Administration at the club, Richard

Garlick, drew attention to the dilemma. He pointed out that the annual wage bill of the club of £74 million should mean that the Albion would finish in a final league position of somewhere between 9th and 14th. The club were at the time of the sacking only in 17th place. They were performing below expectations, they had won just twice in their last 21 league games. Those making decisions at the club went along with the "conventional wisdom" of the time, namely that results will get better if you sack the manager. They appointed Alan Pardew, an experienced manager and one with a reputation as a firefighter. But results did not improve, in Pardew's first 13 games in charge they only won one game and were in last place in the League. There was much talk about his dismissal, not just because of the results but also because of his relationship with the players. Four of the players got into trouble with the police in Spain, where they were on a club midweek holiday.

Perhaps it was not the manager that was underperforming at the club. The owners, in February 2018, sacked the club chairman, John Williams and the chief executive Martin Goodman. In doing so they demonstrated where the power lay in a football club. Williams was an experienced and well respected football executive who had enjoyed success at Blackburn Rovers before being sacked by that club's new and unsuccessful Indian owners. The reason given by the Chinese owners of WBA for sacking these two executives was that it was they who were responsible for appointing Pardew. What a mess, not so different to what had happened at Aston Villa a year earlier.

It is the owner of a club that is now the main person responsible for the money the club has to spend. Success will bring rewards to the club, a share of the Premier League's broadcasting revenue, possibly qualification for the lucrative European wide competitions and big name sponsors, but the club needs to invest to be able to compete at this top level. The financial gap between the haves and have nots of football grows each year. Access to funds might be a necessary condition for success, but it is not a sufficient condition. The owner has to know how to spend his money wisely in the football business, there are many examples of owners who have lost money on their investment. A good person in charge of the football team, a leader, is also important, whether he is called manager or coach. The wage bill might explain in the region of 80% of the final league position but this is not 100%. Investing in football clubs is a high risk business. Randy Lerner was reported to have lost in the region of £300 million on his investment in Aston Villa. When WBA were relegated they needed to plan for a very large reduction in broadcasting income. Whilst in the Championship they would receive parachute payments for three years but this still meant that the cost of relegation to the club would be in excess of £200 million. It is not surprising therefore that Southampton paid a £2 million bonus to Mark Hughes, their manager, for keeping that club in the Premier League. Aston Villa's final Championship play-off game was worth over £200 million to the winner. It is these high risks that owners use to justify their short term decision making, to the hasty hiring and firing of managers.

The Manager

A key factor in the success or failure of any business, whether in football or not, is the quality of the leadership. It has been shown that across all business, good leadership will boost performance above what is average by in the region of 15%.[5] The leadership at a football club has, as mentioned above, traditionally come from the manager, with some owners interfering more than others. The manager has traditionally picked the team, motivated them, determined the tactics and has had a big say in which players to buy and which to sell. The most technically advanced study of the influence of the manager "on the success of a football club showed that his contribution amounted to about 15%, almost identical to the influence of a chief executive on a business". This means that given a period of time, and given resources and given a certain amount of freedom the better manager will produce results 15% above that of the average manager.

But it can be hard to decide who is a good manager and who is average. To do so with any accuracy it is necessary to be able to measure the quality of the players the manager has at his disposal. One of the earliest studies in England on this problem was that of Dawson in 2000.[6] Dawson pointed out that the most successful managers are not necessarily the most efficient managers. The study was just covering the period from 1993 to 1998; it is interesting that the two most efficient managers he found for this period were Arsène Wenger at Arsenal (who went on to manage Arsenal for over 20 years) and John Gregory at Aston Villa (who Ellis dismissed).

He based his measure of a player's quality on transfer fees being paid. He found that in the region of 70% of the win ratio of a club could be explained by team quality, with the remaining percentage attributable to random factors and to the contribution of the manager. We now refer to clubs underperforming or over-performing based on the size of their wage bill. Based on this criteria the best performing teams in the 2017/18 season were Brighton, Huddersfield and Burnley. The managers of these clubs deserve much credit for this, but they are not always given the recognition and financial reward their leadership deserves. The managers of the underperforming clubs are, in contrast, quickly identified and removed. A study by Omar Chaudhuri, reported in *The Times* of the 15th May 2018, showed that Brighton and Huddersfield were among the most successful clubs in terms of overachievement in 2017/18. The study was based on actual points obtained during the season compared with those that had been predicted based on wage levels. Manchester City and Tottenham were also major overachievers. Amongst the major under achievers were the three relegated clubs and perhaps surprisingly Arsenal.

We can place managers/head coaches into different categories. There are what can be called celebrity managers, there are elite managers, there are the older experienced managers, the new up and coming managers and those who unfortunately come and go.

The West Midland clubs have experience of managers from all these classifications but not in recent years the elite managers. The clubs have seen celebrity managers, with Gianfranco Zola, Roberto di Matteo and Walter Zenga. All brought to their clubs by foreign owners, usually as the result of a recommendation by an adviser, an expert, an agent. Unfortunately not all big names turn out to be a success.

There are a small group of managers that can be called elite. They manage/coach the clubs that win the top competitions. How many are there in this elite group? How many can continue to deliver above average results? Szymanski in his study into the performance of over 1,000 football managers found that only about 20% "had a positive impact on their club that was statistically significant". Only 1.5% had a statistically significant negative effect – the worst managers are quickly removed. This leads to the conclusion that "most managers make little difference, while a few have a significant impact".[7] Most clubs will achieve almost exactly the league positions that their players' wages would predict. But just a few are able to do significantly better than that. These few elite managers, that is those who have a significant impact, are now very well paid, the highest paid manager in England in 2017 being Pep Guardiola at Manchester City, receiving £15 million per annum with Jose Mourinho second highest with a salary of £13.8 million. Both have held the title of FIFA Coach of the Year. This again demonstrates the importance of money for the success of a club. It also helps explain why the Greater Birmingham clubs have not enjoyed success. The average salary for managers in the Premier League in that year was £4 million. Tony Pulis was being paid in the region of £2 million.

The tendency with local clubs is to appoint an experienced person who they believe will be a safe appointment. There are a number of managers that have been around for some time that have developed a reputation for being able to keep a team afloat with limited resources. They are sometimes called impact managers (although they do not always have a positive impact).

Owners turn to them in the hope that they will provide a steady hand, to provide strong and stable leadership – in the short term (such names as Sam Allardyce, Tony Pulis, Alan Pardew, Roy Hodgson, Ian Holloway and Harry Redknapp). These and a number of other names well known at local clubs are members of the "League Management Associations 1,000 Club" – the number indicating the number of games they have managed. They have certainly survived. They move from club to club, they are engaged in the game of musical chairs. The owners of the clubs too often turn to them rather than give a chance to a younger less well-known manager.

There are managers in this experienced category who might be thought to be unlucky, Martin O'Neill for example, who might have achieved much more if he had been given more money to spend. He became manager of Ireland. Villa have also been managed by Graham Taylor, under whose leadership they finished in second place in the top league. He left them to manage England. The Albion have also been managed by a respected England manager, namely Roy Hodgson, and the Wolves by Glen Hoddle. It is not always easy to decide who is good and who is elite. Some good managers might have been considered elite given the opportunity, but some managers who might be thought to be elite struggle without the financial resources to back them up.

An interesting case of an elite manager encountering problems is Rafael Benitez. He was UEFA Manager of the Year for two successive seasons. He was manager of Liverpool when they won the UEFA Champions League in 2005. But he fell out with the owners of Liverpool because they would not back him in the transfer market. He left the club by "mutual consent" in 2010. In March 2016 he took on the task of trying to restore Newcastle United to its former glory. The club finished in top place in the Championship in 2016/17 but in the following season struggled against relegation from the Premier League. The owner of the club Mike Ashley was not making available the finance Benitez thought he needed. Ashley was being prudent, he had let it be known he was willing to sell the club. But as Randy Lerner discovered at the Villa, being too prudent can cost the owner a lot of money.

The relationship between the owner and the manager, however good he may be, is "critical and can create or destroy a club's chance of success". Martin O'Neill refers to it being of paramount importance. Gerard Houllier explains how it can have a direct impact on a team's performance.[8] But with so much money at stake the relationship has changed. In 2002 Chris Green wrote a book entitled "The Sack Race".[9] He was concerned even then about the short term tenure managers (who he refers to as the gaffers) were being given to prove themselves. With football being a results business, if things go wrong the manager is the easy target. Michael Calvin, writing on the same topic, in a book entitled "Living on the Volcano" points out that the new breed of owners demand success whatever the human consequences.[10] Most managers now have little chance to prove they are talented leaders. Steve Bruce who has been a manager for many decades has recently said that he would not wish to enter into football management as it is now.

Owners of clubs, even of successful clubs, now frequently change managers. Chelsea have had ten managers/head coaches in fourteen successful years. Perhaps Aston Villa have not been too bad! Sir Alex Ferguson has referred to the present rate of turnover of managers as preposterous.[11] A number of managers are involved in a game of musical chairs. The average tenure of a football manager in the Premier League is now less than 18 months, with that of a manager in the Championship more like 9 months. What sort of leadership can a manager demonstrate in that time? All the evidence is that a manager needs in the region of 2 to 3 years to have a significant impact. But with so much money at stake most of the modern owners are not prepared to wait that long for results. This leads to a breakdown in the traditional leadership structure. Now 35% of management dismissals are the result of a breakdown in relationship between the manager and the owner (or the Chairman). The leadership is more and more coming from the owner, with advice from "super" agents and consultants. Managers come and go, they can easily be hired and fired. Over one half of first time managers after being dismissed fail to get another management job.

It is becoming more and more common for the owner to sack his manager at any sign of a problem. This is despite the fact that the evidence shows that the sacking of the manager does not necessarily lead to better results.[12] During the 2017/18 season up to the end of March 2018 amongst the 92 League clubs 39 had changed their managers. Amongst the Premier League clubs nine had changed their managers with three of the new appointments being non-British. The three overseas managers were successful, their clubs remained in the Premier League. Of the six British managers, all experienced in fire-fighting, one half were successful, they kept their clubs in the top tier, one half were not successful. The issue of sacking managers will be returned to in the chapter on Aston Villa.

One can see why the local teams have not been successful. The clubs have either not had owners who could provide sufficient funds to enable the club to compete at the highest level, or if the owners have had the funds they have made poor appointments at managerial level. There has also been a problem in that most of the owners were not willing to take risks, they were prudent. They did not, perhaps they could not, appoint the elite managers. One can contrast what has happened with the local teams with what happened at Leicester City in the 2015/16 season. As a local Leicester journalists observed "To win the league by ten points is down to much more than luck. It is down to good leadership and wise investment from the owners, good management from the board, brilliant leadership from Claudio Ranieri, and immaculate attention to detail from all staff".[13]

The Leicester story illustrates what might have happened, but it also illustrates a problem. How do owners and football "experts" identify good managers? Ranieri was voted "Coach of the Year" in England for 2015/16, he was a hero. But in February 2017 he was sacked, he was judged by the Leicester owners (and some of the players) to be the villain. Jose Mourinho blamed the sacking on "selfish players", it was rumoured that a secret meeting had taken place at which some of the players and the owner were present. That is not the end of the story, the man appointed to replace Ranieri, his former assistant Craig Shakespeare, was sacked in October 2017. The up and down life of a manager.

The Region

With the West Midlands clubs not having enjoyed success over recent years, they have not been in a position to attract the big multinational companies as sponsors. They have not been able to sell themselves in the global market. The owners of the clubs for many decades were usually local businessmen who were proud to be associated with the clubs, it gave them a status in the local community. They were not expecting to make very much money from their investments. How things have changed. The future of the local clubs is now in the hands of little known foreign businessmen, decisions that will determine the success or failure of the clubs are being made 6,000 or so miles away. Globalisation has affected these clubs in the same way that it has affected many local business.

Dr Xia became the new owner and chairman of the Villa in 2016. He promised to make Villa one of the elite clubs in Europe and to make them one of the best supported teams in China. The trouble is that local football fans are sceptical. A few years earlier similar claims were being made by another Chinese businessman who had just taken over Birmingham City. He did not deliver what he had promised, he was not what he claimed to be and he finished up in prison.

Birmingham was once a proud city, famous around the world. In the 1970s it experienced difficult times, some the result of changes beyond its control. Some the result of decisions made locally. The region is fighting back seeking to rebuild its reputation. It has been said that "the standard of a city's sport is an important benchmark by which to judge and measure numerous aspects of its culture, quality of life and ultimately competitiveness and success as a city. National and international sporting success is pivotal to what any major city would like to achieve".[14] Like it or not football is now the most high profile of sports. The leader of the Manchester Council has referred to the enormous contribution made to that city by the success of their football clubs. He pointed out that the success gives an enormous competitive advantage when competing with other cities for inward investment and jobs.[15]

In this book it will be argued that success in sport can benefit a city, a region. It is good for its image, it is good for its reputation, it is good for the people who live in the region and it helps give them a sense of identity. Clearly Manchester is a city where this is the case. But success in sport, does not necessarily bring benefits to a city. Liverpool were the top team in Europe in the 1980s but the economy did not benefit. At a different level, Brazil have been the best footballing country in the world for some time but its economy has not benefited from its football success, or from having hosted both the World Cup and the Olympic Games. The corruption and inefficiencies associated with football in Brazil and with the hosting of sporting events have done more harm than good.[16]

Has sport helped Birmingham? One hundred years ago (even 50 years ago) Birmingham was a respected city. It was still a major manufacturing city. It had a skilled labour force. It had a pioneering and much admired municipal administration. It was home to what was for a short time the top football club in the world. Where is the city now? The decline in the fortunes of the football clubs mirrors the decline in many other local industries. With the large businesses that remain, the future, for many, is dependent upon decisions being made in boardrooms many miles away. A similar decline has happened in other regions. In "Up There – The North East Football Boom and Bust" Michael Walker examines the relationship between the downturn in the coal and steel industry and the decline of the once famous football clubs from that region.[17]

The plan of this book is that in the next chapter we will attempt to answer the question of whether or not sport does matter. In the following few chapters the varying fortunes of the Birmingham and other West Midlands football clubs will be explored. The history of each team will be divided into two parts. First, the recent history, that is since the start of the Premier League in 1992, and the second part covering the earlier days. The reason for the two parts is that the football business has changed fundamentally with the formation of this new League – a League which it has been said was "developed by and for television". In chapter 7 the recent history and current standing of the City of Birmingham will be examined. In the following chapter, to provide a comparison, the history of the City of Manchester and of its two football clubs will be considered. Finally influences, changes beyond the control of the decision makers at the football clubs and at the city councils will be discussed – namely, globalisation and national politics. Finally, we will consider whether or not it is likely that at least one of the clubs from the region will ever join the elite and be in a position to bring benefits to the region.

1

DOES SPORT MATTER?

The answer is "yes". But unfortunately Birmingham and the region has up until now, hardly benefited from the dramatic growth in this industry. Success in sport brings rewards. There can be economic benefits, there can be a psychological impact (a feel good factor) a feeling of pride, there can be an impact on people's health. Being home to a successful club can boost the image (the reputation), the brand value, of a city. Hosting a successful sporting event adds to the prestige of a city. Birmingham will in 2022 have an opportunity to show what it can do.

From an economic point of view, sport is one of the top 15 business sectors in the country. In 2010 it was estimated that it contributed over £20 billion to the national economy. Sport is now big business. Football is the biggest sport, but it is more than a business. The success of football clubs has become a key component in sustaining a city's identity. The importance, the significance, of sport to a city was demonstrated in 2017 in Manchester in the days after the terrorist bombing. The success of one of the city's football clubs in the European Championship two days after the bombing was used to make people feel good about themselves, to make them feel united as a community. This was followed two days later by the "City games", again bringing together the people. Manchester showed the potential power of sport not as an opportunity to make money, but to make people feel they belong, to bring them together. In Barcelona the local football team is seen by some as the symbol of a region's political identity.

Sporting success can not only brings prestige to a city, it can also bring financial rewards. A study on the economy of Greater Manchester estimated that in 2011 football contributed around £330 million in gross value added to that region's economy.[1] In addition the success of that city's football team adds to the brand value of the name Manchester. It was estimated that the success of the clubs adds each year an amount equivalent to that obtained from £100 million, per annum, of advertising expenditure. One example of football leading to inward investment is the case of the owners of Manchester City who entered into a £1 billion deal to fund the buildings of 6,000 new homes in a part of the city that needed redevelopment. No such inward investment has resulted from the ownership of the Birmingham clubs.

Leicester City's success in winning the Premier League in the 2015/16 season is estimated to have boosted the economy of that city by over £140 million in gross value added. Of this sum over £100 million is referred to as a direct benefit. This is the additional money received by the club and by businesses in the city as a result of match day tourism. In qualifying for the following season's UEFA Champions League it meant a further boost to the local economy. In the 2016/17 season an estimated 10,000 additional international visitors travelled to the city, spending money and supporting jobs. The prize money for the club as a result of reaching the quarter finals of the Champions League was over £70 million. This money helped fund additional investment in the club's stadium and training facilities.

In 2011 Swansea were promoted to the Premier League. It was estimated that this would be worth an extra £58 million to the local economy in a year and would create 400 jobs. There are in addition to this less easily quantifiable benefits in terms of adding to the reputation of the city. Huddersfield, who were promoted to the Premier League in 2017 were hoping that the local economy would benefit by similar amounts and that it would give much needed publicity to the town.

Throughout history, success in sporting competitions has brought pride to those associated with the winning team. From the time of the original Olympic Games, through the period of fascist governments in Europe, through the period of communism in China and Eastern Europe, sports success has been used to boost the status of the system, and bring pride to the community. It still is; the present leadership in China is investing heavily in an attempt to be the leading soccer nation by the year 2050.

A Successful Club

Football has taken on an importance many people believe greater than it deserves. Thirty years ago it was seen by those in power as a rough working class sport. Now politicians, Prime Ministers and even royalty claim to be fans of the game. It is said that when political leaders meet anywhere in the world, the subject of football is often the first talking point, an ice breaker. For a community it helps to create a bond. It is an escape from the mundane realities of everyday life, it is an escape from politics.

One reason why the people in and around Manchester have been happy to be identified with "Greater Manchester" is because the name is associated globally with success. The growing confidence and success of the city of Manchester has gone hand in glove with the success of the football teams. The reasons why the investors from Abu Dhabi purchased Manchester City was because around the world the name Manchester was associated with success in football. They are said to have looked at Aston Villa and turned away. The two Manchester teams have between them been champions of the Premier League (Premiership) in 16 of its 26 years. Unfortunately in this period Birmingham teams have not helped the reputation of the region.

It is interesting that the name of a city can be associated with the success of a club even though the club may be owned by foreigners, the managers may be foreign and most, sometimes all, the players are foreign. All the city provides is a venue and some loyal local fans. The link between the success of a club and the city may be illogical but it is a fact. The Manchester clubs have been good at seizing onto football as a business opportunity. Many large companies want to

3

be identified with the club, to be so called business partners. On TV, sportswear, beer, banks, betting opportunities and cars can be advertised before a vast global audience (of any age). Football is media friendly. Football matches can be dramatic, they are not too long in terms of time. Different competitions can be hyped. The players can be heroes, they can be villains. The rules are easy to understand, language is not a problem.

Much of the media is beholden to sport. In the old days local newspapers would rush out late editions on Saturday evenings to satisfy the needs of the local community. Now it is TV that supplies the up to date information. Sky would be a much smaller business without football, a number of newspapers would be out of business without their sports sections. Unfortunately it is not the West Midlands clubs that attract interest from the global audience.

It is now accepted that professional football is driven by money. Those involved on the supply side of the business seek to obtain as much money as they can from the consumers. There is a product to be sold, those involved with the production include the media, sponsors, the brand partners, sports goods manufacturers and of course the players, managers and owners. The consumers are the traditional fans and the TV based fans. Football is a product that has to compete with other sports, with other forms of entertainment to attract consumers' money. It has done a very good job but the way the money earned has been distributed has been criticised, it is very uneven. The rich are getting richer and the less rich are struggling to keep up.

For a long time the game marketed itself as the beautiful game, but there are now many who refer to it as the ugly game.[2] Scandals that have been rumoured about for some time have been exposed. Gambling linked to the game has become a concern. There have been proven cases of match fixing and FIFA officials have been found guilty of accepting bribes. The influence of agents has been criticised. The inflow of funds from secret offshore accounts has increased. But the sport seems able to handle the scandals, the TV money pours in, dubious owners take over the clubs, more sponsorship funds are available, local fans become of less relevance to the clubs but the demand for the sport continues to grow.

The Premier League is the third largest sports league in the World (behind the Basketball and American Football leagues in the USA). The clubs in the league, the league itself and the players in 2013/14 contributed over £2.4 billion in taxes to the Exchequer (over one half of this was the tax and national insurance contributions paid by the players and other employees). The league created over 100,000 jobs and contributed £3.4 billion to national GDP.[3] In that year there were two Birmingham teams bringing a share of this wealth to the local economy. But by 2016/17 there was only one team at this level.

Sport gives pleasure to many millions, but there is a limit to how much time an individual can devote to watching sport, this is called 'Sports Space'. Money follows the sport that attracts the most attention, that dominated this sports space. People around the world want to watch the best teams, the best players. Unfortunately sport clubs in Birmingham do not attract the stars.

A City of Sport?

One way in which a city can benefit from sport is by hosting a major sports event. Manchester tried on three occasions to attract major sporting events to the city. It failed the first two times, namely in their bids for the 1996 and 2000 Olympics. One of the lessons the council learned from these failed attempts was the need for central government support for their bid. They learned the lessons and were successful in bringing the 2002 Commonwealth Games to the city.[4]

Those who govern Birmingham decided some time ago that the city would benefit from hosting international sporting occasions. Up until 2017 they had had some success in attracting international events to the city but they had been in the less high profile sports. They had tried but had failed to attract one of the, so called, mega events. The city continued to try and in December 2017 it was announced that they would host the 2022 Commonwealth Games.

In the past the city had suffered from at least one drawback when trying to attract such events. They had no big sporting venue. Villa Park was the largest stadium, but that only seated 42,000. The Council have for a long time talked about the building of a City of Birmingham Stadium. There were plans in 1973 for an arena to be built in the Snow Hill area. This became linked to the bids for the 1982 Commonwealth Games and the 1992 and 1996 Olympic Games.[5] A later proposal was to build a National Football Stadium near to the NEC. This proposal not surprisingly failed, Wembley was said to be the home of football in the country. Birmingham did however have some success with support for the National Indoor Arena (1991) and before that for the development of the new Alexander Stadium (1978). It is this Stadium, enlarged, that will be the venue for the opening and closing ceremonies and the athletic and field events at the 2022 Commonwealth Games.

One plan for a Birmingham stadium was to be a public/private venture. This was to be located in Saltley in what was known as Wheels Park; it was to comprise both a casino and sports stadium. The Blues were to move there from St Andrews, the proposal had enthusiastic support of the club's directors. The proposal collapsed, a casino was to be involved and the idea of a casino upset local councillors (the casino was in the end built on the NEC site). The next proposal was very ambitious, a joint sports stadium shared by the "Blues" and Warwickshire County Cricket Club. Such a stadium for both football and cricket had proved to be very successful (indeed world famous) in Melbourne. The proposal failed. A little later, Blues now with new owners proposed to develop a new stadium, but with Carson Yeung's financial position so uncertain, it got nowhere. To be fair, the Chief Executive of the club at the time, Peter Pannu, did raise the question as to whether such a stadium was necessary when Blues could not even fill a 30,000 seater stadium.

The failed bid to host the 1992 Olympics illustrated another of Birmingham's problems. The International Olympic Committee decision on where to hold these Games was made in

1986, a good time for Birmingham when it was being successful in its redevelopment. The UK Olympic Committee had chosen Birmingham over London and Manchester to be the UK's nominated City. Unfortunately, although Birmingham had easily defeated its national rivals in obtaining the support of the UK Olympic officials it failed badly when it came to the international decision. In the vote on who would be the host city only one city being considered obtained less support. It was generally agreed that the Birmingham bid was technically excellent, and the bidding team was very well led by (Sir) Dennis Howell, a former Minister of Sport and a Birmingham man. But at the international level the bid did not attract support. One reason why was because the bid received little support from the British government. Westminster let the city down, it did not appear to care. If Birmingham had been chosen as the city to host the 1992 Olympics, what a difference it could have made to its future. The city chosen for 1992 was Barcelona.

When a number of years later, London was the UK's nominated city for the 2012 Games the support from Westminster at the international level was somewhat different. For the 2022 Commonwealth Games to come to Birmingham it was necessary to have UK Government support. It was estimated that the Games would cost over £600 million, with the Treasury being required to meet 75% of the cost. This time the Treasury did support the bid believing that such an outlay represented value for money.

In 2013 Birmingham had felt overlooked when UK Sport announced that £27 million of national lottery funds money would be made available to bring more than 70 major sporting events to Britain over the following 6 years. Unfortunately Birmingham was not one of the cities listed to benefit from this. Birmingham had obtained national financial support for the building of the £51 million National Indoor Arena, but that was in the 1980s. At the time it was the largest sports building of its type in the country. It does host international sporting championships, the World Indoor Athletic Championships being held there in 2018. Another success was the development of the Alexander Stadium. Its early development was linked to Birmingham's unsuccessful bid to host the 1982 Commonwealth Games. It has hosted a number of national and international athletic championships. It has been referred to as the home of UK athletics. One reason Birmingham was chosen to host the 2022 Games was said to be the high quality of the existing facilities.

Private sector sports clubs have been reasonably successful in attracting major national and international events to the city. In cricket Edgbaston has been host for test matches for many decades. It managed to retain its Test Match status as the result of the redevelopment of the stadium in 2011. But it was only able to afford the cost of redevelopment because it received a loan of £20 million from the City Council. The loan was supposed to be repayable over a 25 year period at a fixed rate of 5% interest. It was supposed to be repayable in equal instalments over time by what are known as bullet repayments. But the Warwickshire cricket club could not afford to repay the City Council who had in fact been very generous even though they themselves were short of money. As at the end of 2016 none of the loan has been repaid, all the Council receives is the annual interest payment of just over £1 million. This is an example of a public subsidy for a sporting event. The idea of a public private sector partnership to fund a stadium in a city is very common in the United States. In tennis the Edgbaston Priory Club have staged international tennis competitions from 1982, but they are not now attracting top international players. Villa Park was once a regular venue for FA Cup semi-final games and the occasional international match. Not now, the new Wembley Stadium which belongs to the FA which attracted £120 million of lottery money now stages as many events as it can, but even then it struggles to pay its way.

Birmingham has been losing its share of both the national and global sports market. It claims to have been the first city in the UK to be named a 'National City of Sports', and to have hosted more World and European sports events than any other city in the country. The problem is that the city is big in minority sports, and small in major sports. If Birmingham wishes to improve its global status and to be widely known as a city of sport, it needs to have its name associated with the sports watched by the largest number of people. It is these sports that dominate the world media and attract the largest amounts of sponsorship and commercial income. The Commonwealth Games attract much less world coverage than the Olympics, but it is the fifth largest sporting event in the world, it will help promote the city in many parts of the world.

The Cricket Champions Trophy in 2013 contributed in the region of £13 million to the local economy. Some of the test matches took place at the Edgbaston ground. The city wished to ensure that the name Birmingham received prominence in the TV coverage of the matches; not everyone being aware that Edgbaston is in Birmingham. The 'City End' became the 'Birmingham End' and the twenty over team became the Birmingham Bears.

Those responsible for marketing Birmingham were proud to be able to announce that the city's involvement with the 2015 Rugby World Cup would boost the local economy by £56 million. The city was acting as hosts to two matches at Villa Park. This figure was based on the estimated expenditure of visitors to the city and to a possible long term economic impact. It was argued that the value of the brand Birmingham would benefit from the increased exposure to a global TV audience. One has to hope that those living outside the UK realised that Villa Park is located in Birmingham. There is a problem, with identification for some clubs and some grounds.

The £56 million that came to Birmingham from the Rugby World Cup was good but it was swamped in comparison with the boost that Manchester receives from its two football clubs, now estimated to be in the region of £500 million each year. Sports tourism is becoming increasingly important. It has been estimated that one million overseas football fans visit the UK each year. Football fans are particularly lucrative to the local economy.

Surprisingly the fans from overseas spend an average of £1000 on each trip. Do they come to Birmingham? Unfortunately Villa Park ranks as only the tenth most visited ground in the country. The numbers are far behind those who visit the grounds of the London, Manchester and Liverpool clubs.

The Decision as to who will Host major sports event

Sport clearly matters to those governing many big cities. The evidence for this is the trouble that they will go to in order to attract major sporting events.

At the end of September 2017 the Executive Board of the Commonwealth Games Federation announced that the application by the City of Birmingham to host the 2022 Games "was not fully compliant". At that date, which was said to be the closing date for applications, Birmingham was the only city offering to host the event. The Board announced that they would take another two months before they could make a decision, this they said would enable other cities to develop propositions. But when the end of November arrived they said they needed yet more time and hoped to be able to make a decision by the end of the year. Birmingham had to wait anxiously through the last few months of 2017 to hear whether or not the CGF would award the city the 2022 games.

There were some people, those familiar with the murky history of decision making surrounding major sporting events, who were concerned about the delay. What did the members of the Executive Board of the CGF want from Birmingham? The public had become cynical following a number of scandals over host city decisions for mega sports events. There had long been concerns about corruption within FIFA and the International Olympic Committee. Recent evidence of this being the decision to award the 2022 World Cup to Qatar. This did at last lead to legal action being taken.[6] The decision of the International Olympic Committee to award the 2002 winter Olympics to Salt Lake City had been shown to be corrupt, with members of the IOC having taken bribes from members of the host city bidding committee.[7]

In theory the decision making process to select which city should host a major sporting event should be sound. The council of the sports governing body, say the IOC set up a sub-committee to evaluate the bids from the cities competing to host the games. The sub-committee prepare a technical report based on certain criteria such as the suitability of the proposed venues, the tournament infra-structure and financial viability. Each of the members of the full council or of an executive committee, having received the sub-committees evaluation report will then vote on which city they wish to support.

The outcome of a vote often comes as a surprise, even to those closely involved. Sepp Blatter, President of FIFA at the time the decision was announced on who would host the 2022 World Cup was expecting the USA to be awarded the event, not Qatar. The bookmakers' favourite to host the 2012 Olympic Games was not London but Paris. South Africa were expecting to be the hosts for the 2023 Rugby World Cup, not France. Those compiling the technical report, presumably the experts, recommended that the Games be held in South Africa. There was the usual behind the scene lobbying and hidden deal making and the delegates in the end decided on Paris. There was no suggestion, with this particular event, that any of the delegates were themselves accepting bribes. The rationale for the change in heart was that France guaranteed the World Rugby Council a £350 million surplus from the games, but South Africa had only promised £270 million. The delegates had voted for the money, but hopefully money to be put back into sport.

On occasions the national delegates on the councils of the international sporting bodies who have a vote, base their vote, not on what is best for the sport, but on the amount of money or other rewards that they or their home country will receive. Lucrative commercial contracts including the award of television rights have been shown to influence delegates decisions, as have old fashioned cash in brown envelope type transactions.

It was not clear what was delaying the CGF decision on a host city for 2022. The chair of the Evaluation panel said that they needed to be "fully satisfied that the ultimate host for 2022 is capable of staging a Games that fully delivers for Commonwealth athletes and host communities". As usual they talked about legacy objectives. But the amount of money available to finance the Games was clearly an important issue for the Panel to consider. They had been let down by the city of Durban's late withdrawal from hosting the 2022 games on the grounds that they would not be able to afford to cover the costs. The CGF could not make another mistake. The UK government were willing to support the Birmingham bid financially, and the local councils were also willing to provide support.

FIFA

It has been known for a number of decades that certain of the decisions made at FIFA have been the result of bribery and of corruption. A number of once high ranking FIFA officials are currently facing criminal charges or have already been found guilty. Jack Warner from Trinidad, once Vice President of the Association was at the end of 2017 fighting an extradition order to be sent to the USA to answer corruption charges relating to FIFA business.

The story goes back to the year 2000, when a decision was being made as to who would host the 2006 World Cup.[8] The decision was to be made by the 24 members of the FIFA Executive. The final choice lay between South Africa and Germany. Blatter wanted the Cup to be held in South Africa. As President he would have what might have turned out to be a crucial casting vote as it was believed that the executive would split 12 to 12. Germany were keen to host the event. Their bidding team was led by the well-respected ex-footballer Franz Beckenbauer. To the surprise of most the vote was 12 to Germany and 11 to South Africa. The Oceania delegate abstained. The enquiry that followed concentrated on the delegates who had voted for Germany and why. Jack Warner was a key man. He could deliver three votes, those of the Federations from the Caribbean and North and

Central America. These votes were cast in favour of Germany. The US authorities have brought charges against Warner connected with money he received from the sale of television rights to this World Cup and the movement of cash, intended for the use of national football associations, into accounts that he personally controlled.

Jack Warner has been involved in a number of scandals at FIFA. It was alleged that he received a $10 million bribe from South Africa to buy his support for the bid to host the 2010 World Cup. Another key figure in the corruption at FIFA has been Chuck Blazer from the USA who was also a member of the FIFA executive committee. In 2016 the US authorities found him guilty of accepting bribes in connection with FIFA business. He became an informer and helped the FBI to obtain evidence of corruption by wearing a wire-tap at meetings.

In 2017 three former FIFA executives from South American were on trial in New York accused of taking bribes in connection with FIFA business. One of the three had been the head of Brazil's Football Association, another the head of Peru's association, the third from Paraquay, a former Vice President of FIFA. The troubles for certain FIFA executives and officials started when in 2015 the Swiss police raided premises in Zurich. Following the raid more than 40 people were charged with over one half being found guilty.

In 2017 police were investigating bribery allegations against Nasser al-Khelaifi who as well as being chairman of PSG was also a minister without portfolio in Qatar. He was heavily involved in the decisions to award the World Cup to Russia in 2018 and to Qatar in 2022. Influencing a decision might not always involve the transfer of cash, it can be the result of political pressure. With the Qatar decision, it is known that the French President asked Michel Platini, the head of UEFA, to look after the interests of France when casting his vote. Platini did vote to host the Cup in Qatar. Following the FIFA decision, Qatar did invest large sums of money in France and they did purchase and invest heavily in the top French football team PSG. The US authorities are still investigating corruption surrounding this particular host country decision. Clearly there have been many problems at FIFA over the years. But Sepp Blatter still argues that it is not bribery that influences the delegates when voting on host country issues, rather it is political pressure.

A further FIFA scandal concerning Platini came to light in 2016 when he received a payment from FIFA of 2 million Swiss Francs that could not be properly explained. There was a further scandal involving another executive member, this time from Cyprus, a key ally of Platini, following the award of the games to Qatar. This member was lucky enough to receive £32 million from the Qatar Investment Authority from the sale of land that he owned. The sale of land was said to be nothing to do with his vote to support that country.

Those representing England have at times been involved in some dubious attempts to obtain the support of FIFA executives. They wooed Warner in their unsuccessful attempts to obtain support for their bids to host the 2006 and the 2018 World Cups. The Garcia Report into corruption at FIFA said that Warner showered England's bid team with inappropriate requests and that the bid team "often accommodated his wishes in apparent violation of bidding rules and FIFA's code of ethics".[9] The bid team found jobs in English football for some of Warner's contacts and provided cash to support certain projects in the Caribbean. The Garcia Report also revealed that the Australian bidding team paid $500,000 into Warner's personal account, the money was meant to finance a sports centre, it was also, according to the report, intended to influence the way Warner would vote.

Olympic Games

One of the stated objectives of the International Olympic Committee is to build a better world through sport. A worthy ambition. The Games certainly provide a spectacular showcase for sports people from all over the world to compete. Unfortunately over the years the IOC have attracted much bad publicity resulting from such issues as failing to be able to control drug use by some athletes and from their soft approach to countries that have been found to be complicit with the cheating. There have also been financial scandals but less attention has been paid to these.

London was successful in their bid to host the 2012 Games. This was said to be the cleanest of all contests between candidate cities as to who would be the chosen host. The reason for this was because new rules had been introduced following the scandals surrounding the award of the 2002 Winter Olympics to Salt Lake City. It was found that certain IOC members when visiting Salt Lake to evaluate its suitability as a host, received luxury gifts and the promise of scholarships at US colleges for their children. These were given in return for their votes. Ten members of IOC were forced to resign. It was found that representatives from Salt Lake City had paid agents to acquire the votes of certain delegates. This came to light when an IOC member from Switzerland blew the whistle. The whistle-blower suggested the members were the victims and not the villains and it was the representatives from the competing cities that should be blamed. It also came to light that Sydney, who had hosted the games in 2000, had received an offer from an unknown agent to supply the votes of certain delegates. Agents had also been active in selling votes for the support of Atlanta, as host for the 1996 Games.

Following these scandals new rules were introduced to restrict the contact between IOC members and host city representatives. But what about agents? A scandal did break out over the London bid for the 2012 Games. A Panorama TV programme showed four so called agents who claimed that they could secure the votes of certain IOC members in return for a cash payment. "It was said that up to £1.9 million would be needed for between 15 and 20 votes – plus an agent's fee of nearly £600,000." It was feared this disclosure would harm the London bid. There was no suggestion however that any member of the London bidding team was involved with the proposed deal. It was a TV team that set up the scam.

The outcome of the vote on the host city for the 2012 games came as a surprise to many. Paris were the bookmakers favourite. It was said that there was much goodwill amongst delegates towards Paris after their failure to attract the 1992 and 2008 Games. The London team made an impressive case, they needed to. In the first round of voting London received 22 votes, Paris 21, Madrid 20 and New York 19. This illustrates how important the vote of one delegate can be. The London lobbying campaign was said to have been run like a military operation. Two of the stars at the crucial IOC meeting in Singapore helping to sell the London case were David Beckham and Tony Blair (Paris did not send any heavyweights.) The 2016 Olympics were held in Brazil: they were a financial disaster with many scandals.

The Commonwealth Games

There have been relatively few scandals surrounding these Games. There have been, perhaps not surprisingly, political disputes arising over issues such as apartheid. The only financial scandals that have come to light arose in connection with the 2010 Games that were held in India. Following these games certain top Indian officials were charged with corruption. One particular problem arose over the award of construction contracts to a Swiss company with resulting kick-backs from the contractors to the Indian Games officials.

At the time of the Birmingham bid for 2022 there were political problems within the CG Federation. There was much in-fighting. Malaysia wanted the headquarters to be moved from London to Kuala Lumpur. It was said that unless significant changes in the governance and management of the Federation took place the future of the games themselves was in doubt. The city initially chosen to host the 2022 Games was Durban in South Africa. It turned out, however, that following the huge financial loss resulting from holding the football World Cup in that country, public funds were not being made available to support the Durban bid. In fact Birmingham had decided in 2013 not to bid for the

2022 Games on the grounds that they would be too costly. Clearly the city council members changed their minds despite the fact that the city's financial problems had become worse.

Hosting Games (The Benefits)

To be the host city, to be the host country, for an international event can in fact be a mixed blessing. Many people benefit, building contractors, executives, hoteliers, sports people and local politicians. But does the host city benefit? The majority of Olympic Games have lost money for the country that was host but many have benefited the host city. The London 2012 Olympics was an example of this. Financially it was not a success for the UK. Of the £9 billion plus cost of the games, London provided less than £1 billion; the balance was paid for by the rest of the country. Certainly the East of London was physically transformed and the local football club, WHU, benefited from the national investment.[10]

It is now accepted that most Olympic Games lose money, despite the claims made before the event. There are benefits, but many of these are only short term. It was estimated that the average Londoner has a boost in happiness resulting from hosting the Games, equivalent to £8,000; this was a feel good factor. But this only lasted for one year and it is doubtful whether the citizens of say Wigan or Hull benefited by anywhere near this amount. The games did attract foreign investment and did create employment but mainly for those in London and the South East.

The financial arrangements concerning the Olympic Stadium turned out to be a farce. It is the same story as that of stadiums built to host many other mega sports events, the latest being the stadiums built to host the Games in Brazil.[11] With the London Olympics the country was left to pay for the conversion of the Olympic Stadium into a football stadium. The stadium cost over £430 million to construct but a further £300 million was needed to be spent in order to convert this venue into a football ground. Of this conversion cost, WHU contributed only £15 million. The club pay only a modest annual rental of £2.5 million (reduced to

£1.25 million if they are relegated from the Premier League) to be able to use the stadium. They do not have to pay for stewarding and policing. They have use of the stadium for 99 years.

So to host a sports event can be uneconomic from a national point of view but good for the host city and very good for the owners of a club that can use the facilities after the event. One reason why the investors from Abu Dhabi, were happy to purchase Manchester City, was that they could take over a new stadium paid for with public money. The irony in the West Ham case is that the fans do not appear to like their new home.

The House of Lords Select Committee that investigated the 'Legacy' of the London Olympics concluded that it was an outstanding success but they did point out that there was little evidence of it leading to an increased participation in sport and there was an uneven distribution of economic benefits across the UK.[12] It revealed that the event created 10 times more jobs in the South East than in the West Midlands. The games did attract additional foreign investment resulting in 31,000 new jobs, but the West Midlands only benefited by 3.7% of this total. The benefits to the North East and North West were even lower than those to the West Midlands. The legacy "faltered" outside London.

Even in London there are doubts as to the benefits. In 2017 the Mayor of London revealed that the Olympic Stadium was expected to make a loss of £24 million in 2017/18 and to continue to lose money after that. This was partly the result of "bungled" decision making from 2011, which resulted in "the taxpayer taking all the risks and footing almost all the whole bill". There was talk of trying to renegotiate the contracts relating to the use of the stadium.

The government department responsible for promoting UK business claimed that the Games benefited the UK economy by £9.9 billion.[13] But many are sceptical of this figure including the Federation of Small Businesses who expressed the view that the impact of the games had been disappointing. The contracts that small businesses had been expecting often did not materialise. The

Government department claimed that of the total benefits £2.5 billion was additional inward investment. The problem is estimating what is additional; nobody knows what would have happened without the games. At the beginning of any bidding process the costs of staging a games are underestimated. At the start the public were told that the London games would only cost £2.4 billion. The figure soon changed, officially the cost was £9 billion but many believe it was nearer £11 billion. As always the finance provided by the private sector was less than expected with the result that for the London Olympics the cost to the public sector more than tripled.

As Andrew Zimbalist, a leading sports economist points out the problems with mega sporting events start with the bidding process.[14] To host such an event one city competes with another city to be the national candidate. The selected national candidate then competes with other cities from other countries. The bidding process is expensive and has been shown to be corrupt on some occasions. The local organising committee are invariably motivated by private business and political interests. The bidding process is hijacked by private interest. This can result in over building. The Barcelona Olympics were generally regarded as a huge success but there are many other stories of disaster. Hosting the 2004 Olympics in Greece helped bankrupt the country. In Montreal it took over 30 years to pay off the debts incurred in hosting the 1976 Olympics. The stadium built for the Sydney Olympics in 2000 still costs the city £18 million a year to maintain. The stadium used in Beijing costs £10 million a year to maintain and is little used.

The 2014 Commonwealth Games held in Glasgow was the largest ever multisport event held in Scotland. The lessons learned from this event should be relevant to Birmingham. The 2014 games were generally regarded as a success. The City of Glasgow was able to claim a near £100 million boost to the city's economy, but the official report on the games pointed out that Scotland as a country did not enjoy any specific advantages.[15]

The Glasgow Games cost close to £550 million, of this £372 million came from public funds, that is the Scottish government, the host city and Lottery money. The remaining costs were mainly covered by sponsorship income and ticket sales. The organisers of the games did well and produced a small surplus which was invested in the Scottish NHS. There were many who argued that the country as a whole would have benefited more if all the money spent on the games had been spent on schools and health. The games illustrate the gains being made by the host city, not the country.

With sporting events there is always much talk about legacy. The Scottish government report produced one year after the Glasgow games discusses future benefits. It mentions that existing much improved arenas and stadiums can be used to host future events. They estimated the economic impact to the city for the one year following the games was £18.5 million. In addition to the economic impact on sport there were benefits from improved infrastructure and increased tourism. It does mention that there was a non-financial impact, in particular the effect on civic pride, on culture and on community programmes. A further benefit expected was a higher profile for the host city internationally, just what Birmingham needs.

There are many examples of failure. In football the World Cup in South Africa is estimated to have cost the country over £3 billion and it only received back £380 million, a huge financial loss. The expected tourists did not turn up in South Africa to watch the events. The country was however able to boast that it was the first country in Africa to host the World Cup but whether it was worth it seems doubtful. The games gave a temporary boost to South Africa's reputation and to its brand value but this only lasted for a short time. The 2014 World Cup in Brazil was also a financial disaster. After the games £300 million of tax payers' money needed to be paid to rebuild the Maracanã Stadium. There had been the usual problems with inflated budgets and corruption. The stadium was too big for the needs of the country after the games. From a transport point of view the stadium is not linked to the rest of the country. For both South Africa and Brazil, not too wealthy countries, it could be argued that the money could have been better spent on other things. They both are left with underutilised stadiums.

The success of a local team in sport can bring lasting benefits to a city as long as the team stays at the top but the evidence on the benefits of hosting a major sporting event is inconclusive. There is much hype about legacy and sustainability. Hosting a mega sporting event does give a short term boost to tourism and valuable TV exposure. There are those who do benefit, such as the national sports organisations, the local politicians, those involved in construction and tourism. But there have been many white elephants and somebody has to pay for them.

There is, in fact, some disagreement as to whether the presence a sports team in a city gives a boost to the local community.[16] It is a big issue in the USA where in many cities local politicians lobby for public sector funding for new stadiums. It has been found that many of the claims of large intangible benefits do not withstand scrutiny. It is one thing to argue whether or not the presence of any team benefits a city and another to argue that the presence of a highly successful team benefits the city. It is being argued in this book that a winning reputation brings intangible benefits. It is this that Birmingham needs. The inhabitants of the city need to feel pride, not to feel second best.

What can one conclude? A successful club is good for a city, for its image and for the economic rewards. A city can benefit from hosting a mega sport event. There are those in the private sector who benefit and the host city should benefit, but there is usually a cost for someone else to carry. The Birmingham City Council have been very active in trying to attract international sporting competitions to the city, they wish to promote the city as one of sport, not just business. They have had some minor success in the past, they kept trying and did in the end succeed in attracting a mega event.

It is perhaps unfortunate that Birmingham has been awarded the Commonwealth Games just at the time when many people are questioning the Games relevance. Two questions are being asked, one being the relevance of the Commonwealth in the 21st century, and the other whether or not these Games matter as a sporting contest. The moral justification for the old Empire has been discredited, and the economic relevance of the Commonwealth is unclear. With the UK's planned departure from the EU it could be that the old links between the Commonwealth countries become important once again. All Birmingham can do is to go ahead as planned and hope to do its best.

After the Games the City would not be left with a large stadium. The plan being for the showpiece venue, the Alexander Stadium, to be enlarged to a 40,000 seater venue for the Games but then to be reduced to a 20,000 seater stadium. Whether such a venue would be commercially viable in the future was uncertain. To host an exciting games would however do much to boost the image of the City.

A City of Football?

In 2016 Sport England surprisingly awarded the title of City of Football to Nottingham. They were very impressed with what that city was doing to encourage the people in the local community to play football and to become involved. One aspect of the project was to attract the British Asian community to play the game. It was felt that the many Asians in Nottingham (and indeed elsewhere) were keen to play the game but were not being catered for. Nottingham had decided to take the game to them.

The politicians and football establishment in Manchester were disappointed that they were not officially named the City of Football. They believed they had a right to this title, their bid being backed by two of the top teams in the country. Sport England were however keen to re-establish the links between the local community and football.

What about a case for Birmingham to be named as the City of Football? Those involved at the city level and at the club level would not have been surprised that the city missed out. The professional clubs had not been exciting. For a city the size of Birmingham the size of the crowds they attract to their games is disappointing. The clubs have been active in community activity, but apparently did not make such a good case as Nottingham.

The business history of the local clubs reveals what has gone wrong. From the early days the clubs have struggled financially. They have too often been mismanaged. Only just over 10 years ago Villa were writing about the need to be prudent, at a time when football had taken off. The owners of the clubs have been risk averse. They have changed managers far too quickly. A comparison of the history of the Birmingham clubs with the Manchester clubs is revealing.

When football was a small business, success or failure only really mattered to the local fans. But from the late 1990s, with the market opening up to new commercial opportunities, big money came into the game. Success on the pitch now depended more than ever on access to money. A new type of owner appeared, some were good, some bad. The Birmingham clubs did attract international investors – but not those who understood the football business. Four of the local clubs are now owned by little known Chinese businesses. What have football fans in the Birmingham region to look forward to? Possibly not very much, that is unless they have decided to support clubs from the North West or from London.

In his fascinating book "The Game of our Lives", David Goldblatt discusses the changes in fortune of football in the different regions in England.[17] He looks at the relative decline of football in the Midlands and finds that the malaise is at its grimmest in Birmingham. He believes that the city should have been more successful in football as it should have been in a number of other aspects of cultural and economic life.

Football has become something of a Soap Opera. The public tend to see it as a game with heroes and villains. The heroes are the players in the team one supports. The baddies are the players at most of the other clubs. Books are written about a club's "legends". Little boys (and sometimes big boys) wear shirts with the name of their heroes on the back. But there are another set of goodies and baddies in football clubs, the owners. Success of the club depends more and more about money and those who have the money and control it, they determine the fate of the club. The owners are the real power at a club. Money is a necessary condition for success but not a sufficient condition. The individuals that provide (or fail to provide) the money are often very interesting. Sometimes their lives are much more intriguing than the so called legends. The contribution of such owners to the success or failure of the local clubs will be explored.

This book is a football book but not one that offers a nostalgic look at the great players and past glories of the local teams. In fact the book could have been called "The Lost Teams of the Midlands" but for the fact that this title has already been used by Mike Bradbury in his fascinating book on football in the region.[18] He was writing about the lost teams of 100 years ago – let us hope he will not soon be publishing a second edition of the book dealing with the lost teams of more recent years.

Sport is important at many levels. Football, as the most high profile sport is important not just to the followers of the game, but to a community, to a city.

2

ASTON VILLA

In 2016 Aston Villa was the subject of headlines in of all places 'The Wall Street Journal'. The article was entitled "The Ignominity of Aston Villa".[1] It pointed out that relegation from the Premier League for the club would be ugly, not just because of lost revenue and lost fans but because of lost relevance and lost prestige. The article reminded its readers that Villa was once one of England's legendry clubs "during the reign of Queen Victoria Villa was huge". But Queen Victoria was dead; what happened to Villa in the 100 or so years since her death to change the club from being the best in the country to being a second tier club?

Danny Blanchflower, one of the most respected and successful Villa players in the second half of the 20th century, made some challenging comments about the condition of Aston Villa in the 1950s and 1960. "The whole place was crying out for soccer leadership and guidance and I eventually tired of the complacency there. Villa has a tremendous potential and still has but I am not sure how it can be realised".[2] This was before the Doug Ellis era, before the Randy Lerner era. In 2003 Graham Taylor when leaving his position as manager of the Villa to become the England manager, said "I believe that changes are necessary". "The structure of the club has to be looked at on and off the field".[3]

What happened? Thirty years after Blanchflower's comments another successful footballer, Paul Merson who played for a time at Villa gave his views on the club. "It is not good enough. We have had bad runs but it's four years on the trot now".[4] Four years for

Merson, but for the fans there were to be more bad years. Villa talked big but with the exception of a brief period at the end of the 1980s and early 1990s they failed to deliver. In the early 2000s they had a chance once again to become an elite club, when for three seasons running they finished as the sixth best team in the country. They are now very far removed from such status.

When Doug Ellis, took over control of the club in December 1968, he referred to encountering the results of "years of neglect and decline" (similar to words used by Karren Brady at Birmingham City over 20 years later). He believed an immense financial balancing act was required to keep the club going: "it was dying on its feet". The club had £180,000 of debt, (about £3 million at today's values). He did save the club. He was the most important man at the club for 38 years, there was some success but not a lot. He was criticised for being too prudent. Fans were pleased when he sold the club in 2006 to a wealthy American, perhaps the club could now join the elite. But in 2010, after only four years in charge, the new owner Randy Lerner said the club's aim was to be as competitive as possible given their size and resources. The club was no longer thinking big.

Lerner in fact was generous in providing resources to the club. In the Lerner era the owner provided the club with £242 million by way of loans and with over £70 million through new equity finance. But the money was not well spent, the club was being badly led. It was not running efficiently. Villa were relegated in 2016. Early in the 2015/16 season they had started to prepare for life in the second tier. The scouts had apparently been told to look out for cheap new recruits who knew what it was like to play in the Championship. The manager was living in rented accommodation, with a short term lease.

The financial accounts for the last year of the Lerner era show a loss of £81 million. This was partly due to decisions that were made to carry out certain accounting adjustments, in particular to recognise what are called exceptional items. Those in charge of the club when the accounts were being prepared, decided to write down the value of the stadium by £45 million and of the playing squad by £35 million. One reason why such adjustments are made at a particular point of time is to make it easier for the club to look good in the future, from a financial point of view. Of interest is the fact that over the Lerner era the club had paid out £23 million as compensation to sacked managers, such payments were becoming unexceptional.

In 2016/17 the first year in which the new Chinese owners were in charge, the club finished in 13th place in the Championship and made a loss of £15 million. This was after receiving a parachute payment of £41 million. Parachute payments would be received for two more seasons but would fall to £33 million in the 2017/18 season and £15 million in the next. The club, unless they were promoted to the Premiership, would face financial problems.

The club had failed to gain promotion in 2017 and failed again in 2018. In 2018 they lost 0-1 in the play-off final, in what was said to be the 'the most valuable match in the world'. If they had won the final their revenue in 2018/19 would have been at least £85 million higher than it had been in 2017/18. This being their guaranteed share of the Premier League's broadcasting revenue for one season (less the £15 million parachute payment they would have received in the lower league). If they had won the play-off game, been promoted and then relegated after just one season in the Premier League they would have received parachute payments in each of the next three season amounting in total to about £75 million. Playing in the top tier would also of course have meant higher match day income and better sponsorship deals.

A missed opportunity both on the pitch and off it. If the club had won the game it would have been good for the City of Birmingham, for the fans, for the manager and the owner: Dr Xia and his associates would have been £200 million or so richer.

Steve Bruce, the manager in 2018, had on four occasions led teams from the second tier into the first tier, twice with the Blues and twice with Hull. The fans hoped that this game against Fulham would prove to be the fifth time. The Wembley final was watched by the current owner, by Doug Ellis and by over 30,000 of their fans, including the Duke of Cambridge. They lost and the consequences were serious.

Steve Bruce had warned of the problems that would follow defeat. He was already operating on a tight budget; much of the success of the team had been based on the performances of players on loan, wages would need to be cut, and it was most likely that these loan players would leave the club. Bruce talked of a tight recruitment budget, he had only spent just over £2.5 million on transfers during 2017/18 and had raised £18 million from sales. Not easy times ahead.

We will look at the history of the club over two periods. The first part will consider the most recent years. That is the years from the beginning of the Premier League (the Premiership) in 1992. This includes some of the Doug Ellis era. It includes the 'Lerner era' and the short period with Dr Xia in charge. Then the second part will look at earlier years.

Part A: The Recent History – From The 1990s

The Final Years of the Doug Ellis Era

The 1990s were a time when the Villa should have established themselves as one of the top three or four teams in the country. The Premier League was bringing large sums of money into the game, the Villa should have been taking advantage of their position as the top club in the second city in the country, a club with a long proud history.

Of course to the younger generation of football followers history does not mean a great deal. Villa are not a glamorous club. But in the first year of the Premiership Villa finished in second place – excellent, a promising start. Manchester United were Champions and continued to remain at or near the top. Villa just became a middle of the table club, more likely to be relegated than win the league. The relative failure from the 1990s could not be blamed on a divided board of directors, which had been a problem a few years earlier. In fact the club's performance could have been predicted based on the policies of the Board.

In the difficult years of the mid 1980s, Ellis had made his objective clear. The "current problems of football throughout the country are likely to persist but the aim will be to continue to operate at a profit". As Ellis explained in his autobiography, he had helped "salvage" the club and had "steered it towards more stable financial waters".[5] The first lesson he said that he would offer to new managers would be to "let modern businessmen run the business and football experts run the football". The trouble with this lesson was what was meant by the expression a 'modern' businessman. A person who was successful in the business climate of the 1950s and 1960s, and who was good at cutting back on costs in the difficult years of the 1980s, might not be the 'modern' businessman needed to take advantage of the opportunities of the 1990s.

In the early years of the 1990s the club were financially sound, but were not investing enough for the future. They were not borrowing. They could survive without borrowing, so why borrow? They were relying on retained profits "as a primary source of funding". (This was a traditional West Midlands conservative business policy). Arsenal had at the time loans of £4.6 million, Tottenham had bank borrowing of over £4 million, and even Norwich a loan of £1.5 million.

Relying on profits to finance growth can be seen as a safe policy. It does not involve asking either bankers or equity investors to produce new funds. Such a policy does, however, limit the rate of growth of a company. The borrowing potential of Villa was high, but was not being used. Villa could have obtained more funds and could have invested more; it is necessary to invest to be successful. Doug Ellis' business philosophy was "Generate income before you spend it"; it is true that borrowing, particularly in a declining market, can be risky, but the market was growing, not declining.

In 1997, Villa, together with a number of other clubs, raised new equity funds on the stock market. This, from the club's point of view, was a sensible move. Football club shares were popular, in fact there was a stock market 'bubble', particularly in football club shares. The club issued new shares which they sold to raise money for the club, and, as is usual on an initial public offer, the directors sold some of the shares they owned to raise money for themselves. This is known as an 'exit route' and it enables the directors, who have through their past efforts helped build up the company, to cash in some of their investments. Aston Villa raised £15.2 million of new money from the new issue. Some of the shares had been sold to selected investors (a placing), with other shares offered to the public. At the time the club had its shares listed on the market, the capitalised value of the club was in the region of £83 million.

But the stock market soon became disillusioned with football club shares (the bubble burst), and by the end of 1997 the price of Villa shares had fallen from their peak by 34.8%. (The FTSE index had risen by 11.3% over this period). The directors witnessed a considerable decline in the value of the shares they had retained, but had made handsome gains on the shares that they sold. Ellis had bought a 47% stake in the club in 1982, and sold 14% of the club's shares at this time of the 1997 flotation.[6] He obtained £11 million from the sale of a part of his holding. Whilst the share price was still high, his remaining holding of shares was worth about £30 million, but the value dropped to approximately £3 million in 2000. This (with the £11 million already realised) still showed a good return on an investment estimated to have been less than £0.45 million. Ellis, in his autobiography, points out that not only he benefited from the 1997 public listing, others to benefit were those supporters and other directors who had bought shares in an earlier issue.

Ellis had doubts about floating the Villa shares on the market, because he was concerned about "the treadmill that one could get onto whereby the banks, investment houses, brokers, whatever are telling you how to run the club". He was persuaded, however, because Villa needed money for stadium improvements and to be able to give Brian Little further support in the transfer market.

When he was criticised by fans for the club's lack of success on the pitch his reply was that although the fans might be his customers "my duty is to look after shareholders interests". He was the major shareholder.

On the pitch the club were having only mixed success. After finishing second in 1992/93 they finished in 18th position (out of 20) in 1995 – only avoiding relegation by one place. The manager from July 1991 to November 1994 was the popular Ron Atkinson, who was sacked despite the fact that the team won the League Cup in 1994.

Ron Atkinson found Ellis very difficult to work with – not a person with whom he found easy to have a close relationship. Atkinson states that from day one of his management of Aston Villa, he and Ellis were "destined not to get on with each other". Atkinson was very critical. He writes that Ellis was "a classic case of a man full of his own importance. The people he claimed as friends always looked like toadies to me".[7]

Atkinson believes that he would have remained as Villa manager for much longer if he had been less forceful. To work with Ellis for a longer period meant he would have to be subservient, to bow and scrape to placate his huge ego, to be a yes man. Atkinson admits that "in reality, apart from the odd inevitable collision" he did not have too much conflict with Ellis. This was for the simple reason that Atkinson did not seek it. The problem for Atkinson was that Ellis "wished to be involved with team selection and tactics".

It is fairly obvious why the two men did not get on. Both had large 'egos', both liked to do things their own way. Atkinson is an extrovert who enjoys public attention. Ellis refers to Atkinson as "just a big boy at heart". Ellis did, however, speak well of Atkinson's role in the 1993-94 Coca Cola Cup final win over Manchester United. "His personality, experience and self-confidence were of great benefit to the team in terms of leadership".[8]

Ellis came to the conclusion in the summer of 1994 that there was no way that Ron Atkinson and he would ever forge a constructive working relationship in moving the club forward. Ellis believed the opportunity was there for the club to move forward. The club was in a European competition and "financial stability was there in terms of resources, available for the right kind of signings". Ellis complains that Atkinson "desired no manager-chairman relationship whatsoever if he could avoid it". This communication issue was obviously a key factor in the breakdown of the working relationship. Both write passionately about it in their autobiographies. The team performed badly in the early months of the 1994 season. Atkinson was removed, and replaced by Brian Little.

Ellis got on well with Little and is reported to have said that Little would remain as manager of the club as long as he, Ellis, was chairman. During Little's term as manager the club won the League Cup in 1996 but, then to Ellis' surprise Little resigned in February 1998. John Gregory was appointed as the next manager, and remained at the club for four years. The club did not win anything during this period, but Gregory did attract a lot of attention, not for the right reasons. The club found themselves in problems over the use of agents.

In the final chapter of this book certain current problems in the game will be discussed, one is the use of agents. Doug Ellis has said that he had never trusted the football agents but that he was, over his thirty years in the game, forced to deal with them. In 1993 Villa bought Mark Bosnich, an Australian, who found it necessary, in order to play in England, to marry an English woman to obtain citizenship. It was Bosnich's agent, Graham Smith, who suggested this strategy. Ellis knew it was wrong but went along with the proposal and the purchase of the player. Smith was paid £150,000 for his involvement, but denied this was an agent's fee, preferring to call it a consultancy fee. When the details became known, Aston Villa were fined £20,000 for irregular dealings with an agent. Ellis claims he "only broke the rules slightly".

Ellis' problems with agents became much greater when John Gregory became manager. One thing that Gregory was proud of during his early days at the club was the fact that all of the players in his Villa team were British. Most Premier League teams had acquired a number of foreign players. After a number of months the fortunes of the team changed, and Gregory suggested to Ellis that, to overcome the problems, the club "should buy some foreign players". This led to Aston Villa becoming involved in dealing with British and foreign agents and led to further transfer scandals. These problems will be returned to at the end of this chapter.

The 2000s

The departure of Gregory was not the end of managerial problems at the club. Graham Taylor was appointed in February 2002 to be the next manager, but this was seen by many as a move which was not taking the club forward. Taylor had been Villa's manager from 1987 to 1990, he then left to become England manager. His term as England manager was not particularly successful. He was cruelly treated by the press.

It is generally agreed that Taylor was a good person, a good manager, but he did leave himself open to press criticism. In 1997 after leaving his post as manager of Watford, where he had some success, one of the papers ran the headline "He will not work in this country again". In 2001 Taylor did say that he had retired from football club management. He said at the time "I will not become manager again. Not even for a week. I cannot be any clearer". He did come back, he first became a director of Aston Villa, and then when the manager post became vacant Ellis persuaded him to take on the job.[9]

Taylor and the Villa Board announced that their approach for the first decade of the 21st century was to bring forward many of the players from the excellent youth team the club had developed. In 2001/02 the club were winners of the FA Youth Cup, and a number of the winning team soon played in the Premier League. After their experience with Gregory, the club were understandably wary about purchasing expensive foreign players.

In May 2003 Graham Taylor resigned as manager. The season 2002/03 had been a disaster for the Villa, not only were they towards the end of the season in danger of being relegated from the Premiership, but they lost twice during the season to Birmingham City. Taylor was not popular with the fans, and was booed at the last match of the season. It appears that he had also lost the support of Doug Ellis.

At the time of his resignation, Taylor made clear he was leaving not because of the club's bad results, but that "modern football, with its well-publicised financial pressures, involved much wider issues than mere playing matters, and those are a major factor in my decision." He clearly resigned over a disagreement with the Board over the financial strategy of the club.

Taylor as a manager had a plan. He wished to bring along the talented youngsters at the club, but knew that in order to succeed you needed to combine them with experienced players. The Villa board were reluctant to spend much money on such players. They had had a bad experience with Gregory's purchases.

Ellis expressed sadness at Taylor's resignation. The general feeling was that Taylor was a good, honest man but he had taken on an impossible task; he had inherited a group of "over paid, under achieving players". Because of the collapse of prices in the transfer market he was unable to sell at a "reasonable" price. As with other Villa managers he had found it difficult to work with the board of directors and their attitude towards finance.

Taylor had said from the beginning of his second period as manager of the club that his plans would take time. He had said that in football it is not possible to change things overnight, that changing a structure takes time. His lack of success in the short term meant that he was not given that time. When he resigned he did not publicly criticise any individuals but made the point that the structure of the club needed to be looked at, that radical change was necessary, and that if you get things right at the top "there is a good chance it flows down".

David O'Leary in May 2003 became the next Villa manager, having been the manager of Leeds United from 1998 to 2002. Whilst at Leeds he had kept the club near the top of the

Premiership but had spent more than £90 million on buying players and had written a controversial book about the players at the club. O'Leary did not achieve success for Aston Villa.

There was pressure on Doug Ellis to remove yet another manager. By 2005 O'Leary was complaining about the lack of finance that had been made available to him to buy new players, but the fans were not impressed. He had purchased a number of biggish name international players, but they had performed badly – international mercenaries. O'Leary had referred in April 2005 to the club needing to act big. He believed that big name targets would have a positive impact at the club. They did not. The manager said that there were excellent players coming through the youth academy programme, but for how long could the club wait? David O'Leary's contract as manager lasted until 2008, the chairman seemed reluctant to sack yet another manager and to pay yet more expensive compensation.

O'Leary had not made himself popular, he at first complained about the quality of the players he inherited, but in the 2005/06 season he had to admit the squad who were playing badly were the players he had chosen. He had bought together a squad of experienced internationals. He also had a number of good young players who had come through the club's youth programme. The fact that they did not play well together was the manager's fault. O'Leary blamed a chronic injury list but also blamed poor refereeing. He criticised the local media for being negative – but what did he expect after poor performances? He fell out with one of the local papers. He was running out of excuses. The club clearly had governance problems. Ellis continued to dominate. In 2005, the Chief Executive, Bruce Langham and the commercial manager Abdul Rashid left the club. Langham resigned after serious disagreements with the chairman over club policy.

In the 2005 close season the club told its shareholders at the AGM that it had spent £15 million for six new players. This was true but it had received £5 million from the sale of two key players. The club was able to obtain two new 'first team' players on loan.

This was a solid investment by the Board, not great, but it should have been enough. The fans were therefore disappointed to see such a poor 2005/06 season, which included a 3-0 defeat to Doncaster Rovers (from the third tier).

Club for Sale

In the early 2000s it became known that Ellis was willing to sell the club. He was over 80 years old, his health was not good, and the club was stagnating. There were a number of interested parties. One investor who appeared on the scene was Jack Petchy, through his company Treffick. At the end of July 2004, Petchy held 19% of the club's shares. This made him the second biggest shareholder in the club. Petchy was wealthy, being ranked 19th in the 2004 Football Rich List. He started life as a cabby and then became an investor in a number of different industries including football. He had, in the past, been a director of West Ham and of Watford and in 2004 played a key part in the financial restructuring of Leeds United. He lent Leeds £10 million to help them overcome a liquidity crisis, but he charged a high rate of interest and set the club a deadline as to when he was to be repaid. He was a football man but a market raider. Not exactly what Villa needed.

A number of offers were being received for the club. One approach in 2004 was from "Messrs Ranson and Thompson". It was the unanimous view of the directors, having taken advice from the club's advisors, that this approach significantly undervalued the company. The initial Ranson consortium offer was a bid of £33 million, this was rejected. It was a year later when they came back. Ellis had indicated that he believed the club to be worth in excess of £60 million. The second Ranson bid of £47 million was therefore in the eyes of the major shareholder still undervaluing the club. At the end of 2005 the stock market valued the club at about £55 million; this price had risen on expectations of a takeover bid. It was said that the Ranson bid got nowhere because Ellis did not in the end want to sell, and to stop working – despite a triple heart bypass operation and cancer.

In October 2005 it was reported that two Irish property owners, the Comer brothers, and a front man Michael Neville (a lifelong Villa fan) were attempting to put funds in place for a bid for the club. There were rumours that the bid would be worth £64 million. In Jan 2006 Neville said that he was "optimistic of clinching this transaction". But many months later still nothing had happened. There were those who blamed the Comers, but some blamed Ellis for the lack of progress.

By July 2006 even the players were becoming frustrated, they criticised publicly the financial policy of the club. The first team squad issued a statement expressing concern with the lack of investment, and the cost cutting policies of the directors. Ellis had announced in October 2005 that the club was available for sale. The manager was told that he must sell in order to buy. The statement that was issued was "unattributed" to individual players. It said that if the club wished to be a big club, the chairman needed to start doing something about it. The players said that they were doing all they could, but that leadership needed to start coming from the top. This was a time when other big clubs were being purchased by wealthy foreign investors.

There was a suggestion that the manager had been involved with the players in the release of the statement. O'Leary denied this. The Villa directors launched an investigation following which the club announced that the manager's contract had been terminated by mutual agreement. This was the termination of Ellis' twelfth manager's contract. The club were not able to prove that O'Leary had been involved in the 'revolt' and so had to pay him compensation for the early termination of his contract. The exact amount O'Leary received was not announced, it was reported by some as being £0.5 million and by others as being £2 million. Not bad, following his removal from Leeds United four years earlier, with over £3.8 million compensation.

Doug Ellis was devoted to the club but was not popular with fans. In fact he did Villa one final big favour by rejecting an offer from one potential purchaser, George Gillett, a US investor.

Gillett and his partner Hicks failed to convince Ellis that they would be suitable owners. Gillett and his partner went on to take over Liverpool. They were financial wheeler dealers who specialised in buying businesses with the help of large amounts of borrowed money.[10] The cash flow to be generated from the business acquired would be used to repay the loan and the owners would then sell out at a profit. This is called financial leverage. They were not successful as owners of Liverpool. The financial markets collapsed in 2008 not giving them the financial gains expected and their team were not successful on the pitch.

Gillett had been seeking to purchase a top club for some time. He said that he was looking for a club that had a strong fan base, Villa were an obvious target. An independent valuation of Aston Villa at the time was £115 million but as Ellis later said as he thought he was on his death bed, he reduced the asking price by £20 million. Gillett and Hicks were willing to pay the £85 million but Ellis was not willing to accept. He believed that with a community club such as the Villa the owners should have a local interest and the second reason he gave for rejecting the offer, was that he did not believe in borrowing. He did not believe that borrowing large sums was the way a football club should be run. When Gillett and Hicks had purchased Liverpool they made promises that they would not keep; their objective was short term financial gain. Ellis saved the club from these cowboy capitalists. He did go on to sell to an American, one that did not have local links but one that did not need to borrow.

Whilst there was much talk of takeover, the club continued to fight on in the Premier League. After many years in which the club underperformed the supporters at the beginning of the 2006/07 season had at last something to look forward to. They had a new manager at the club, the much respected Martin O'Neill, who was being heralded as the new Brian Clough. The club had had new managers before, many times but this time there was an additional factor that raised expectations. It was believed that the chairman and major shareholder, Doug Ellis, would be leaving. At last there might be real changes.

In October 2006 Randy Lerner bought the equity of Aston Villa for £62.6 million, but some Villa fans were worried. Lerner had owned Cleveland Browns for seven years and in that time the club had achieved nothing. In the seven years they had never won the division of the NFL in which they played and in two of the years they finished bottom. Another worry was that Lerner was bringing Americans onto the board of Aston Villa who had no knowledge about soccer.

The Lerner Era

When Lerner purchased Villa in 2006 there was relief that at last Ellis had gone, He was hailed as one of the new breed of rich foreign owners. Lerner began by supporting the manager, pleasing the fans and acknowledging the heritage of the club (renovating The Holte Hotel). It was thought there was now a chance that Villa would catch up with the likes of Liverpool. He was seen as a "benign" purchaser, he was educated, cultured and it was known how he had obtained his money and where it was coming from. He was not buying the club for personal glory or for political reasons, he seemed genuinely interested. He was not burdening the club with debt in order to finance the acquisition. The future looked promising. The days of Deadly Doug were over. *The Daily Mail* described Lerner as 'the right sort of American', (presumably to distinguish him from the Americans interested in Manchester United and Liverpool.) Unfortunately it is not always the good who win. The club had one of the best managers in the country and were knocking on the door of entry to the lucrative European competitions.

Randy Lerner was a wealthy businessman. When he took over the club he was said to be worth in excess of £1 billion. He had inherited the money from his father, Al Lerner. The father after a number of years' service in the US Marines and then a period selling furniture, (where he was paid $75 a week) set about building up the family fortune. Under his leadership, MBNA, became the second biggest credit card business in the USA. It was the father who purchased the franchise rights to the Cleveland Browns. When the father died Randy inherited the shares in MBNA and became the bank chairman. Four years later he sold the company. He took over the control of the Browns. He sold the club ten years later. When he purchased Villa in 2006 he had little experience of running a successful sports business. The people he brought in with him to be directors of the Villa were all known to him and were close to him. Perhaps he needed a more critical input. They were certainly not knowledgeable about soccer.

One of the directors had been successful on the battlefield, one in sports marketing and one in finance: they had no experience of what was needed to run a successful football club. They did not appear to appreciate that financial success for a club would follow from success on the pitch. They made some poor appointments. Villa's lack of success soon led to an emphasis on cost cutting, and searching for bargain buys and commercial deals. The result has been a disaster in football terms and also a financial disaster.

The total investment by Lerner over his time at the club was in excess of £300 million. He sold it for £65 million. Poor leadership led to strange managerial appointments, to inefficiency and an unfathomable transfer policy. Before looking in more detail at these mistakes, it is worth pointing to the changes in the personal circumstances of Randy Lerner during the period of his ownership of the club and to the change in his attitude. After purchasing the club his personal situation did change. He experienced an expensive divorce and the collapse of share prices on the New York Stock Exchange in 2008 affected the value of his shareholdings. He appeared less and less at Villa Park. Even Doug Ellis said that it was sad he did not give more of his time to come and see the club play.

Managers

Martin O'Neill was manager when Lerner took over the club. He was very well respected, he remained at Villa for four years (2006-2010), and the club were reasonably successful. The performance of the team on the pitch was one that would have been expected based on the level of expenditure, but unfortunately O'Neill could not lead the club into the lucrative European competitions. Lerner wished to cut back on expenditure and the manager was frustrated that he was not being allowed to spend the money that the club received from the sale of players. He believed that the club needed to spend just to stand still. The manager and owner fell out. O'Neill resigned. In September 2010 he was replaced by Gerard Houllier a respected manager who had had a successful record at other clubs. Unfortunately after nine months he had to resign following health problems. From then on the club began to fail. The club appointed 4 managers in the next 4 years. A mistake – the club finished in 16th place in 2012, in 15th place the following season, and then in 2014 and 2015 finishing in 17th place. Finally in 2015/16 they finished in 20th place with the worst record ever in Premier League history.

Lerner with his executive team swapped managers frequently. Houllier lasted 33 games, McLeish 38, Lambert 101, Sherwood 23, Garde 20. However good or bad these managers were, they were not being given much time to show what they could achieve. If the managers were so obviously poor, the question arises; why had the directors appointed them in the first place?

In 2011 following Houllier came Alex McLeish. This appointment shocked the fans. He had been manager of the Blues and had been in charge when they were relegated at the end of the 2010/11 season. Only five days after leaving the Blues, Lerner appointed McLeish as the Villa manager. He was dismissed within a year, the club having won only seven out of 38 games over that time. McLeish argued that if you do not have the players at a club you will not succeed. The owner had said that he wanted the wage bill to be cut whilst remaining competitive. The next manager was Paul Lambert who had the reputation of being a quiet, reserved person. Lerner initially backed him but shortly after giving him a new three and a half year contract he was dismissed. This dismissal was expensive in terms of compensation. Lambert also argued that new, quality players were needed. The most expensive signing he made was Christian Benteke for £7 million. Lambert had to rely on young inexperienced players or well-known players past their best. He did not succeed. Lambert believed that there was something fundamentally wrong with the club. The chief executive Paul Faulkner had also become frustrated and left the club.

A new CEO, Tom Fox, was appointed. He soon dismissed Lambert and appointed Tim Sherwood to replace him. This appeared to be an interesting appointment. He was confident, full of ideas and had a reputation for being outspoken. He did lead Villa to the FA Cup final in 2015. But he often disagreed with the other members of the executive team on questions such as which players should be purchased. He was only at the club for 9 months when he was sacked. The club were at the bottom of the league.

The final appointment, in November 2015, as manager in the Lerner era was Remi Garde. He had no experience of football in England. He had had some success as a manager in France. Lerner thought highly of him and said: "Remi arrived with honesty, humour and a steely sense of what it will take for Aston Villa to be what it is meant to be – hard-working, tireless, and creative and unwilling to concede".

Unfortunately Garde only lasted 147 days. The club won only two of the 20 games with him in charge. He was not given a real chance, the club were already planning for relegation at the time he was trying to achieve results. Not one player was signed in the January 2016 transfer window. Garde was dismissed in March 2016.

Changing Managers – The Effect

Both Doug Ellis and Randy Lerner had a reputation for quickly removing managers, either because of a few bad results or because of disagreements. There has been a great deal of research on the subject of football managers and their impact on the performance of a team.[11] The results show that in general their impact on a club's performance can only be accurately assessed over the medium to long term. But with the present financial reward system in the game many owners are not prepared to wait for the medium term to give managers a chance to prove themselves. There is a myth in football that changing the manager of a poorly performing club will lead to improved results. There is some anecdotal evidence to support this belief – for example the appointment of Harry Redknapp at the Blues in the 2016/17 season and Sam Allardyce at Everton late in 2017. But there are also cases where the outcome has been the opposite – for example Frank de Boer, in 2017, who was only given 5 matches in charge at Crystal Palace to show what he could achieve. Many owners believe, or perhaps more accurately hope, that changing managers will save them.

Some managers are just victims of misfortune, they are sacked not because they are doing badly, but just because of a change in owner. An example of this was Allardyce being sacked by Blackburn. A new owner, who knew nothing about football, advised by an agent who had his own agenda, decided that they could make changes that would be for the good of the club. They were not.

It appears more and more that the owners of the clubs, the people they pay to advise them, and many of the so called experts are not that good at identifying who will be a good manager for a club. It appears to be very much a hit and miss process. In fact the results of a series of matches over a short period of time can be a matter of chance. Some managers who the experts think will succeed in fact fail and some who they believe will fail do succeed. Football is in the short run more influenced by chance than the experts are prepared to admit. Perhaps football is less scientific than the football analysts would lead us and the club owners to believe.

Some clubs more than others seem to believe that a change in managers will bring about a change in fortune. Sunderland who in ten years moved from the first tier of English football to the third tier, had ten managers over this period. QPR had fourteen managers over a ten year period. Swansea had six managers in a two year period. All these clubs had at some time in their recent history had foreign owners. Watford following the Pozzo family acquisition of the club had ten managers in six years. The sacking of managers after only a short period in charge could be seen as evidence of poor recruitment and a damning indictment of the owners.

It is not only at the unsuccessful clubs where there is a frequent change of managers. It is becoming more common for successful clubs also to have a high turnover of managers/coaches. Chelsea are an example of such a club. They have removed more than one manager in the season following success. During the 2017/18 there was continuing speculation as to whether the "elite" manager/coach Antonio Conte would leave the club. Some owners appear to believe that uncertainty is good, that continual change is good. Some owners have different ambitions to their managers. Conte said that those running Chelsea needed to show more ambition. He said that he had "great" ambition but that he was not given the money he needed by the club. He had complained about the club's perceived ability to compete at the top end of the transfer market. Chelsea's net transfer expenditure in the 2017/18 season was £68 million, whereas that of Manchester City was £192 million and that of Manchester United £127 million. If life is tough for the managers and coaches of Roman Abramovich's club, what is it like for everyone else?

The situation is getting worse. In the 2017/18 season, nine of the Premier League clubs changed managers during the season. Three of these nine at the end of the season dismissed the manager they had appointed only a few months earlier. In addition, at the end of the season, at least two other clubs were thinking about changing managers. Arsenal did so, Chelsea were not sure. This meant that the owners of over half the clubs in the League were at some stage in the season dissatisfied with the person they had appointed as manager.

Sir Alex Ferguson has made the comment that the behaviour of many owners has become "silly" because "there is no evidence that the frequent sacking of a manager leads to better results".[12] What the statistical evidence shows is that on average a club's results do not improve following the change of manager. Starting from any date, the performance of some clubs will get better in the immediate future, but for other clubs it will get worse. This is what one would expect to happen whether or not there is a change in manager. "The idea that sacking managers is a panacea for a team's ills is a placebo. It is an expensive illusion". This was the conclusion of Anderson and Sally following an analysis of all the available evidence.[13] Nevertheless, at the first sign of trouble new managers are appointed, hopefully to turn things around?

There are at least three reasons why we should not be surprised at this finding. One is money, the second is time and the third is the random nature of a football match. As mentioned in the Introduction the key factor leading to the success or failure of a club is money. Somewhere between 80% and 90% of the final league position of a club can be explained by the size of its wage bill. The manager, the coach, is not a super hero, if he has not got the right players he cannot consistently deliver good results. Sacking a manager when the club is having a run of poor results might indicate to the fans that the owner is trying to put things right. Sometimes it might work, sometimes not – money would help.

A second reason why a change of manager should not be expected to automatically lead to improved results is that managers need time. Some managers are better than others but even a good manager needs time – perhaps some more than others. Mourinho said that he believed it takes three years to put a football club that has been in difficult times back on track. He believes that it takes that long to re-build a club, to have an influence on the team on the pitch and to develop a good management team behind the scenes. He believes that that was the situation at Manchester United in the troubled years following the departure of Alex Ferguson. It was also the situation when Ferguson arrived at United. Changing a behind the scene management team can be very difficult, especially now with so many "executives" at a club.

There are however a small number of managers who have a reputation for being able to quickly improve a team's performance. They have developed a reputation of being able to move into a troubled club and quickly improve the performance of the team. They are thought to be able to improve the morale at the club, to revitalise it, to reinvigorate it. They may need to change the style of play of the team. They are not going to turn the club into one of the elite, but possibly they are able to save the club from relegation. With relegation from the Premier League now meaning a loss in annual revenue of a £100 million or so, owners are willing to give them a chance and as mentioned above and in the Introduction to the book there are a number of managers with this reputation. There is a certain irony in the way that some managers are treated. Mark Hughes was sacked by Stoke in January 2018. Those running the club believed that a change in management might save them from relegation. They appointed Paul Lambert. He did not save them, the club only won two matches of the 15 played under his leadership and he was sacked at the end of the season. Meanwhile Mark Hughes who was seen as a failure at Stoke was appointed as manager of Southampton. That club was also in danger of relegation. Under his leadership Southampton avoided relegation. Hughes was of course well rewarded.

Sam Allardyce, from Dudley in the West Midlands, has had management experience at more than 10 clubs. At Newcastle in the 10 games before he became manager the club had only earned 7 points, in the 10 games after his appointment they earned 17 points. At Blackburn it was 3 points in 10 games before Sam and 14 in the 10 games after. But managers such as Big Sam have their failures as well as their successes.[14] He succeeded at Bolton and QPR, but was sacked at Blackburn and Newcastle He had success at West Ham, but had problems with some of the club's fans, the owners did not renew his contract. For a short time in 2016 he was the England manager, but had to resign following tales concerning corruption.

In 2017/18 Allardyce was manager of Everton, and the club finished in 8th place in the Premier League. But the owners and fans were not satisfied. Sam Allardyce's contract was not renewed at the end of the season. He was replaced by the former manager of Watford whose team had finished six places below Everton in the 2017/18 season. An odd world.

David Moyes had been a success at Everton but then had problems at Manchester United, Real Sociedad and Sunderland. Moyes was appointed as West Ham manager in November 2017 at a time when the club were in the relegation zone. They finished the season in 13th place in the League, which might have been thought of as an achievement. There were in fact many things wrong with West Ham but it was only the manager who was sacked. He was replaced by Manuel Pellegrini, who had in 2013 been appointed as manager at Manchester City. Pellegrini's contract at that club expired in 2016 and the directors of the club decided not to renew it, despite the fact that the club had been Premier League champions and had won the League Cup whilst he was in charge. So much for the merry-go-round.

A further reason, the third, why it is hard to know what the impact of a new manager will be is that football is sometimes a random game, a 50/50 game. The results of a match can many times depend upon luck. Anderson and Sally point out that football fans find it hard to accept this statistical finding. Fans prefer to believe that results depend upon something explicable, such as skill and tactics.[15] But the result of an individual game can depend on luck, good luck for the one team, bad luck for the other. It could be that a deflected shot wins a game or a bad refereeing decision gives one team the game. It is a fact that 30% of all games end with either no goal being scored or with just one goal. The one crucial goal can be attributable to good fortune.

This means that on the day a weaker team can beat a stronger team. One such match took place in November 2010 when Chelsea managed to lose a match against Birmingham City, by a score 0-1. On that day Chelsea had 25 shots on goal and Birmingham had only one. It was the one Birmingham shot that resulted in a goal. This was of course only one game. At the end of the season Chelsea finished in second place and Birmingham finished in 18th place and were relegated from the Premier

League. Of course we do know that over time the better team, the team with the more skilful players will finish higher than the weaker team. Luck balances out over time. But a new manager might not be given time for the luck to balance out.

Clearly some players are better than others and they are financially rewarded for their skills. Clearly some managers are better than others and they are also now financially well rewarded for their abilities. There are good managers and exceptionally good managers. It is said that only one in five managers can over time continue to deliver an above average performance.[16] None of the ten highest paid managers in the Premier League in 2017 were British. But paying managers high salaries does not guarantee success. In the early months of 2017/18 season the Everton manager, Ronald Koeman was sacked, he had been earning £6 million per annum. At about the same time the highly paid foreign managers of Leicester City and WHU were also dismissed. As with players, money is necessary to obtain the services of the best managers, but it is not sufficient to achieve success.

What are the qualities required of a good manager? Alex Ferguson has written a book on leadership. He does point out that a manager needs time to prove himself. He was given this in his early days in United when he was not particularly successful. He needed three years before the club obtained its first trophy under his leadership. The average tenure of a Premier League manager is now less than one and a half years (in 1992 it was 3 years).

Ferguson emphasises that success depends on a good working relationship with the owner of the club. He believes there are four things that a manager wants from an owner, no meddling, money to buy players when needed, support and fair compensation. Ferguson was lucky, he was given the support he felt he needed by Martin Edwards and later by the Glazers. He emphasises that despite the bad reputation of the Glazers he found them to be good owners. It is doubtful if he would have been given the support he needed, particularly the lack of meddling, by the Villa owners. He believes that there were, and still are plenty of inept owners of clubs in the country, and does refer to Birmingham City as one such club.

Most of the leading managers in the Premier League are at present, not British. The last English manager to win the top league in England was in 1992 with Howard Wilkinson. Ferguson is keen to point out that Scottish managers have had success in England with Kenny Dalglish and Ferguson himself leading clubs to the top of the Premier League. He points out that there have also been a number of other successful managers from Scotland in English football and that many of them were raised in the Glasgow area. When asked what qualities these Glaswegians had in common the reply was "dower grit, stubbornness and determination".[17]

From 1974 to 1982 Ron Saunders was the Villa manager; nearly 8 years, a very long time. He had the characteristics of someone from Glasgow. The club were reasonably successful. But then over the next 35 years they had 18 different managers, these were the years of Ellis and Lerner. Only six of these managers were at the club for more than three years, with only one, Martin O'Neill, for more than four years. Jose Mourinho would not think the managers were being given a chance to turn the club around.

Managers are sacked when the results are poor, but it is not always the manager's fault, particularly now when a collegiate approach is adopted to decision making. There are now only a few autocratic managers, most have to work with directors of this and directors of that. It is the chairman and the board who appoint the managers and his advisers. It is they who are continuing to make the mistakes and yet they are not being removed. Harry Redknapp has expressed the view that it is whoever is in charge of recruitment at the clubs that should lose their jobs and not the manager. It is however, an easy step for directors to take to change managers.

At the first sign of trouble new managers are appointed, hopefully to turn things around. Often the new appointments are the old familiar faces, moving from one job to another. As one leading sports journalist explained it is the case of "the same old managers, the same ideas circulating from club to club". Matthew Syed was referring to

British managers, he believes that the game in England would "benefit from the flow of ideas from overseas with footloose coaches travelling here with fresh thinking". (*The Times* – 13 Sept, 2017) Some less kind journalists have referred to the merry-go-round that is taking place as an exercise in recycling managers.

The Directors and Executives

Lerner was being advised in the decision making process by directors, executives and senior backroom staff. It is now accepted that one reason for the demise in Villa was because there was not enough knowledge amongst this group about the running of a football team. They made bad managerial appointments and their policy with regard to the purchase and sale of players was a disaster. Who were the directors of the club?

Randy Lerner, when his father died in 2002, inherited the shares of a large banking business, MBNA and he became the chairman of the bank. At the time of purchasing the Villa he had little experience of running a business. His own background had been in law and investment. His first mistake was not to appoint people who had knowledge of soccer as directors. Certain appointments were bizarre. One director was General Charles Krulak, a distinguished US general who had fought in Vietnam and who has commanded a group of US marines who had fought in Iraq. He was a proven leader of men, but not of footballers. The advice he offered to the Villa players at the end of 2015 when they had failed to win a match for three months and were bottom of the Premier League was that they should "summon the spirit of the US Marines". He obviously believed that such spirit could lead to victory on a football pitch. In Iraq his company were in trenches, with massive artillery fire raining down on them and they were in the middle of mine fields. The troops survived. The Villa players did not survive, the club were relegated. Krulak remained as a director of the club through the Lerner years.

Lerner brought three other US directors to the club. One was Michael Martin, who was only a director for two years, he like

Krulak was a personal friend of Lerner: he was President of an Asset and Investment company that looked after the Lerner family's wealth. Another of the new directors was Robert Kain. He did know something about sport having been a CEO of a sports and lifestyle marketing firm. He also only remained for two years.

Two key members of the executive team that Lerner brought into the club were Robin Russell and Paul Faulkner. Neither at the time of their appointments at Villa were football men. Russell had been on Lerner's payroll for twenty years. He was made company secretary of Villa in May 2007 and became chief financial officer of the club in 2010. Faulkner's background was in banking where he had worked for Lerner at MBNA as the relationships manager and chairman. At the Villa he became chief executive officer in 2010. Faulkner became unhappy with the way the club was being run, he saw the need for new players. He resigned in July 2014. He and Lerner parted on good terms. He became CEO of Nottingham Forest, but resigned after a few months. He was not happy with the way the Kuwaiti owner of that club sacked the manager, Stuart Pearce. Paul Faulkner was well respected in the Birmingham community and became chief executive of the local Chamber of Commerce.

As well as appointing football managers, the directors needed to be involved in making appointments at executive level. It is now out of favour to have an autocratic manager. Clubs have executive teams with titles such as "Director of Football", "Head of Scouting", "Head of Analytics" and "Technical Director". The role of the team manager has changed, there are few with the power and authority of those of a few years ago. A collegiate approach to buying and selling players is fashionable with transfer policy dictated by collective wisdom.

With Villa's performance on and off the pitch on the decline changes needed to be made. Paul Faulkner was replaced by Alan Fox, who came to the club from Arsenal where he was highly regarded having pulled off a number of big business deals. But he had not been in a position where he hired and fired managers.

Amongst his early tasks at Villa was to fire Lambert which he is reported to have done by email. Lambert had been manager for 2 years 8 months, a long time by Villa standards. During this time the team has been winning in the region of 30% of their matches, more successful than McLeish (with 21% of games as wins) but way behind O'Neill (with 42% wins).

Fox was not a football man. He had been in the sports marketing industry for over 25 years before becoming commercial director at Arsenal. In a BBC radio interview he agreed the results of the Villa on the pitch had not been good whilst he was in charge but pointed to the successes on the commercial side. He pointed out that he had succeeded in obtaining a good shirt and kit sponsorship deal and he was keeping down costs. He regarded this as making progress. His commercial successes could not, however, compensate for the loss of over £50 million per annum of TV income following relegation.

Fox was keen to distance himself from the past. Soon after he was appointed he pointed out that his new management team would have a difficult job undoing what had gone wrong in the previous five or six years. He agreed that in recent years the club had failed in its recruitment policy and had failed to integrate the players being purchased. It is not really surprising with 27 new players being signed during Lambert's years in charge.

The first manager appointed by Fox was Tim Sherwood, but he only lasted for 9 months being replaced by a strange appointment Remi Garde. The club had spent £55 million during Sherwood's brief period in charge, but they did receive £40 million from the sale of players. Sherwood was keen to point out that many of the new players acquired were not of his choosing, they were chosen by the new team of 'Technical Analysts' at the club. Fox was proud that the club were using the new approach, technical analysis, to decide which players to buy and which to sell, but so were all the other clubs. More and more data was being collected in an attempt to be more successful in the transfer market. But the analysis of data is no guarantee of success in a sport. Sherwood's view was that nobody at the club seemed to take responsibility for what was happening. Ten players were purchased in the summer of 2015 and their performance ranged from average to poor. One example of such a player was Adama Traoré a £7 million signing from Barcelona. He had been successful in Spain in youth football up to the 19 age level. He had pace, he played 12 times for Villa but was in the end dropped from the squad for his lack of discipline. Presumably the analytics did not pick up on this character flaw.

In July 2015 Villa appointed Hendrik Almstadt as "Sports Director". He came to the club from Arsenal, a club that was said to be big supporters of the use of statistical analysis, although it is far from certain that Arsène Wenger was completely taken in by analysis of data. His club did however purchase a sports analysis company in 2012 for over £2 million. The data collected would, in theory, enable the club to identify and value the best recruits. It is reported that the club bought the company on the recommendation of Fox who was at the time the club's commercial director. It is said that Fox was viewed with some suspicion by the 'old school' members of the coaching and scouting staff at Arsenal, and that they were not disappointed when he left the club in 2016 to move to the Villa.

Villa made another interesting appointment in November 2014. Paddy Reilly became head of scouting and player recruitment. It was hoped that he would bring about better value for money signings. He had links with the Villa going back a number of years, having left the club following O'Neill's departure to become scouting co-ordinator at Liverpool. Unfortunately the new technical team at Villa did not achieve the desired result. They spent over £55 million on new players in the summer of 2015. The manager Sherwood was said to be not happy with one half of the players recruited. They were said to be mainly Reilly's targets. In the next available window, January 2016, the club spent nothing.

The new back room team had not been successful with their transfer policy. The quartet said to be responsible were Lerner, Fox, Hendrik and Reilly with one hopes the manager. They had access to all the data they thought they needed. With this analytical approach data is collected, on every player that the club might be interested in. Inputs on such factors as the player's heart rate, his number of assists and miles covered in a match, are analysed to decide who is good value for money. This technical approach received a big boost following the success of a weak US baseball team that adopted this approach, the results are discussed in a book called "Moneyball".[18] The problem is that now all the top football clubs are using this approach; when only a few teams used analytics it did give them a comparative advantage. When the US baseball team, the subject of the "Moneyball" book, adopted this approach they were the only team using it, they did have a comparative advantage. Surprisingly the man behind Moneyball, namely Billy Beane, in 2017 was involved in the consortium seeking to take over Barnsley football club.

Football is not a science. Human beings are hard to measure. They are hard to categorise in numbers. Running and jumping abilities can be given a meaningful number but attributes such as a hunger to win, a desire, guts, courage, temper, body language and complacency cannot be easily measured. At best they can be placed on a scale, and given an ordinal number but such numbers cannot be added together. Analytics can employ drones at training sessions, they can interview those with knowledge of a player but combining all the data collected in a meaningful way, cannot be done.

Clubs that are successful claim that analytics has helped them with their acquisitions. Leicester City and other clubs claim it enables them to succeed. The so called Black Box at Southampton is said to be the envy of many a club, with its array of computers, with interactive touch screens giving the club's scouts and analysts access to statistics on players from all over the world. But failed clubs, such as Villa also claim they use analytics, obviously not so successfully, and Southampton have only had limited success.

The Financial Decisions

Randy Lerner was, intentionally or not, an extremely generous benefactor, with only two or three Premier League club owners having invested more of their own money in their clubs. His reign was, however, a story of poor decision making. He put too much faith in the people around him who did not have enough football experience. As explained above one major mistake was with regard to managerial appointments, a second was the transfer strategy and a third was the financial management. One finance expert referred to the club as a circus.[19]

Lerner personally lost in excess of £200 million as a result of buying Villa. The folklore is that during the 2007/8 to 2010/11 seasons the club overspent on player acquisitions. The plan was gambling on breaking into the lucrative European competitions. When O'Neill left the club, having failed to get into Europe, they cut back on expenditure in the transfer market and on wages. The average annual net expenditure on acquisitions between 2006 and 2011 was £18 million, the average annual net expenditure on acquisitions for the five years from 2011 was only £7 million. The club did continue to buy players but the focus seemed to be on quantity rather than quality. The analysts must have been very busy. In Lambert's period they spent £53 million on new players but this was the cost of 26 new players. The recruitment record in the latter years was based on free transfers, loan players and low price deals. Sherwood said "we sold a lot of players and we brought in a lot of money".

If the transfer policy over Villa's later Premier League years was inconsistent and a mess, so was the wage policy. In 2011 the wages were 91% of revenue, the highest rate in the league. No wonder the club was making losses. One way to bring down a high wage ratio is to increase revenue – but the club were not able to do this. They initially cut back on wages. The ratio falling to a manageable 54% in 2014 but increasing to 72% in 2015 (the second highest in the league, only the Albion being higher) and to over 80% in 2016.

What were those running the club doing wrong? In February 2017 a *Financial Times* study to ascertain who were the smartest spenders on wages among the top 69 clubs in Europe over the 2011-2015 period found that of the clubs from England, the Villa were not very smart but not quite the most stupid.[20] They were ranked 63rd out of the 69, in terms of obtaining value for money (Queens Park Rangers were the worst English Club). The study was based on the fact that the best predictor of a team's position in the league is its wage bill. The study calculated the margin by which each of the clubs exceeded (or fell short) of the league position that would have been predicted on the basis solely of its wage bill.

The study concluded that to underperform, to deviate from a ranking based on the size of the wage bill, could be attributed to one or two things. Either bad luck or poor management. In Villa's case bad luck could be ruled out because the under-performance has been going on for such a long time. The size of the wage bill as a predictor of the final league position in a season is not perfect but it can be useful. The change in the wage bill from year to year relative to the change of other clubs should also indicate the direction in which a club is moving. In 2008/09 Villa's wage bill was 7th highest and they finished in 6th place in the Premier League. In 2009/10 wages 6th highest, league position 6th. In other words the club was performing as well on the pitch as would be predicted. Unfortunately the club was losing money, it was not generating enough revenue to support the level of wages it was paying. Andy Lerner and his executive team decided that something would need to change. Surprisingly they hardly cut back in their total wage bill. They changed their transfer policy, with more players coming and going. In 2010/11 their wage bill was 7th highest, they finished in 9th place. In the next season they paid the 7th highest amount of wages, and finished in 12th place in the league. This was followed by 8th highest wages and 15th place, then 9th highest wages and 17th in the League. In 2014/15, 8th highest wages and 17th league place. Finally in 2015/16 the club's wage bill was the 7th highest in the league and they finished in 20th place and were relegated.

Who were the people at the club receiving the wages? The total wage bill in 2013/14 was £71 million, this went up to £84 million in 2014/15. In the year of relegation, 2015/16 the wage bill was even higher; £93 million. This is the total bill for all employees not just the football players. It might come as a surprise to some fans to know that the club employed 535 full time staff during the 2014/15 season (up from 496 the previous season). The number of playing and coaching staff during 2014/15 numbered 185 (up from 173).

It should not be assumed that all the non-footballing staff are modestly paid. The highest paid director in 2014/15 received a £1.25 million salary package, quite an increase from the previous year when the highest paid director received £0.27 million. One can assume that the highest paid director in 2015 was Fox and in 2014 Faulkner. Fox in fact only took up his appointment as a director in November 2014 so the figure mentioned above relates to only 7 months service. In 2015/16 the highest paid director, again presumably Fox, received £2.9 million. Not a bad rate of pay for a person who was only at the club for 19 months and was in charge while the club was on its way to relegation and whose reign at the Villa has been referred to as disastrous. It was said that he would be remembered for his lack of football knowledge.[21] To be fair receiving a large bumper salary as a farewell present has happened before. When Blues were relegated Karren Brady received over £1 million in salary. Carson Young when he discovered what had happened brought a legal case against Brady and the directors of Blues. He lost.

At the Villa, Lerner was having to fund the losses, he was having to fund the high wage levels being paid. The revenue figures of Villa were disappointing. In 2013/14 their annual revenue was £117 million, the following season only £116 million. But even though the level of revenue was not growing the club should have done better with the money they were generating. In 2014/15 they were generating the 10th highest level of revenue in the league but the club were fighting against relegation.

The revenue should have been higher for a second city team. They were not attracting crowds; Southampton had higher match day receipts than Villa. Villa Park is not a big stadium but the club have had difficulty in filling what they do have. The occupancy rate being almost the lowest in the league. In 2007/8 the average attendance was 40,000 in 2014/15, only 34,000. The commercial and sponsorship income for Liverpool in 2014/15 was £116 million by way of a contrast for Villa it was £28 million.

The growth in commercial income was disappointing, especially for a club that believed itself to be a big club. Nevertheless their commercial income figure was the 7th or 8th highest in the league. Their shirt sponsors have not been global brands. In July 2017 they announced a shirt sponsorship deal with 'Unibet', an online gambling operation. Their shirt sponsors for the previous two seasons had been Intuit Quickbooks an accounting software supplier for the small business sector. That deal was worth about £5 million a year. Prior to this they had a similar size deal with Dafabet and before that a £8 million deal with Genting. (The Manchester United deal with Chevrolet is worth about £40 million per annum). The club in 2014/15 employed 261 people working on merchandising and general operations, an increase from 232 the previous year.

Lerner when he acquired the club announced that he hoped to bring in a £100 million sponsorship deal which would provide funds for O'Neill to buy players. It never happened. Instead the club basically had to rely on Lerner's money to fund their lifestyle.

A Little Too Late

By the end of 2015 Lerner had had enough. He had been trying for some time to sell the club. He resigned as chairman of the club expressing the view that perhaps he should have done so earlier. The new chairman was Steve Hollis, a well-respected and well liked member of the local business community. He had said that Birmingham as a city should have more self-belief and that 'Brummies' need to swagger more like Scousers.[21]

His background was in finance and he had a reputation for being able to turn round unsuccessful businesses. He was only appointed in January 2016 so he was in no way responsible for the decisions that had been made in the past at the club. As would be expected he was optimistic about saving the club and said that he had no fear of relegation. He might not have had fear but the fans certainly did. They had seen what had happened to other clubs that thought they were too big to fail, Leeds and Sheffield Wednesday for example.

Lerner should have personally had concerns about failure. Relegation would cost him a lot of money. Clubs in the Premier League were to receive from 2016/17 a large boost in TV income. This would have meant that Villa in that year in the top league would have generated a total revenue of about £150 million. Valuing a Premier League club on the basis of say twice annual revenue (an average valuation ratio) would have meant that the club was worth about £300 million. Lerner sold the club for £76 million. Through poor investment in the transfer market, in one season the owner lost over £200 million.

With Steve Hollis as chairman and with the ex-governor of the Bank of England, Lord Mervyn King appointed as a director the changes being made at the beginning of 2016 seemed to promise a bright future. Lord King had been a serious Villa fan for over 50 years, he cared passionately about the club. As well as these two top financial men other directors were appointed who were knowledgeable football men. Adrian Bevington was brought in as an adviser. He had been an FA executive. Unfortunately he resigned after only 2 months, the club were on the way to relegation and he felt that a huge amount of work lay ahead and that it was crucial that the club "made the right calls on the big decisions". Unfortunately they did not.

Another new member of the top team was David Bernstein. He had been a former FA chairman and had been chairman of Manchester City for five years. He also left after only a few weeks. He had been brought in to review the football side of the club but at the time of resigning, pointed out that "it had proved impossible to implement the agreed structure" and that his own position had become "untenable". "The issues at the club were fundamental and the solutions were radical". He had set up a four man football board but encountered problems with the line of reporting and the acceptance of the lines of authority delegated to the board. This highlighted what had been going wrong at Villa for over 8 years. Lord King also resigned. Apparently King and Bernstein had clashed with Lerner. The two new directors had been in touch with each other by email and Lerner found out that they had been critical of his methods. As a result of Lerner's response the two prestigious directors resigned. A third football man had been appointed as an adviser, namely Brian Little, a respected ex Villa footballer. He was well liked by the fans. He survived the Lerner changes. Randy Lerner had given the impression that things were going to change when he resigned as chairman. He did bring into the club outstanding people but unfortunately the final decision always remained with Lerner. It was not until he sold the club in May 2016 that things could really change.

Doug Ellis had failed the Villa because he made some bad managerial appointments and he was not able to work well with the better managers. He was financially very prudent. He personally did make money out of the club. Randy Lerner failed because he also made disappointing appointments, but he did not manage his wealth wisely and lost money.

The early years of Randy Lerner were good. He invested money in the club, they finished in 6th position in the League for three years in succession but unfortunately they did not break through into the elite group who benefited financially from the European competitions.

In the years just before Ellis sold, little had been spent acquiring new players. The net transfer spending averaged £5 million per season. The net transfer spending in the first four seasons of Lerner's ownership with Martin O'Neill as manager was in the region of £20 million a season. The annual wage bill increased from £22.5 million in 2006/07 to £80 million in 2009/10. Lerner did try to break into the elite group. Unfortunately the club was operating at a loss, which was £2.8 million in 2006/07 increasing to £4 million in 2011/12, and to £81 million in 2015/16. Lerner was supporting the club and underwriting the necessary borrowing.

Lerner never intended to be a sugar daddy and at some point he lost interest in the club. He must have become tired of spending money with little to show for it. With the amount spent on buying the club from Ellis, with the loans he made to the club and with the loans he converted into equity shares he had spent over £300 million on the club. He had been trying to sell it for over two year but failed. In January 2016 he had assured supporters that he would not sell the club until it was back on track. He handed over a search for a buyer to the new chairman Steve Hollis and to the chief executive Fox. The club did not get back on track and he did sell. He sold his interest in the club for £76 million, but he would receive an additional £25 million if the club were promoted back to the Premier League within the next three years.

Lerner had been in charge of the club for nearly 10 years. He was a generous owner but as the person in charge he was ultimately responsible for the flawed decision making. He took bad advice, made some bad appointments and wasted his own money. This of course he is entitled to do but unfortunately he did little for the club. At a time when they should have been joining the elite group of clubs he steered them into the second tier. He did nothing for the reputation of the City of Birmingham, he did nothing for the Villa fans.

The New Era

In May 2016 Villa were purchased by the Recon Group, a Chinese company owned and controlled by Tony Xia. Dr Xia has obtained a doctorate from Harvard University where he studied landscape design. Initially football fans were told that he was the youngest ever person to be a professor at Harvard, his claim was later watered down to one of being the youngest ever assistant to a professor.[22] The supporters were told that he was a very rich man and that he had developed a passion for Villa whilst studying for a few months at Oxford University.

He took over the Recon Group in 2004 and he built it up as an umbrella organisation for his interests. It was initially claimed that his company Recon Group owned five listed companies in China. When this fact was challenged the claim was reduced to the Recon Group owning 75% of one listed company namely the Lotus Health Group. This Health Group had made a loss of £53 million in 2015. The overall profitability of the Recon Group is not known because it is a private company and so does not have to publish its accounts. Xia blamed the media for exaggerating his academic record and for the miscommunication about his business interests.

The Birmingham Post Rich List for 2017 ranked Dr Xia as the 6th richest person with West Midlands interests. He talks big, he communicates with fans by Twitter, and he plans to put Villa amongst the top three clubs in the world within 10 years. This would be quite an achievement.[23] The revenue of Villa in 2016/17 was in the region of £60 million that of Manchester United was £500 million. Much investment would be required to catch up. Xia's plan is to make the Villa the cornerstone of the sports, leisure and tourism part of Recon.

A company Recon Sports was established in the UK to act as the parent company for the Villa. The company at the beginning, that is at the 27th May 2016 had as one of its directors, Tracy Gu. She was a trusted associate of Dr Xia. A Vice President of Human Resources in the Recon Group, brought into the football club to help introduce modern management ideas. The Lerner team of executives must have thought that they had been using modern methods.

One other director Xia brought to the club was Chris Samuelson, which was an intriguing and perhaps revealing appointment. He only remained a director for a few days. When foreign investors wish to purchase an English football club it is quite usual and understandable to employ an agent, sometimes called a super-agent, or a financial advisor to help smooth this process. Samuelson had a track record of taking on this roll at other clubs. In Dr Xia's acquisition of Villa, Samuelson appears to have taken on such a role.

Samuelson has been described as an offshore financial advisor. He is based in Switzerland. He provides corporate services and these included helping investors manage their funds and helping companies set up offices in tax (and secrecy) havens. He has acted for many of the controversial super rich from Russia. He has been a subject of numerous money laundering investigations in the USA and Europe. He has been involved with football, in particular with the contentious takeover of Reading in 2012 by Russian investors.[24] Reading was acquired by a company, TSI, established in Gibraltar. The beneficial shareholder was Anton Zingarevich. Samuelson had helped set up the deal. He was made a director of the football club and for a time was the acceptable public face of the new owners. The identity of the other shareholders was kept secret. Samuelson justifies protecting the privacy of clients if they want it on the grounds that they are often high net worth people who live in danger. They need privacy for their own safety. This Samuelson provides. Zingarevich said that the money to buy the club was family money. In 2014 he disappeared from the scene at Reading leaving the club in a financial mess. Samuelson ceased to be a director.[25] What was Samuelson's role in Xia's takeover of the Villa?

It is easy to see why the Chinese involvement in European football is good for China. The country has ambitions to be the top footballing country in the World by 2050. The President of the country is a football fan and has ensured that the country had invested heavily in the sport from grassroots level to their own Super League. But is Chinese ownership good for the foreign clubs involved? They own clubs across Europe, not just underperforming teams in the West Midlands. In Italy in 2016 a group of Chinese investors wished to take over Milan FC. The owner, Silvio Berlusconi was happy to sell for £450 million but the investors had trouble raising the finance. One problem with these acquisitions is the uncertainty surrounding the investors. For example are the Recon Group all they claim to be? *The Financial Times* (26/6/2016) reported that the Lotus Health

Group (Xia's listed company) was at the centre of "a mysterious episode last December when it announced and then two days later retracted the appointment of Chinese President Xi Jinping's cousin to its Board of Directors". There is always some confusion with large Chinese businesses as to how much a company is government controlled and how much is in private hands. There was even rumour following the Villa takeover of some Chinese Government involvement. There is also uncertainty in the Villa case as to whether the misunderstandings about the background of Dr Xia were just an accident or whether there were deliberate attempts to mislead. *The Daily Telegraph* reported that a company controlled by Dr Xia had been criticised in 2007 by China's Ministry of Construction for providing false information when it attempted to secure an industry standard certificate.[26]

The Financial Times (10 Nov 2017) in an article on the Chinese ownership of European clubs point out that the investors involved range from prominent tycoons such as Mr Guo of Fosum (owners of the Wolves) to little known businessmen like Tony Xia. It refers to 'Mr' Xia as a "quirky character" who runs a range of businesses from food additives to the design of smart cities.[27]

But whatever the background of Dr Xia, whatever his other interests, whatever his motives he cannot be blamed for the demise of Villa. He deserved a chance to show what he could do.

The new owners did as promised, spend money prior to the start of the 2016/17 season. They twice broke the record for the most expensive transfer in the Championship. Unfortunately they made a poor decision over the appointment of a new manager – repeating the mistakes of the previous owner. They decided to appoint a man with a global reputation namely the experienced Roberto Di Matteo, who had formerly been manager of Chelsea (when they won the European Championship in 2012) and formerly the manager of WBA. Di Matteo did point out that his new job at Villa would be tough. He made the usual comments about being at a big club and that he and his backroom staff were excited to take on the challenge.

Unfortunately he did not realise how tough it would be. He was appointed in June 2016 and dismissed in October 2016. During that time the team only won one match in the Championship. This was surprising; the club had just spent £50 million on new players. There had been mixed views over the appointment of Di Matteo who had been dismissed by WBA in 2011. He was however strongly supported by the new owner. The two had talked about a two year plan to rebuild the club. Plans are easy to produce, it is meeting the plan that is hard.

The new owners appointed a new chief executive Keith Wyness. He had held this position at Everton for 5 years, and was well respected. Through his involvement with Everton he had many contacts in China. He made the usual optimistic statements about the future of the club, claiming in March 2017 that "The club has probably never been in better financial shape than it is right now". This was after reporting the record loss in the final year of the Lerner era. Most of this loss was however the result of writing down the value of some of the club's assets. In 2016/17 the club would be receiving a parachute payment and supporters were told that the new owner would fund future growth.

The club appointed Steve Bruce as the new manager, which was a popular choice with the fans. Bruce was experienced; he had managed nine clubs and had managed over 400 games in the Premier League. He had been successful, leading more teams from the Championship to the Premier League than any other manager. In 2018 he was competing for promotion with another old war horse namely Neil Warnock at the time manager of Cardiff City. Warnock had started his career as a manager over forty years earlier, managing non-league clubs. Over his career he had managed 14 league clubs. He had led teams from the Championship to the Premier League twice.

The club did invest in many new players. They did however have a problem; as a result of the big financial loss the previous season there was the danger that they would break the Championships Financial Fair Play rules. The rules are complicated but basically say that a club should not have losses over 3 seasons of more than £83 million. The Villa had made losses of £81 million in one season. The club had to try to balance its books, it sold players for £18 million and brought in players on loan and with free transfers. It did however buy some new players, including one, Hogan, costing £15 million. The future looked quite promising, they were the bookmakers' favourites for promotion from the Championship. Unfortunately they did not get off to a very good start, but by the end of the season they were challenging for a play-off place.

The club were not promoted. It soon became clear how much the owners had gambled on obtaining promotion. Villa only lost the play-off final game by one goal. If events in that game had turned out a little differently, say perhaps a deflected shot, a mistake by the referee or an injury. As it was with defeat the company faced the prospect of administration and being wound up. Such is "Casino" capitalism. A chance to win big, a chance to fail badly. At the beginning Dr Xia like all gamblers talked big. The club had invested £88 million in new players in 2016/17 in an attempt to achieve promotion.

Many clubs during a season can find themselves in a situation where they have cash problems but Villa's situation in 2018 was particularly dangerous. They had missed a £4.2 million tax payment. For a football club to upset the HMRC is dangerous: a number of clubs have been issued with a winding up partition as a result of being unable to pay their tax bills. The club had found it difficult to find the cash to pay the players wages for the month of May. They also needed to find £11 million by the end of June to pay an instalment on a player they had purchased. They owed money to WBA, Brentford and Bristol City amongst others. The players acquired had generally been paid for in instalments and the club were needing to borrow from banks to pay these instalments.

The club not only had cash flow problems, it had governance problems. The experienced chief executive Keith Wyness fell out with the owner, left the club and sued them for over £6 million for wrongful dismissal. There was also uncertainty as to whether Steve Bruce would remain as manager. If he was dismissed he was entitled to a £1.5 million payoff. This would add to cash flow difficulties. The club were talking about selling land that they owned near the ground for £4.5 million.

The club were in a serious financial problem. Tony Xia was said to not be in a position to invest more in the club because China had introduced new laws that made it difficult to transfer funds out of China. There were however Chinese investors who did not need to transfer money out of their own country because they already had it invested in accounts in tax havens. Xia drafted in a respected financial expert, Trevor Birch, to help solve the problems. Birch was an ex footballer who was now an insolvency expert. He had once been chief executive of Chelsea and was involved with the administrative deals that kept the Portsmouth club alive. It was to be hoped that he could do something to help Villa. The club would not find it easy to produce a plan for 2018/19 to satisfy the FFP requirements. With large accumulated losses, with receipts from parachute payments reduced, new money was needed. The club were desperately seeking investors who were prepared to invest £40 million or so in the Villa. One problem was what percentage of the club's equity would the investors want to own before they were prepared to invest in the club and would they be happy with Xia to continue as the majority shareholder.

The outcome was that two wealthy businessmen paid Tony Xia £30 million for a 55% stake in Aston Villa. They promised to make much needed funds available to the club. Xia would receive more if Villa are promoted. The two new shareholders who each own 27.5% are Nassef Sawiris from Egypt and Wes Edens from the USA. Xia continued to own 45% of the club's shares and became co-chairman. Nassef Sawiris became executive chairman.

Part B: The Early Years

1874 to the 1940s
Aston, once a village referred to in the Domesday Book, later a suburb of Birmingham, has a long sporting history. The 'Aston

Lower Grounds' were a section of a park on what was then the edge of Birmingham, and were "the acknowledged headquarters of Midlands sports". The 'Grounds', as well as a venue for football matches, also held athletics events and cricket matches. England played Australia in cricket at the Grounds, with W.G. Grace a member of the England team.[28]

The first major Association Football club in the city was Calthorpe FC founded in 1873 by the Birmingham Clerks Association. They initially played on a pitch just south of the city centre, at Calthorpe Park. The Calthorpe club declined because, under the terms of their ground rental agreement with Lord Calthorpe, they were not allowed to charge for admission to watch their matches.

The Aston Villa club was founded in the winter of 1874 by a group of cricketing enthusiasts at the Villa Cross Wesleyan Chapel. Perhaps the major contribution Calthorpe FC made to football in the Midlands was to provide Aston Villa with one of their best footballers; namely Archie Hunter. The Calthorpe team on a tour of Scotland played against Hunter who impressed them. A year later Archie came to Birmingham with his brother Andy to find work and to play for Calthorpe. They could not find the Calthorpe club's ground and were directed to the Aston Villa ground (which was at Perry Barr at the time). There the Hunters joined fellow Scott, George Ramsay. They formed the basis of the most successful team in the country. If the Hunter brothers had been directed to Small Heath or to Aston Trinity, it might have been these other teams that achieved success.

Aston Villa became one of twelve founder members of the Football League. The club's first Chairman, William McGregor has been called the father of the League. It was Ramsay, together with William McGregor, who led Aston Villa from obscurity to be the top team in the country. They did this in a ten-year period. McGregor first saw football played in the 1850s, as a boy in Scotland. In the 1870s he moved south to Birmingham, then in the midst of a trade boom. He was not a good footballer, but was a good leader. He later became the Birmingham representative on the FA Council, where he became a leading advocate of professionalism.

During the first twenty-seven years of the Football League (1888-1915) Aston Villa were the best team in the country. During this time they were Division One champions six times, runners up six times, and won the FA Cup on five occasions. They achieved the double in 1896/97.

The fortunes of the club changed after the First World War. Through the 1920s they did win the FA Cup once but in the league the best position achieved was 5th in Division One. They were no longer among the elite, but there was an arrogance about the directors of the club. In 1925 they voted off the board, Frederick Rinder, who had been an important and wise figure at the club for many years. The club did not appoint their first manager until 1934. Other clubs, notably Arsenal with Herbert Chapman as manager, were showing what could be achieved with a modern approach. The Aston Villa board argued that they had done well in the past with the directors running team matters, so why should they change? The club performed well in the early 1930s, but relegation in 1935/36 led to two years in Division Two.

Although the club achieved little playing success in the inter-war years, they did attract good crowds, home gates in the 1930s averaging 37,000. Crowds remained at this level in the 1940s and 1950s despite the team's poor performance.

The 1940s, 50s and 60s

These were not good years for Aston Villa. They were relegated to Division Two in 1958/59, but promoted again the next year. They continued to struggle, were relegated again in 1966/67, and then (a complete humiliation) relegated to Division Three in 1969/70. The highest position they achieved during these three decades was sixth in Division One.

The entire period from the resumption of league football after the Second World War through to mid-1970s was in fact one of under-performance by this once great club. Peter Morris, writing in 1960, refers to the club as "wallowing" along in the First Division, fighting off relegation.[29] This, he points out, had been the pattern since the 1940s. They had not once over this period at any point in a season occupied one of the top five positions in the league. Who was to blame? Whitehead asked the same question: "At what point in the preceding half-century did Aston Villa cease to be a force in English football?" He and others placed the blame at the top level of the club.[30]

By the 1950s Aston Villa were no longer the top club in the West Midlands. Danny Blanchflower (the best player they had during this period) left the club because he believed those in charge were "fooling around". He refers to the "pathetic manner of their approach" and to the fact that it was a club with a big potential "but it wasn't chasing its big opportunities the right way". The club was lucky to stay in the top division in 1955-56, retaining their place only on the basis of a slightly superior goal average. They did, however, win the FA Cup competition in that season, their first appearance in that final for 33 years. As an indication of the lack of ambition at the club, they turned down the opportunity to join with Birmingham City to enter a joint team in the new European wide competition the Inter-Cities Fairs Cup.

The club were heavily in debt, and the level of debt was increasing. Morris refers to the 'muddled politics' of the Board of Directors. A Shareholders Association tried unsuccessfully at an EGM in 1958 to replace two of the retiring directors with their own nominations – they did not have enough votes, however, and the retiring directors were re-elected. One problem was that at the beginning of the 1960s, four of these six directors were aged over 70.

What were they doing wrong in the late '50s and '60s? Birmingham was a booming city. The motor industry in the city was successful, the unemployment was low, wage levels were high. People in the City were confident – old buildings were being pulled down, new roads constructed. Manchester and Liverpool as cities were not as prosperous. Why could the biggest football team in Birmingham not benefit from this prosperity? Through the 1960s the City of Birmingham was booming, but Aston Villa were not. "They were a club in freefall, short of inspiration, confidence, talent, and crucially, money". (Whitehead). Here was a time when Aston Villa should have benefited from the growth in confidence in the city. It was a time when both the Wolves and WBA were successful.

Villa were moving from one crisis to another. One manager was sacked in 1958 and Joe Mercer, a most respected manager, was appointed. Even though Joe Mercer was popular with the public, he left the club in 1964, by mutual consent; he was suffering from 'hypertension' partly brought on by his relationship with the club directors.

The club even handled his departure in a clumsy manner, which made matters worse and Mercer suffered a nervous breakdown. Was the lack of success Mercer's fault or the directors? As is usual when a club is unsuccessful, it is the manager who leaves the club before the directors. In fact Mercer came back to football a few years later as manager of Manchester City and was successful. Villa struggled in the Division One for another 3 years after Mercer's departure, before being relegated in 1966/67.

"The root of the problems lay in the boardroom ... The men in charge of Aston Villa in the 1960s belonged not so much in another decade as another age entirely". A respected player, Charlie Aitken, made the comment that "the place was run like a family business, like a corner shop. Everyone was content with the way things went on". Of course there is nothing wrong with a family business – the Edwards family were developing a very successful meat business in Manchester and the Moores a very successful mail order business in Liverpool at the same time as Villa were on the decline. The problem was that Villa directors did not see the need for change at a time when the football business was changing dramatically. There had been little change in the Villa board over the last 20 years but things began to happen in 1964. Douglas Ellis was approached to see if he would join the Board. He was willing but there was a problem.

Ellis was born in Cheshire in 1924. He claimed that he became more and more of an Aston Villa supporter from the time of his arrival in Birmingham in 1948. When he arrived he purchased season tickets at both Aston Villa and Birmingham City – as a football enthusiast he liked to watch a match every Saturday. He also purchased "a couple of shares" in each club.

He was by the 1960s a successful businessman, having in the 1950s built up a package foreign holiday business at just the time such holidays were beginning to become affordable and popular. He also developed business interests in hotels, a brewery, house building and land development. Ownership of a football club would fit in well with his portfolio of business activities. He would have become a director of Aston Villa when asked in 1964 (and therefore never have joined the Blues Board) but for a division of opinion on the Aston Villa Board over his appointment. There were some directors of the club who were happy that he wanted to join them, particularly as he was willing to invest £30,000 in the club (which was an amount equal to that invested by any other Board member). But not all the directors were happy with Ellis' approach.

One point made was that Ellis could do nothing for the club that was not already being done. Ellis could not understand this comment. His view was that "The directors were extremely dignified and courteous gentlemen. They were honest and full of old-world charm – but they were not leading the club anywhere". Ellis was correct. Over the next 4 seasons they did not move forward. In 1966/67 they were relegated and in 1967/68 they finished 17th in Division Two. The club were sinking in a football sense and also in a financial sense.

Norman Smith was Chairman in the late 1960s, he had first joined the Board in 1939. He was a well-liked and modest gentleman, who travelled to Villa home games on a public bus. No one doubted that he and his fellow directors were good people, devoted to their football club, but they did not have the abilities to run a football club. One of the players, Fred Turnbull, who sometimes travelled to games in the same corporation bus as the

Chairman, describes the directors as being similar in appearance to those in "old-fashioned photographs with their bowler hats and the like".

The directors did not know how to handle the financial and management problems the club encountered. In fact, they seemed to believe that they did not need to do anything, that Aston Villa had a right to be amongst the football elite. Even traditionally unfashionable clubs from medium sized towns such as Coventry were showing the Villa how to market themselves in the new era. The directors did not realise how the game had changed. In 1968 they paid £60,000 to purchase a player, a club record fee. At about the same time Leicester City paid £150,000 for a player. Norman Smith made it clear that Villa did not have that type of money to spend on transfers.

The embattled Board again took the easy way out and sacked another manager (a similar story to that 40 years later). Some of the directors wished to raise new equity finance. Bruce Normansall, the vice-chairman, stated, "I am not going to say we are over blessed with cash but we are meeting our commitments". By this he presumably meant that the club could pay its debts, but it did not mean they could not meet their commitment to produce a good football team. The club desperately needed money.

In 1968 the club were facing a financial disaster, and the team were fighting against being relegated into the Third Division. As ten years earlier, angry shareholders were holding meetings aimed to remove the existing Board of Directors. Unlike ten years earlier, the directors had indicated that they were now prepared to stand down and to sell their shares.

The question was who would buy shares in Aston Villa. Who was prepared to take over the club? One candidate was Ron Harrison, who was at the time Chairman of Walsall Football Club. Another possible buyer was a group from Atlanta in the USA. One offer came from a Midland based financier, Pat Matthews. He was managing director of a fast growing merchant bank. He offered to purchase the shares owned by the directors, to provide the club with a bridging loan, and to use his contacts to find other wealthy businessmen who would be willing to buy a place on the Villa Board. He said that he was not doing all this to make a profit, he was doing this "to put something back into Birmingham"; believing "it is impossible to make a profit out of football". The existing Villa directors were frightened of Matthews. Matthews did, however, have a significant influence on Villa in that he arranged a £50,000 overdraft for the club and became a major influence in the financial restructuring of the football club. It was he, who with the club president, had talks with Doug Ellis that led to the Ellis takeover. It was he who approached Tommy Docherty to be the new manager, and he did this before Ellis was appointed as Chairman. It was Matthews who advised on the financial restructuring of the club and who helped persuade the existing directors to reluctantly sell their shares and to agree to the appointment of Ellis as Chairman.

The Doug Ellis Era: In The Beginning – 1968 to 1992

Steps were taken to bring new money into the club. Ellis made the club an interest free loan of £100,000 (approximately £1.6 million at today's prices). New shares were to be issued at a price of £5 per share and each director was to purchase 5,000 of these shares. The intention was that no director should own more than 5% of the company – there would be seven directors. Supporters and investors would own the remaining 65% of shares. Ellis made a statement on this planned distribution of the new shares at a meeting of shareholders and supporters in 1968. The existing shares were upgraded becoming special shares, each of which carried 15 votes and which became very valuable.

The new shares were issued in March 1969 and just over £205,000 was raised. This was less than hoped for, but was nevertheless an important cash inflow at a time when the annual turnover was only £150,000.

At the end of the 1960s it appeared that, from a financial point of view, the position of Aston Villa was improving. They had appointed an impressive commercial manager Eric Woodward, who had been involved in selling soccer in the USA. The club had a new Board of Directors, had additional money and a "new" manager. But in 1968/69 they were still near the bottom of Division Two, and were relegated to Division Three the following year.

What had gone wrong? More boardroom problems. Unfortunately, over the next few years it emerged that there were many differences of opinion in the boardroom on key issues. One was the sacking in 1970 of Tommy Docherty; another was the youth recruitment policy. A major clash occurred over the proposal of Doug Ellis to remove Harry Parkes as a director. Parkes was popular with the fans; he was an ex-Villa player and the owner of a well known city centre sports shop. Parkes was also popular with the other directors, who fought to keep Parkes on the board and pointed out that Ellis, in trying to restructure the board, was acting on his own initiative and in his own interests. Ellis commented that he "had serious differences of view with Mr Parkes over a variety of matters, and that the board was not united". The board was clearly not united, for they did not agree with Ellis.

One reason why there was a problem was that the other directors "believed that they had not received enough public recognition for their part in the successful relaunch of the club". It was always the "charismatic and dynamic Chairman" who received the publicity.[31] A number of years later, looking back at these troubles, Ellis admitted, "I was a devil for saying I. It was making a mistake I suppose. I tried to run the Board as a Chairman should run the Board, but someone has to take the initiative." But from the point of view of hogging the limelight nothing seemed to change very much at Villa Park.

The other directors tried to have Ellis removed from the Board. The football team was, however, just about to be promoted back to the Second Division and the fans, now enjoying a 'feel good factor' were not against Ellis. Ellis won the day.

The 1970s

From a corporate governance point of view, the period can be divided into three: 1970-75 with Ellis as Chairman, 1975-78 with William

Dugdale as Chairman, and 1978-80 with Kartz as Chairman. From a football point of view, after two years in Division Three in 1971/72 the club were promoted back to the Division Two, and in the following year (1972/73), promoted back to Division One. In 1976/77 they finished fourth in the top Division – their highest position since the end of the Second World War. In 1980/81 they won the First Division, and in the following year they won the European Cup. What had happened to change the fortunes of the club in just over 10 years, from Division Three to Champions of Europe?

In a book written about Aston Villa in the 1970s, with the optimistic title of 'Children of the Revolution', Richard Whitehead concludes "At the end (of the 1970s) Aston Villa was poised for its greatest moment(s) in the twentieth century". If Whitehead meant 'moment' he was correct – if he meant 'moments' he was not.

What happened at Villa Park that led to success? One key factor was the appointment of one good manager followed by another. The decade had begun with Tommy Docherty as manager, but he did not last long and Vic Crowe replaced him in January 1970. Docherty was never really Ellis' choice and with Docherty as manager the team had been relegated to Division Three. It took a year or two with Crowe as manager before the performance of the team improved. They did reach the final of the League Cup. Ron Saunders replaced Crowe in 1974, and in 1974/75 they were promoted back to Division One.

Despite the team's success, there were still many problems at boardroom level. There was no stability, yet at this time they achieved their greatest football success for many decades. The success of the club was achieved despite a divided Board. In fact there were more in and outs at Board level in the '70s and early '80s than at any other time in the club's history. Ellis, who had saved the club financially in 1968, fell out with other directors and was forced to resign as Chairman in 1975. Sir William Dugdale replaced him as Chairman.

The takeover by Ellis of Aston Villa in 1968 had been referred to as a "re-birth". A re-birth had been needed. Improvements needed to be made to the ground and to the team. The response of supporters to the 1968 takeover was dramatic. The size of the home crowd before the takeover had been for some games as low as 12,000, but by Boxing Day 1968, it had soared to 41,000.

Ellis claimed that he saved the club from disaster.[32] He might well have done so but unfortunately this did not satisfy some of his fellow directors. During the 1974/75 season Ellis had discussions with Ron Bendall, who was an Aston Villa shareholder who wished to invest more money in the club. Bendall was the head of an accounting firm that specialised in handling receivership cases. He was successful and had become a tax exile who now spent most of his time in the Isle of Man.

Ron Bendall wished to increase his shareholding in the club and to become a director. A vacancy existed on the Board so Bendall was invited to join. Sometime later problems arose over his wish to buy more shares in the club. He knew of the promise that had been made at the meeting with supporters at the time of the floatation in 1969, namely that the shareholdings of each director and his family should not exceed 5,000 shares. After Bendall became a director, certain shares became available in the market and Bendall and his family acquired these to push up the family holding to 27.2%. To Ellis this was an example of boardroom disunity. Ellis pointed out that Bendall had accepted the 5% limit at the time of becoming a director.

Ellis had had the opportunity to increase his own shareholding. As already mentioned, when the club had been short of finance Ellis had lent the club £100,000 (interest free). One condition attached to the loan was that Ellis had the option to convert the loan into equity shares. In the early 1970s the financial position of the club improved, and they were promoted. Ellis was encouraged by other board members to allow the club to repay the loan and to rescind the option to convert the loan into equity. He did so. If he had converted the loan to equity shares he would have subsequently been in a stronger position to defend his position on the board.

Following the AGM in 1975, it became clear that the other directors wished to relieve Ellis of Chairmanship, and replace him with Sir William Dugdale. Ellis reluctantly had to accept this but continued as a director. What had Bendall and the other directors got against Ellis? The club had just been promoted and had won the League Cup. Sir William Dugdale was in many ways the "most intriguing character ever to have occupied the chairman's seat at Villa Park".[33] He was an Old Etonian, an Oxford graduate, and an ex-Grenadier Guard. He was a very well-respected figure in the local community, being Sheriff of the County of Warwickshire, and Chairman of Severn Trent Water Authority. He had been an Aston Villa supporter since the age of 10; he had ridden a horse in the Grand National, and had flown in an air race from England to Australia. He was a member of the landed gentry, a member of some of the top Gentlemen's Clubs in London. He was certainly not a typical football club director.

Ellis expresses the view that the Villa directors, whilst Dugdale was chairman, allowed the manager, Ron Saunders to "rule his staff by fear". Ellis believed that Dugdale was also weak in dealing with the architects, the builders, and the other commercial enterprises who were involved with the redeveloping Villa Park. Whatever Ellis' views, the other directors believed in Dugdale and elected him chairman, but the club was not doing well financially. The ground required major investments, football was declining in popularity (partly due to the growing hooligan problem) and TV money was insignificant.

In 1978 Ron Bendall wished his son Donald to become a director of the club. The father was the major shareholder in the club but as a tax exile was finding it difficult to keep an eye on what was happening at the club. Sir William Dugdale (after three years as chairman), and two other directors resigned from the Board. Ron Bendall proposed that his son Donald become a director, and that Harry Kartz become chairman. The proposal was accepted.

In late 1979 the not unexpected confrontation took place between Ellis and Ron Bendall. Ellis called an EGM, "with the objective of getting Ronald and Donald Bendall along with Harry Kartz removed from the board". Ellis was making an attempt to re-establish himself as the top person. He was criticising his fellow directors for being undemocratic. Ellis was narrowly defeated by 44% of the votes to 42%. Having been defeated in a vote to remove the chairman who was the largest shareholder, it would have been difficult for Ellis to remain on the Board. He resigned and sold his 5% shareholding to Ron Bendall, on condition that should Bendall ever wish to sell his shares, it would be to Ellis.

So the 1970s finish a decade of incredible disunity on the Board, with fighting between powerful egocentric businessmen for control of the club. Despite the troubles in the boardroom, the team became Division One champions for the first time in 50 years and went on to win the European Cup in 1982. Ellis was not a director over the period when the club won the First Division and European Cup.

What of Ellis' claim that a united board is necessary for success? There was no unity in the '70s, but there was success. Infighting continued at Board level and harmony was not restored until well into the '80s, and from then on the performance of the team was at first good, then 'mediocre', and then disappointing. They were relegated to the Second Division in 1986/87. Strange, the 1980s and later the 1990s was a period of unity – but no success.

The 1980s

Problems arose in 1981 when the manager, Ron Saunders, resigned over a rolling contract dispute. He wanted such a contract, but the board would not agree.[34] Saunders was effectively sacked. He complained that he was being treated by the board as an office boy. It was the usual problem of power. Bendall said that Saunders wanted complete control and that the directors were not prepared to give it to him. Saunders, in fact, walked out of the job at Villa and walked into the manager's position at Birmingham City, the club's closest rival. There were nasty undertones to this move. Jim Smith had been a popular manager at the Blues, but in 1982 the chairman, Keith Coombs, removed him to bring in Saunders. The move did not prove to be successful. Birmingham City remained near the bottom of Division One, and were relegated in 1984/85.

In November 1982 Ron Bendall sold his shareholding in the club (just under 40% of all the shares), to Doug Ellis. Ellis came back as chairman. The club had a debt of £1.6 million, despite the fact that the club had won Division One and the European Championship.

The club finished sixth in the First Division in 1982/83, then mid table for three years, before being relegated in 1986/87. The club were relegated 6 years after being European champions. It was during this period that Ellis acquired the nickname 'Deadly Doug'. Tony Barton was manager when Ellis came back in 1982 but was sacked in 1984. Then came Graham Turner who was sacked in 1986. Next came Billy McNeill, who was manager when they were relegated, and who was sacked in 1987. Next was Graham Taylor who led the club back to Division One then to second place in the top division before resigning to become England's manager.

One particularly interesting appointment of manager was that of Dr Jozef Vengloš in 1990. Dr Jozef was from Czechoslovakia, he had been a successful manager of the national team. He also had experience of managing club teams across Europe. In making the appointment Villa were leading the way, he was the first manager born outside the UK or Ireland to manage a top English club. Unfortunately the appointment did not work out too well, he left after one season.

Doug Ellis developed a reputation for being hard on managers, removing them after a relatively short stay at the club. In his autobiography he defends the decisions he has made and believes his reputation for being 'deadly' was not justified. Ellis could point out that the club had a history of being 'deadly' before he became chairman. Perhaps it is coincidence rather than a club culture, but as mentioned earlier in the chapter, Villa have a record of only keeping managers for short periods of time. In their nearly 80 seasons with team managers there have been 22 appointments, an average of a new manager every 3 years. The chairmen do not change so often.

What had been happening to the club's finances during the years of infighting at Boardroom level? Through to the mid-1970s, the club had been making reasonable profits, revenue was just about growing in real terms, and wages were only taking up about 50% of total revenue.

The latter half of the 1970s were however not such good times. In the 1970s and 1980s attendances at football matches were on the decline. Wage bills were steadily increasing. There was not a lot of money available to fund the purchase of new players, and money needed to be invested in ground improvements and ground safety. When Villa briefly reached the top in Europe it was not at a time when they could cash in on their success; TV were not paying large sums for the right to show football matches.

Over the 1970s and 1980s Aston Villa failed to attract the crowds one would expect for the major team in the country's second largest city. Not surprisingly, when in the lower divisions they had had poor crowds, but in 1980, when at the top of the First Division, they were attracting crowds of less than 40,000. "My biggest regret at the moment is that we are not getting the crowds we would like." As Woodward points out, the club received bigger gates in Division Three than when at the top of the First. Woodward pointed out, Liverpool and Manchester had similar hooligan and recession problems but still attracted bigger crowds.[35]

The club in 1981 was close to bankruptcy. When Ellis returned as Chairman in 1982 it was at a time of increasing problems for football. Ellis immediately began to cut back on the wage bill. In 1982/83 it was £1,146,000 the following year £1,025,000 then £963,000, then £762,000, and in the following year, 1986/87, the club was relegated. Financially the club was being improved, but at the expense of its performance on the pitch.

Ground Improvements

Ellis was a key figure in the redevelopment of Villa Park. It became one of the best grounds in the country. The 1980s, were a time when clubs were being required to spend money on ground improvements. Because of new Safety Regulations and later, problems associated with hooliganism, clubs were required to invest in their grounds at a time when many of them were short of cash. It was at the time that the Safety Laws and the Police were controlling much of the investment that was taking place at grounds.

Tentative planning for changes at the Witton End of Villa Park had begun in 1973. Ellis was, however (as always) cautious. He told the 1973 AGM, "We cannot afford a stand before we reach the First Division." The problem was that "We cannot afford to be without one when we get there." They were in the Second Division at the time.

In retrospect, Ellis was right to be cautious. Many of the clubs that embarked on major ground improvements during the 1970s, were to suffer major financial problems. Wolves, Chelsea, Spurs and Sheffield United in particular. These clubs built up huge debts to pay for ground developments at a time when interest rates were very high. The development of the Aston Villa Sports and Leisure Centre was, however, a huge success and the income from leasing out car park land funded the building of what was named the North Stand at Villa Park.

Work began on this stand in January 1977. This new stand at the Witton End was the first major construction at Villa Park since 1922 (a development that at the time had led to a financial crisis at the club). Fortunately, the construction of the North Stand did not threaten the financial survival of the club, but it did result in a financial scandal, resulting in police prosecutions. The financial arrangements with regard to the construction of the stand were sound, but a few of the people involved with the project were not.

The police were involved in an investigation into £725,000 that was paid for unaccounted for work. The architect of the stand, Harry Marsden, admitted to having conspired with Ron Bendall (the ex-chairman) to obtain money by deception from the Football Trust by inflating claims of costs involved in building the stand. An Aston Villa employee, the Stadium manager, admitted that he also was involved in the false accounting. He was involved in authorising unjustified payments. The case was not settled until February 1985. Bendall, who of course had resigned as a director of the club, was very ill and died in April 1986.

Aston Villa had continued to invest in their ground. A new stand had been built on the Witton Lane side of the ground and was named the Doug Ellis Stand. Next it was planned to rebuild the major stand in the ground, the Trinity Road Stand.

The existing stand was old, with no executive boxes, and plans were to redevelop it and increase its income generating capacity. Ellis had to battle with the local authority, but did win in the end. Ken Bates' comment was "They're building another stand at Villa Park. They're going to call it 'the other Doug Ellis Stand'." [36] In fact, whilst Ellis was a director of the club, the stands and terraces on all four sides of the ground were rebuilt. Ken Bates and Doug Ellis were survivors from the old generation of owners, they did not particularly respect each other. Bates is alleged to have said about Ellis that "he was old, offered nothing for the future, he was surrounded by no talent and his teams attracted poor crowds".

Problems with Agents

During John Gregory's four year period as manager, the club spent £71.5 million on players, and recouped £46 million from the sale of players. Three particular purchases of foreign players seemed, after the event, to have been unwise, from a footballing and a financial point of view. The three players concerned in total cost the club over £20 million; they were Boško Balaban (£6 million), Juan Pablo Angel (£9.5 million) and Alpay Özalan (£5.6 million).

Angel was from Argentina. Where did the money go that Villa paid? Angel was half owned by a company, it being quite common in South America for companies to purchase a 50% stake (for as little as £100) in promising young footballers, hoping that one day if the player was successful, they would be able to share in the transfer fees. Angel's South American corporate owners, therefore, received a large part of the fee. Ellis has said that the player's agent and those involved in Argentina wanted him to pay "the money in different proportions into four different banks in three different countries". He refused to do so. He paid the sum in one amount to the FA in England who transferred the money to the Argentinian FA. What happened to it after that is uncertain. The chairman of the Argentinian FA was also the chairman of the club selling Angel. Ellis was reportedly concerned about Gregory's own financial interests in this deal, but apparently all the financial aspects of the deal were negotiated with Ellis, not with Gregory.

Ellis was also concerned about the arrangements involving the purchase from Turkey of Alpay Özalan. In this case, two payments were deposited in Swiss bank accounts, and five agents were involved in sharing the commission including two of those involved in the Angel transfer.

Doug Ellis had made clear in his autobiography that he personally was responsible for all money matters at the club; he signed the cheques, and he negotiated transfer deals. Mamie, the Croatian agent of Balaban, stated, "the transfer was carried out solely through Doug Ellis and Villa finance director, Mark Ansell. John Gregory was not involved at all and I cannot understand why the club has not made that clear". The club co-operated with an FA enquiry but did not respond publicly to the comment of Balaban's agent.

Gregory had stated that if he as manager "recommended a purchase it was because he believed it was in the best interests of the club".[37] It was not clear whether or not John Gregory had recommended the purchase of Balaban. There were tensions between the chairman and the manager at the time. The player's agent, Mamie, visited Villa Park on a number of occasions. He stated "Balaban arrived at Aston Villa on the exclusive wish of

Doug Ellis and Mark Ansell and not Gregory". "I spoke with Doug Ellis on three separate occasions over the transfer, but with Gregory not at all. There was a conflict between the manager and the chairman at the time and that was clear with all of us dealing with the club". Mamie believed that the tensions resulted from differences of opinion as to which players to purchase. Gregory wanted a player that the chairman did not want and Ellis wanted a player that Gregory did not want. One interpretation of what happened is that the chairman had his way and Balaban joined the club. The manager, however, had his revenge by not selecting the player to play in matches. The old familiar story of a clash between the chairman and the manager.

Although Balaban must have been disappointed at not being a success on the football field, he did not lose financially. "It was pretty obvious that an enormous part of the fee went to the player and his management company", said Mladen Pretreski, a Croatian agent not connected with the deal. "The transfer was publicly announced as £6 million but it was pretty open and transparent that the player ended up with 80% of the transfer fee paid to him. Only 20% was retained by the club". If this is what happened, it was breaking UEFA rules. There are alternative stories about how the fee was divided; one being that the selling club received £1.5 million and that the balance was divided between Balaban and his agent Mamie (who was also an executive at the player's Croatian club).

An important issue in transfers was then and still is how the money that is paid to acquire the services of a player is divided between the interested parties. The selling club will receive a part of the fee, so might the player being transferred, so will the agent or agents of the player and so might any other stakeholders in the player. Vast sums of money have come into football over the last 25 years, and many people have benefited from this. It has been argued that some agents have taken money out of the game and contributed very little. Large amounts have been siphoned out of the game. The rhetoric is that the Premier League is the best league in the world and that the stadiums and merchandise offer supporters value for money. Unfortunately there is also a murky side to football, which the football authorities and football club chairmen are keen to cover up.

To be successful in football it is obviously necessary for clubs to deal with agents. One particular agent who contributed to the breakdown in the chairman-manager relationship at Aston Villa was Paul Stretford. Stretford was John Gregory's friend, his agent and Gregory owned shares in Stretford's company, Proactive. It was he who successfully renegotiated the manager's contract with Aston Villa and who arranged for Gregory to eventually move to Derby County. The question asked was whether Gregory had a conflict of interest in transfer dealings when as Villa's manager he was buying and selling players, for whom Stretford was the agent, and were such transfers carried out at 'arm's length' prices? Did Stretford have a conflict of interest, he was the manager's agent and at the same time earning fees from the transfer of players to and from the club?

Stretford was a successful agent and had dealings with Villa before Gregory became manager – he was agent for Stan Collymore. Stretford has links with a number of managers, including Kevin Keegan, Peter Reid, Bobby Robson and Graeme Souness, all of whom had owned shares in 'Proactive'. Amongst those Stretford has hired to work for him in his agency business were the son of Freddie Shepherd, the then chairman of Newcastle, and the son of Paul Hart, the then manager of Nottingham Forest.

Paul Stretford's agency did supply a number of players to Villa during Gregory's time as manager and these transfers became an issue that was even discussed in the pages of *Private Eye*, where the question was raised of how many of Villa's transfers were handled by Proactive. The paper claimed that their informants had suggested that "as many as 33 out of 36 transfers to and from the club were made through Proactive".[38] Aston Villa would not confirm or deny the figure, making the point that the issue of who represented individual players during transfer negotiations was a confidential matter.

In the next issue of *Private Eye*, it was mentioned that the paper had received a letter from the lawyers of Proactive, threatening them with legal action because of a "very serious libel". *Private Eye* were used to such letters and announced that they planned to contest the claim on grounds of public interest. The lawyer's letter to *Private Eye* stated that Proactive were involved in only seven transfers involving Aston Villa during Gregory's term as manager, and these transfers involved just four of their clients.

Ellis was not happy with another of the transfers at that time, that of Peter Schmeichel. This player was a client of Proactive and also a shareholder in the company. Ellis said that this was the last time Gregory was to use the services of Stretford. By this time Gregory and Ellis were criticising each other in public and it was no surprise that when Gregory resigned early in 2002. The club compiled a report on Gregory and his relationship with Stretford, which they handed over to the FA Chief Executive. Adam Crozier, said that they would investigate the transfer dealings and the question of whether or not rules had been broken. The FA at the time had troubles of their own and did not want any further scandals. Gregory left the Villa in 2002, but remained in football management. He managed teams in Israel, Kazakhstan and India. In March 2018 the team he managed won the Indian Super League.

So Doug Ellis had his problems in the 1990s, as did Aston Villa. But the club had its successes, they finished in second place in the first year of the new exciting, what was to be super rich Premier League. They won the League Cup in 1994. They should have gone on to do better!

3

THE BLUES

The 17th October 2016 was supposed to have been a significant day in the history of the Birmingham City Football Club. The club wrote to their fans to inform them that this was the "start of a fresh era". The fans were told that the club was now in the expert hands of their new owner, Trillion Trophy Asia Ltd (TTA). The letter from the club referred to "a brighter Blues future off the field and on it, with Gary Rowett and his players". Three months later Gary Rowett was sacked. He had been regarded by many in the game as one of the most promising of the young English managers. At the time he was removed, the Blues were in the Championship, playing well and challenging for a play-off place. The new manager appointed was Gianfranco Zola, on a two and a half year contract. He had been a world class player for Italy and a hero, as a player, at Chelsea. He had however not proven himself as a manager. The Blues played badly under his leadership he was sacked after only three months in charge. The club finished the 2016/17 season escaping relegation on the last day. This was supposed to be the start of a new era. To supporters it felt like the previous one.

Harry Redknapp had been appointed manager with 4 games of the 2016/17 season remaining. He had a key role in saving the Blues from relegation that season. In June 2017 he went to China to have discussions with the new owners about the plans for the 2017/18 season. He came back full of enthusiasm. He said that he had found the owners (TTA) to be good people wanting to move the club forward. Ironically Gary Rowett had returned from China not many months earlier making similar comments. Redknapp had been encouraged by his first meeting with the new owners and believed they were willing to move the club forward. He was sacked a few weeks later.

In September 2017 Steve Cotterill was appointed as manager, the fourth manager in a twelve month period. The 2017/18 season turned out to be another fight against relegation. A few days into 2018 there was talk of Cotterill being sacked. He had a meeting with Zhao Wenqing, the chairman of the clubs holding company, BS Holdings Ltd. Cotterill said that he was encouraged by the meeting, using similar words to those used by the three previous managers just before they were removed. The new "expert" owners, with their advisers did not seem to know what they were doing. All the research on football indicated that it was investing money in the club that would save them, not changing managers every few months. In the period between December 2016 and March 2018, between the sacking of Gary Rowett and the sacking of Steve Cotterill the team had lost 37 games, drawn 15 and won only 13. There is another relevant research finding, namely that in football bad owners often sell to other bad owners.

In March 2018 the club appointed a new manager Gary Monk, he would be their 5th manager in 16 months. Cotterill had not been able to turn the club around, but perhaps the failure over two seasons was not a failure of the manager/coach, but of failure amongst the owners, their football advisors, the directors and executives appointed to run the business. A failure of corporate governance. In March 2018 the owners did recognise that failure could not just be blamed on the manager, the Director of Football was sacked, as were a number of coaches and sports scientists. Equally significant was the decision to no longer use the services of Darren Dein, the agent and consultant who had been advising the owners over the last two years. More on his role later.

The new manager Gary Monk did a good job. Following his appointment the team won five of the final eleven games of the season and avoided relegation. At the final home game of the season when the Blues beat Fulham 3-1, the fans celebrated wildly. It was forgotten that they had only been fighting off relegation. It was in fact another very poor season for the Blues, they had lost more games than any other team in the Championship (26 losses out of 46 games) and no club in the division had scored less goals.

Gary Monk is one of a promising group of young British managers involved in the football merry-go-round. After a successful career as a player with Swansea he became their manager in 2014. The club finished the 2014/15 season in eighth place in the Premier League which was a great achievement for the club, considering the resources they had available. After a poor start in the early months of the next season he was sacked. Six months later he took on the job as coach/manager of Leeds United. They finished in sixth place in the Championship in the 2015/16 season, in a play-off place. Leeds United have had some strange owners over recent years and following another takeover of the club he resigned unexpectedly in 2017. A few days later, in June 2017 he was appointed as manager of Middlesbrough. The club had high expectations of being promoted from the Championship, they had invested £50 million in new players. After what was regarded by the owners as a disappointing start to the season – they won 12 of the 26 matches with Monk in charge. He left the club in December 2017. He was replaced three days later as manager of Leeds by Tony Pulis who had just been sacked by WBA. The merry-go-round continues.

Who are TTA? Who are the people behind them? Where does their money come from? The club (BCFC) is owned by its UK parent Birmingham City Plc., who are owned by Birmingham Sports Holding (BSH), a company listed on the Hong Kong Stock Exchange, registered in the Cayman Islands. The majority shareholder in BSH, at the time they were purchased from Carson Yeung, was TTA, a company registered in the British Virgin Islands. TTA is owned by Paul Suen.

TTA have reduced their shareholding in BSH. At the end of 2017 they only owned 39.87%. Other companies, such as Ever

Depot Ltd and Dragon Villa have become involved with BSH. These other companies are registered in countries such as Samoa and Cambodia. It is far from clear why they are interested in an underperforming football club from Birmingham. They do however financially support the club, and the club do need the money. It is ultimately Paul Suen and other investors such as Lei Sutong and Vong Pech who control the club and make the major decisions. Welcome to the poorly regulated world of global finance, its reach now extends to Small Heath. The ownership position at the club will be returned to later in the chapter.

The Blues in their 100 plus years history have achieved very little in terms of playing success. They have twice been losing finalists in the FA Cup, they have twice won the League Cup and twice been runners up in the Inter-Cities Fairs Cup. The highest position they have achieved in league football had been sixth in the old Division One (the top tier). They have for a very long time underperformed for a club from a city with the second largest population. They have, however, provided their fans with plenty of excitement. Their story reads like a soap opera with a colourful list of characters, some good and some bad.

We will begin the analysis of the Blues by looking at the recent history, at the period starting from when the Premiership came into existence to the present time. In 1993 the club were taken over by David Sullivan and the Gold brothers. The club were at the time playing in the second tier of football. The new owners expected to be able to lead the club into the Premier league. They did save the club financially and did take them into the top tier. Unfortunately the team were not good enough to be able to stay there. The club were then taken over by Carson Yeung, then the fun and games really began.

Part A: The Recent History

1992-2018

At the beginning of 1992 the club were owned by the Kumar brothers. Their family textile business was suffering financial problems due to a crisis at a bank. The Kumar family had fallen victim to the calamitous collapse of BCCI. This was a large international bank that had roots in Pakistan and the Middle East that had in the UK targeted the British Asian community. It turned out to be a crooked bank with links to drugs and crime. The bank failed losing large sums of clients' money. In November 1992 BRS Kumar Bros Ltd went into receivership. Their controlling shareholding in BCFC was put up for sale. In March 1993 the shares were purchased by Sports Newspapers Ltd.

During the Kumar period the club had performed badly on the pitch. In the season 1992/93 they were in the second tier, having only just come out of three seasons playing in the third tier. In the ten year period between 1984 and 1993 the club had had six different managers. The fans had developed a reputation for hooliganism. The club's ground, St Andrews, was in a mess.

The owners from 1993 to 2009 were David Sullivan and the Gold brothers. They saved the club financially, they improved the ground and built up a team that spent a number of years in the Premier League. When Sullivan and the Golds acquired the club the fans had high hopes, the owners were wealthy, were successful businessmen and they brought to the club an impressive young chief executive, namely Karren Brady.

Karren Brady was aged only 23 when she took over as managing director of the club. Her background in football was limited. She was a young woman in a male dominated environment and there were many who doubted that she had the necessary abilities. She had charm and also had a reputation for business acumen and ruthlessness. She was never worried about her lack of experience in football arguing that it was a business like any other business. In her autobiography she provides a very clear picture of the Blues in 1992. An advertisement had appeared in the *Financial Times* in that year offering a football club for sale. She had visited St Andrews on behalf of David Sullivan, who was interested in new investment opportunities. He was apparently at the time more interested in buying a racehorse than a football club, but was persuaded that BCFC had potential. His partners in the acquisition were David and Ralph Gold, who had been involved in football for a number of years through an interest in West Ham United. They were persuaded that at that time they would have more opportunities at Birmingham City than at West Ham.

Karren Brady reports when she first saw St Andrews she was not so much disappointed as disgusted. It was dirty, lacking paint and the Boardroom was furnished in a 1960s style. The club was in the hands of liquidators. The then Chairman, Jack Wiseman, admitted to Karren Brady that he did not know how long the club could stay afloat, since the books were not available to him. He made the point that he was 70 years old, he was "all on his own at the club, and he was doing his best". The club clearly had been run into the ground. Karren Brady makes the point that the existing directors had been running the club at only a fraction of its potential. She was being kind; the directors for over 40 years had been running the club below its potential. Brady reported to David Sullivan "If we are going to buy a football club this is the one it should be". It was a pity from the point of view of the financial viability of the club that they had not purchased it ten years earlier.

The situation faced by BCFC in the 1980s was similar to that faced by many football clubs. They had been run by a succession of directors who had not been able to handle the changes, the rising costs, the increasing demands of the players, the marketing needs and the move away from the working class roots of the game.

The involvement of those running the game was in some cases because of a love of football and in other cases for an ego boost. They had been willing to put some of their own money in the club, and did not expect much of a return, if any. Unfortunately although they had usually been successful in their own careers, they did not have the skills needed in the new environment in which football now operated.

Sullivan and the Golds through their private company, Sports Newspapers bought the Blues in 1993 (for £1.7 million). They set about rebuilding the team, the club's image and the shabby ground. They demonstrated their long term intentions by approving a project to redevelop two sides of the ground, (part of the cost to be covered by a grant from the Football Trust.) Unfortunately the team were relegated to the third tier at the end of the 1993/94 season. They immediately bounced back and so were in the Championship (the second tier) for the 1995/96 season. In the year of their promotion they won the Auto Windscreens Shield (a competition for teams from the lower divisions). They were now beginning to enjoy some success, but the owners, the directors were experiencing corporate governance problems.

Barry Fry was the manager. He was indiscreet, he was reported to have made critical comments about David Sullivan. Fry was not happy with the amount of money available to spend on new players and about an axe which he imagined was hovering over his head. Sullivan was naturally upset at the remarks which were he regarded as provocative and inaccurate. David Gold "pointed out that board meetings should not be carried out via the press". Karren Brady regarded the end of the 1994/95 season as the worst time of her career. She refers to the "them and us" mentality of the manager, and to his belief that the directors needed him more than he needed them. Fortunately the relationship between Fry and the directors improved a little following promotion to the second tier. Fry's approach to management was sometimes criticised; one of his players, Steve Claridge said that it was not true that you could write down Barry's knowledge of tactics on a postage stamp. Claridge said "You would need to fold the stamp in half".

The squabble between the owners and the manager unfortunately continued and in 1996, Fry was sacked by the Board. Trevor Francis, a former player and hero at the club was brought in as manager. The club appeared to be moving forward, they invested £7.4 million (£12.8 million in today's values) on rebuilding two sides of the ground and they were spending money on acquiring new players. In 1997 the club, decided to raise funds to build a third new stand and to purchase additional players.

Trevor Francis purchased a number of new players (including Steve Bruce from Manchester United) and work was started on the new stand. In 1997/98 the club narrowly missed qualifying for the play-offs for promotion to the Premier League.

In 1998/99 they did qualify for the play-offs but lost to Watford in a penalty shoot-out. In 2000/01 the club for the third time failed at the play-off stage (again losing in a penalty shoot-out). They did, however, that season reach the final of the Worthington League Cup, where they played well but lost to Liverpool on yet another penalty shoot-out. The club could be regarded as having been unlucky, but for how much longer could the Board let this go on? The board had invested £4.5 million in their third new stand. In October 2001 they decided to terminate their contract with Trevor Francis. As David Gold said "You can't go on being nearly men. Eventually you have to make a change".

For a while following the removal of Francis the clash between the directors and the fans was unpleasant and in retrospect unnecessary. The views being expressed were that Sullivan "was just in it for the money and Blues needed an owner with more commitment". The criticisms of Sullivan were understandably getting him down; he felt he had been 'slaughtered' by the fans as a result of arguing with Trevor Francis. He had said things about Francis which were reported in the media, which he admitted did not come over as he had intended.

Trevor Francis left the club, by mutual consent; the expression often used when somebody is sacked. He was of course paid compensation. The fans had remained loyal to Francis, even though in five and a half years he had not taken the team into the Premier League.

Francis was popular amongst the fans because in his playing days at the club he had been seen as a hero. But even before he became manager at the Blues there had been criticism of his man management abilities and of his football tactical wisdom. Nobody doubted his enthusiasm and dedication to the game, but the problem has been not all the players in his teams have shared his single mindedness. Some players had found him inflexible and remote; they have not liked his disciplinarian approach. In turn he has believed that some of his players were not sufficiently dedicated to their team, particularly when the amount they were being paid was taken into account. He had problems in managing some players at QPR and Sheffield Wednesday, the clubs he was at before Birmingham.

There have also been critical comments about the football tactics he has introduced at his clubs. Alan Hudson, the former England international said that "Francis could not, in my opinion, spot a great footballer if the bloke's name had four letters in it, started with a 'P' and ended with an 'E'."

It had been widely thought that Francis would be allowed to stay at Birmingham for the 2001/02 season to see if he could achieve promotion – that this would be his last chance. But the friction between the chairman and Francis was so great, and the results on the pitch so disappointing, that the board believed Francis had to go quickly. Sullivan made a mistake from a public relations point of view when, following the sacking of Francis he criticised him in public. One of the criticisms was that Francis had left the club in a "desperate financial state". "When he arrived wages were 60% of turnover. They are now 90%. We are haemorrhaging money at a rate of £100,000 a week."

The fans were angry that Sullivan had forced Francis out. Sullivan said that all the criticism of him was getting him down. In 2001 he said that he and the Gold brothers would accept £16 million for the 78% shareholding they held in the club, through Sports Newspapers. (*Evening Mail*, October 25, 2001). This was roughly the stock market valuation of the shares at the time. Sullivan emphasised that, in selling, he was not looking for a premium over market price, and contrasted his own attitude with that of Alan Sugar at the Spurs.

A few years earlier, soon after the change in ownership, the football club had needed funds, and obtained loans from Sports Newspapers Ltd. Over the next five years loans of over £13 million were received, this of course transformed the financial position of the club. Some of the early loans had been repaid but new ones were received. In 1997 the company was restructured. A new company was formed, Birmingham City plc, (the Holding Company) and in January 1997 they acquired the whole of the share capital of Birmingham City Football Club. The shares of the holding company were then listed in February 1997 on the smaller of the two UK stock exchanges, the Alternative Investment Market. At the time of listing, 59% of the shares in Birmingham City plc, (the listed company) were held by Sports Newspapers Ltd. Sports Newspapers, was a private company and so its shares, not listed on a stock market, were all held by David Sullivan and the Gold family.

In July 1998 the club decided to raise additional equity finance by selling new shares to the public. The club offered another 30 million shares for sale at a price of 25p per share. The shares of football clubs had been falling in value and so were not now seen as a very attractive investment opportunity. Only 8% of these new shares were taken up by the public and by institutional investors. Neither professional investors nor supporters of the club were prepared to invest very much money in the club. This 1998 share issue was underwritten by Sports Newspapers Ltd and so they had to take up the 27.6 million unissued shares. This raised their holding to 78% of the total. The ultimate parent company in purchasing the shares that other investors did not want, injected another £6.9 million into the club.

The investment of new money (both debt and equity) enabled the club to purchase new players, to increase the wage levels and therefore attract better players (the annual wage bill doubled between 1992 and 1995) and to dramatically improve the ground and training facilities. The transformation of the club was remarkable particularly when it is taken into account that the team were not playing in the Premier League until 2002 – therefore not attracting the big TV money. Comments from supporters at the end of 2001 to the effect that the club needed owners who would show more commitment to the club were strange. It is easy to see why David Sullivan felt insulted. The supporters and other investors had turned down the opportunity in 1998 to invest money in the club. The Blues were at last promoted to the Premier League for the 2002/03 season.

When faced with the possibility of relegation in this their first season back in the Premiership they invested large amounts of money during the January transfer window in order to stay up. But in 2006 when again faced with the possibility of relegation they were not prepared to invest. Did the director believe in 2006 that they were too good to be relegated or were they just not prepared to risk any more of their money? In January 2006, in the crucial window period, Blues only acquired two players, both said to be strikers, one was ageing the other was inexperienced. The club were already in the relegation zone and needed to start scoring goals, if they were to get out of it. Neither of these new players was a success.

They had invested in the region of £10 million in the summer of 2005. But why in January 2006 did they only invest £0.5 million when there was a possibility that they would be relegated? To be relegated would mean a loss in the following season of £30 million in revenue. Perhaps it reflected the owners increasing disillusionment with the club and the city.

The directors would appear to have lost interest in the club during the 2005/6 season. In October 2005, the Blues unveiled plans for a £250 million development which would include a multi-purpose sports stadium, an entertainment complex and a casino. The sports stadium would be such that football, cricket, and basketball could be played there. The new stadium would have seating for 55,000 spectators. The casino was to be a joint venture with Las Vegas Sands (who it was hoped would invest £117 million in the project). The project would, however, only go ahead if the Gaming Commission granted it a 'super casino licence'. The proposed project was to be on the East side of the city, in an area that needed re-generation. A model for the development was the

Melbourne Cricket Ground in Australia where the cricket club shared a stadium with a football team. The plan was that the Blues would share the proposed stadium with the Warwickshire County Cricket Club. The new stadium would have given the Blues a chance to increase its revenue, its earning capacity and given Birmingham a boost to its claim to be a city of sport.

Unfortunately the new East side proposal received its first set back when local counsellors decided not to support the proposal, they did not want a casino in the area. There was an alternative site preferred by many city counsellors on the edge of the city at the National Exhibition Centre. The City Council decided to back the NEC bid as a site for a regional casino; the development went ahead. The sports stadium idea was dropped. It must have become clear to the directors of the Blues, that there was a limit to what they could achieve in Birmingham.

David Sullivan was finding that an involvement with a football club as an owner or supporter was not always satisfying. He was not the only person suggesting that there were some players who were footballing mercenaries, players who would move from club to club, sometimes just on loan for a short period, enjoying very high wages whether or not the club was successful. It was the supporters and owners who had the longer term commitment to the club; they were the ones who suffered most if the club failed. The players could just move to another club.

David Sullivan was clearly not happy with his investment in the club. When they had been relegated he said "I saw it coming … It's sad to say but I said right back in October, and everyone thought I was mad, that every alarm bell was ringing. Unfortunately the team didn't wake up … No one else saw it coming and I think if they had done, then they'd have done something about it. There was too much complacency and overconfidence. Had they realised earlier that we had a serious problem, then we might have got out of it. I feel very let down."

A headline in the *Sports Argus* as early in the season as October 29th 2005, said "Blues continued on a downward spiral towards the Championship." But many in the press, particularly those who had not seen the team play, made the meaningless comment that they were too good to go down. As Sullivan said there was complacency and overconfidence at the club. He said he regretted not having spoken out sooner. His view was that all at the club were partly responsible for the club's failure, the directors, the manager and the players.

Did They Make Money?

The club was sold in 2009. Had it been a good investment for the owners? We now know that the answer is "yes", but for a long time David Sullivan and the Gold brothers were showing a loss on their investment. For a number of years they had wanted to sell their shares but could not find a buyer. As with all investments involving share ownership, gains depend very much on timing and luck. Entrepreneurs who became involved with football clubs in the 1960s and 1970s and sold their shares in the 1990s were able to make a lot of money.

The value of the football club shares held by Sports Newspapers (i.e. held by Sullivan and the Gold brothers) at the end of December 2002 was approximately £7.2 million. They had paid £1.7 million in 1993 for one block of shares and £6.9 million for another block in 1998, a total of £8.6 million. No gain at all. In 2001 they had offered these shares to anyone who wanted to buy them for £16 million, but there were no takers. In May 2006, the price of a share on the Stock Market, following relegation to the Championship, was 13 pence, valuing the combined holding of Sullivan and the Gold brothers at £8.7 million, again no real gain. Share prices are volatile and over 2005/06 the season shares showed a high price of 24 pence and a low of 11 pence. At the high price the Sullivan and Gold holdings were worth £15 million. At this price the owners were showing a gain on their investment, but the price that can be obtained from selling a few shares, is different to the price that can be obtained from selling 62 million. In 2001 nobody would pay £16 million for the club, nor would they in May 2006. Yet three years later a ladies hairdresser from Hong Kong would appear on the scene and pay two to three times what the company was worth.

Where are they all now? Blues, at best are a struggling Championship club. David Sullivan, the Golds, with Karren Brady are running West Ham United. They had pulled off a coup over the use of the Olympic Stadium. They are, however, again unpopular with the fans of the club they own. They have again been attacked by fans at home games. Baroness Brady has a seat in the House of Lords and the investor from Hong Kong is in prison.

The Carson Yeung Era

When Carson's company, Grandtop, acquired the Blues, supporters of the club were quite excited. It was said that he was a billionaire and that he was a lover of football. He had exciting plans for the club. When he purchased his first block of shares in the club they were in the Championship, second tier. When he sold the club they were in the second tier but during the five years of his ownership the fans did have excitement. The Blues were winners of the League Cup beating Arsenal 2-1. They spent two years in the Premier League. Unfortunately these five years were not good for Carson, he lost most of his own assets and some of the assets of other people. He finished up in prison with a six years sentence. When he purchased the Blues, they were not in a bad state financially, they certainly owned their own ground. When he sold the club they were in a perilous state with debts of approaching £16 million with the ground being held as security against the loans. If the loans could not be repaid St Andrews might have to be sold.

In Hong Kong on the 3rd March 2014 Judge Wau brought the Carson Yeung case to a conclusion. His findings were that Yeung had concealed key details of his share dealings, that he had lied in his explanations of how transactions had been processed and crucially he had lied where his money had come from. "The lack of paperwork, the use of third parties to make payments and the contradictory answers he had given had all painted a picture of money laundering." The Judge agreed with the prosecution that the purchase of the Blues had been partly paid for with the proceeds of an indictable offence. Yeung was sentenced to imprisonment. The Court decided that Yeung was a money launderer.

This is a probably how he will be remembered in Birmingham. But was he a bad man? The best researched book on the subject by Ivery and Giles points out that he really was a football fan and he really did care about the Blues. Before his legal problems he made frequent trips from Hong Kong to watch his team play and took pleasure from their success. Unfortunately he was not a good businessman. He was "a man who sunk almost everything he had in the club trying to make it better". Unfortunately he failed. He was a gambler, a high roller, a risk taker. Perhaps too many of his friends and business associates were also gamblers.

He grew up living on a council estate in Hong Kong. He left school at the age of 15 to train as a hairdresser. He opened his first salon at the age of 29. He was successful as a ladies hairdresser attracting many celebrities to his salon. He claimed in court at his trial that much of his wealth had been earned through his hairdressing business. The Judge found this difficult to believe.

As his wealth increased he began to invest in property and to speculate in the Stock Market. He claimed in Court that by 1998 his portfolio was worth in the region of £2.4 million. When asked in Court for details of his share dealings, he was not able to provide the paper work to support his claims. The Judge concluded that there was a deliberate attempt to conceal. Before his 2013 court appearance he already had experienced problems with the law. In 2004 he had been convicted for failure to disclose his beneficial interests in a number of share transactions. He was fined but he was not found guilty of stock manipulation. One other source of Carson's wealth were the casinos of Macau, the biggest gambling centre in the World. He gambled himself in the VIP rooms, was a shareholder in a number of syndicates (Junket operations) and a friend of casino owners, some of whom were leading Triads.

The Takeover

The acquisition of the club by Yeung was a mess. An example of how not to take over a company. It should have been seen as a portent of what was to come. The Carson Yeung years turned out to be a disaster. During 2006 and 2007 Carson and his associates had been looking for an English club to buy. They were pointed in the direction of the Blues by Keith Harris of Seymour Price, an Investment Bank. Yeung was enthusiastic and had his first meeting with Sullivan in the summer of 2007. Six years later at his trial he gave his reasons for wishing to buy the club. He knew the Chinese market could be enormous and he planned to build up the Blues fan base in that country. Yeung did not have enough cash available to him at that time in 2007 to buy all the shares of the club. His plan was to immediately buy 29.9% of the shares (at a price of just over 61 pence per share) and to buy the remainder of the shares before the end of that year. Unfortunately he encountered difficulty in raising the money needed to pay for even the first block of shares. His company Grandtop did find £5.5 million and the balance needed to buy the first tranche was eventually produced personally by Carson. Questions were being asked as to how a ladies hairdresser could obtain these large amounts of money. It was later revealed in the court case that a company, Kingston Finance, had made a personal loan to Carson of nearly £13 million.

No cash appeared to pay for the balance of shares during 2007, again no cash appeared during 2008. Sullivan and the Golds became more and more concerned about who they were dealing with. They were making decisions about the running of the club without consulting Carson. Eventually in the summer of 2009 two years after the initial negotiations, Carson and his associates came back to the owners of Birmingham City Football Club wanting to buy the rest of the shares.

Sullivan was surprised at the unprofessional way the Hong Kong investors handled the purchase. They carried out little due diligence. His comment was that they merely asked us about ten questions and they failed to bring in accountants and auditors. Sullivan made them pay for their amateurish approach and for their lack of knowledge. Sullivan knew that Carson would not want to fail for a second time to complete the purchase of the club. It would have meant a huge loss of face for him within the Hong Kong Chinese community. Sullivan took a chance and asked for £1 per share. Apparently some of the directors of Grandtop wanted to negotiate the price down but Carson agreed to pay the £1 a share. This was valuing the Blues at £81.5 million probably three times what the club was worth.

To obtain the funds to pay the balance of the purchase price, Grandtop issued new shares, by means of a rights issue. They also took out a bridging loan. This loan was provided by The Best China Ltd, a company which was owned by Pollyanna Chu. She was also the controlling shareholder of Kingston, the finance company that helped Yeung to buy the first tranche of shares. Pollyanna Chu was CEO of one of the largest casinos in Macau, the Golden Resort Hotel. She was reputedly one of the wealthiest women in Hong Kong. There were stories at the time about her being the power behind the throne but she never openly became involved with the football club.

In October 2009 Grandtop with Carson as its chairman completed the purchase of the Blues. The Hong Kong company Grandtop changed its name to Birmingham International Holdings (BIH) to reflect its main business interests. They were the parent company with BCFC, the football club their major subsidiary. Yeung proudly announced that he was going to pump money into BCFC, £40 million in the first available transfer window which would be January 2010 with the same amount being available in the summer. Yeung (who was president of the club) and Vico Hui, (who was chairman of the football club for a short time) had passed the Premier League "Fit and Proper person test". This meant they had been evaluated and found to be fit to own a football club in England. All looked good. Yeung said that he wished "to let the Chinese know how an English Premier League club is managed". Hui said "we have very good connections in the China market. We know how it works. We could be the best supported club in the world."

In Yeung's first season in charge 2009/10 the Blues finished the season in 9th place in the Premier League, the highest position they had achieved in over 50 years. In the summer of 2010 Blues went on a pre-season tour to Hong Kong and China. 70,000 spectators watched them play at the former Olympic stadium in Beijing. The club had spent money on new players although not quite as much as Carson indicated. Things were going well. In February 2011 they won the League Cup, their first major trophy win for 48 years. As cup winners, they qualified to play in the lucrative Europa League in the 2011/12 season. The early months of 2011 turned out to be the high point of the Carson era, one of the few high points in the 100 year history of the club. In June 2011 Yeung was arrested.

In May 2011, the club were relegated to the Championship. In the next season, 2011/12, they were nearly promoted back to the Premier League. They finished in 4th place losing in the play-off game to Blackpool. In 2012/13 they finished in 12th place and then embarrassingly in 2013/14 they were nearly relegated to the third tier of English football finishing in 21st place, equal on points with the team just below them. They only escaped relegation on the last day of the season. In the 2014/15 and 2015/16 seasons they finished in 10th place in the Championship. In October 2016 all Yeung's official links with the Blues came to an end.

The Finances

On the pitch the team were up and down, but behind the scene things were bad. In the financial accounts for the year 2009/10 the first year of Carson's ownership, the auditors gave a warning. In their opinion the conditions within the club indicated the existence of "material uncertainty which may cast significant doubt about the group's ability to continue as a going concern". The accounts made clear that the club was reliant on funding from Carson Yeung. He had lent the club £14 million, he was not seeking repayment for at least a year. There were of course doubts as to where Carson Yeung's money was coming from. The club needed still more funding. This 2010 financial warning was at a time when the club was still in the Premier League. The parent company organised a placing of new shares. Carson mortgaged his expensive house on the Peak in Hong Kong to raise money for the club. It was planned that the money raised would be used to reduce the existing debt and to fund the purchase of new players.

To be fair most of the debt that the company had accumulated had been used to finance spending in the transfer market. During their two seasons in the Premier League (2009/10 and 2010/11) they spent, net £36 million on new players, the third highest outlay by a club, only beaten by Chelsea and Manchester City. These other two high spending clubs had of course much richer owners than the Blues and they had annual revenue figures three to four times higher than the Blues. BCFC was clearly being run in a financially dangerous manner. They were also paying the players high wages with no provision for a reduction should the club be relegated.

One problem that arose was that the financial advisors Seymour Pierce who had introduced Carson to the Blues, now that the purchase was complete wanted a £2.2 million fee for their work. The club disputed the fee, they were served with a Writ and in the end had to pay. One further problem arose in connection with the change of ownership. In the last days of the Sullivan Gold era, Karren Brady had been given a £1 million parachute payment plus a car. The two Gold brothers and David Sullivan had each charged the club £420,000 in "advance" management fees. Yeung was surprised when he took over management of the club to find that these amounts had been paid and that in fact the club did have some debts whereas he believed that it was debt free. The club brought a case against the former directors, it was settled out of Court with £3 million being returned to Yeung and his associates.

Less than two years after BIH had taken over the football club, there was dispute at boardroom level. Yeung had been arrested in 2011, as a result the shares in the company were suspended and his assets frozen. Yeung who was chairman of BIH did not want to resign. There were problems with the auditors, with delays in the publication of the accounts. The football club had a transfer embargo. They were selling off their best players, they were factoring their future parachute payments. They had borrowed against the security of their ground.

In August 2013, Yeung agreed to resign as chairman, and the board agreed to invite offers for the club. During his trial and in the early days after his conviction Yeung did try to influence the running of BIH and the club. He still owned the largest block of shares and some of his associates were still directors. Early in 2015 there were contested elections for a place on the board. The English Football League were not happy with a convicted criminal trying to interfere with the running of a football club. Peter Pannu had become a key man in the running of the football club and the holding company. Carson's 18 year old son, Ryan Yeung was made a director of the football club. In February 2015 the Board of BIH appointed Ernst and Young as receivers. This was a voluntary decision by the directors to call in receivers. They were being asked to take over the management of the company and to find a buyer. Yeung did not agree with this move but he could not stop it.

The financial management of the club had been abysmal. The auditors of BIH and of BCFC were never really happy with the financial reporting of the business. The annual accounts for both 2010/11 and 2011/12 were qualified. The auditors had not received all the information they needed to be able to conclude that the accounts were true and fair. They were not convinced that there was sufficient funding available to enable the group to continue as a going concern. Things did not improve.

In 2013/14 the wages to turnover (revenue) ratio was 98%, nearly all the money the club earned was being paid out as wages. Their turnover that year, with the parachute payment was £20 million but the club was struggling. Whilst they were in the Premier League their annual revenue was well over £50 million per annum. In 2011/12 their first year after relegation they made an operating loss of £4 million. But after taking into account the profits on the sale of players and the receipt of a parachute payment they reported a pre-tax profit of £15.7 million. One surprising item in the 2012 accounts was the directors remuneration figure, £687,000 (up from £80,000 the previous year). The largest part of this payment it was assumed was to be a payment to Paul Pannu.

The situation did begin to improve in 2014/15 the wages turnover ratio was reduced to a manageable 67%. The net debt of BIH was down to £19 million. This figure is however high for a company whose principle subsidiary had a turnover of only £21.5 million. The club was not good at generating revenue. Its match attendance figures were, in 2015/16 only the 9th highest in the Championship. Clubs from much smaller towns, such as Ipswich and Derby were attracting much bigger crowds. Their commercial revenue figures were embarrassing, again only the 9th highest in the Championship, for a team based in the second biggest commercial centre in the country.

BIH was put up for sale in June 2015, the receivers announced that their preferred bidder was Trillion Trophy Asia (TTA) an investment company registered in the British Virgin Islands, wholly owned by a Chinese businessman Paul Suen. The receivers granted TTA an exclusivity period during which the details for the transfer of ownership could be worked out. BIH was to be restructured. The shares were to be relisted on the Stock Exchange. The takeover was completed by October 2016.

TTA was to own between 60% and78% of the BIH shares and Carson Yeung and his associates were not to own more than 14%. It was announced that the company was not to be sold to anyone else for two years. This condition was perhaps necessary because Suen had a reputation for being a short term trader of shares and Carson was in jail with his future uncertain.

By 2014/15 the secured bank loan had been repaid but they were able to continue in existence only because TTA had granted them a loan of approximately £19 million, but with a high interest rate of 8%, and with the loan repayable after one year. It was however the willingness of TTA to meet future funding needs that satisfied the English Football League that the club would survive.

The club continued to be dependent upon its parent company BIH who were in turn dependent upon TTA. The BCFC (the football club) accounts for 2015/16 makes the point that £16 million had been provided to the club by BIH and that forecasts indicated that an additional £15 million was required to see the club survive through until November 2017. It was the investment company Trillion Trophy Asia who were providing the BIH with the financial support.

Paul Pannu and Panos Pavlakis

Two interesting directors at the club during the Carson Yeung period were Paul Pannu and Panos Pavlakis. Both had a big influence on the day to day running of the club. Pannu was also a key man in BIH. In fact the 2009 to 2014 period should perhaps be known as the Yeung-Pannu period. With Yeung fighting a court case, Pannu was (he claimed) left in charge of the decision making at the football club. Pannu's career showed he was a man of considerable ability but that he was a difficult person to work with and he seemed to move from one set of troubles to another.

Pannu joined the Hong Kong Police Force at the age of 21. He was a high flyer and rose to the rank of senior inspector. His police work involved investigating Triad activities. In 1993 he was arrested. He had been living a lavish lifestyle and it was found that he had more money in his possession than one would have expected for a police inspector. Pannu argued that it was because of the nature of his work, that he had to spend so much time in the company of leading members of Triad gangs. He was suspended from the Police Force whilst his activities were investigated. The case brought against his was that he had received money from a Triad boss. The boss concerned, who was due to give evidence in court in the Pannu case, was murdered at a F1 Grand Prix motor race meeting in Macau. Another witness decided not to testify. The court acquitted Pannu on the grounds that he could not receive a fair trial. He was suspended from police work for three years. The Triad gang, the Sun Yee, that he was involved with was one that Yeung had also been linked to. Pannu claimed that he was the victim of a vendetta based on race and jealousy. He resigned from the police, believing he would have a difficult future if he remained.

Whilst suspended Pannu did not waste his time. He studied law at the University of London, and became a barrister. He was called to the Bar in Hong Kong in 1997. When Yeung took over BCFC he brought in his old friend Pannu to help run the club. His title was Vice Chairman of Football. Pannu had spent a year studying for a Master's Degree in Management and Business of Football and so it appeared that he was well qualified for this role. He became Acting Chairman of the club in 2010. Carson became preoccupied with his trial which began in 2011. Pannu was made a director of BCFC in June 2011. One of the first problems that he had to deal with were the large payments the club made to Sullivan, Gold and Brady at the time they were selling the club. There were problems with Pannu throughout his stay at Blues.

Pannu had been appointed as a director of the holding company BIH in 2012. He became CEO and managing director of that company. He became one of the highest paid directors in English Football and in addition to that his private company Asia Rays Ltd., was paid £0.46 million for providing consulting services to BIH. From BIH, for 9 months work, he received over half a million pounds in salary. The auditors were not happy with these payments, there was a doubt whether they had been properly authorised. He was fired from the board of BCFC in December 2014 for allegedly exceeding his authority. The receivers Ernst and Young removed him from the post of director of BIH in March 2015.

Obviously a skilled operator but unfortunately he did not use his skills to benefit football clubs. Pannu did not disappear from the scene. In May 2015 he filed claims against BIH on the grounds of constructive dismissal, failure to pay wages, bonuses and a long service reward. He later added a libel claim for damage to his reputation at the time of the termination of his appointment. The receivers made a number of counter claims against Mr Pannu concerning a breach of duties whilst serving at BIH and BCFC.

The auditors had a number of problems with Mr Pannu and BCFC. They were not happy with a dodgy deal that had been arranged with the Chinese Company Xtep, a company involved in the leisure business. There were two sides to the deal. On the one side the Company would arrange to manufacture and sell replica Blues shirts, with the royalties being paid into a tax haven subsidiary of BIH. The other side of the deal involved BIH paying money to Xtep to cover advertising and marketing expenditure. As far as anyone could see there was no benefit to the football club in the arrangements.

Another interesting director was Panos Pavlakis who was appointed to the Board of BIH in December 2013. He resigned from that position in March 2015 following a battle at boardroom level. He had become a director of the football club, BCFC in January 2014 and remained as a director of the football club into 2017; even though there had been dramatic changes in the ownership and leadership of the parent company. One reason why he was interesting was because of his link with Carson Yeung; he had a relationship with a daughter of Carson's half-brother.

The Present

The takeover by TTA went ahead in 2016. Paul Suen, the majority shareholder in TTA was known in Hong Kong as the Penny Stock King. A Penny Stock is a low price share which has a low downside risk, you cannot lose much money and the possible gains are great. Following on any good news a penny stock can easily double in value. Suen is certainly not a sugar daddy. He buys shares in a listed company, improves the situation of that company and then sells and moves on. It helps if he can buy the shares with borrowed money. His interests are wide; at the same time as purchasing the Blues he purchased another Hong Kong company whose major business interest was oil exploration in Argentina. The fans were unsure, he might turn out to be a short time investor who slightly improves the situation and then sells the club to somebody else. He might be a longer term investor wishing to become involved with the new Chinese love affair with football. Unfortunately his first major decision was not good. He made the same mistake as the Chinese owners of Aston Villa by appointing a new manager with an international reputation that he believed would give them global appeal. Zola was brought in as manager, but only lasted for three months.

TTA did provide BIH, and through them the football club with financial backing when they needed it. At the end of 2016 they agreed to provide a loan of £26 million, the money was to be used to explore new ways of generating income. BIH needed to broaden its income stream. Sports education, on-line gaming and entertainment were mentioned.

How much did Paul Suen pay to acquire the Blues? It is not an easy question to answer. He in fact purchased the holding company BIH who owned not only the football club but also a number of other investments, Suen did not simply hand over a sum of money to make the purchase. He had already made loans to BIH (HK$150 million) and had accepted convertible notes which could be converted into equity shares as repayment of the loan. There was also a new issue of equity in which Suen was involved. BIH did need to raise new finance and so they made a rights issue to most of the existing shareholders. However, it was a special rights issue, Carson Yeung and his associates were not allowed to purchase any of the new shares. Suen is believed to have purchased HK$250 million of the shares.

With the loan and the purchase of new equity shares Suen's total investment in BIH was worth approximately HK$400 million (£41 million). However, there is one further complication. Suen agreed to sell some of his shares so that the number being offered to the public was large enough to satisfy the freely available requirement of the stock exchange. This means he will have recouped some of the investment mentioned above (say £10 million). One estimate is therefore that Suen paid in the region of £31 million for the control of BIH and therefore of the Blues. He had control but did not own all of the company's shares.

In March 2017 the board of BIH announced that they proposed to change the name of the company to "Birmingham Sports Holdings Ltd". They believe that the new name would better reflect the current status of the groups business and its direction of future development. The fans of the club saw the reference to future developments as encouraging. The fans had hopes that starting with the 2017/18 season things would get better. The club had new owners, with perhaps more financial muscle. Zola had been sacked and the club had a new very experienced manager. The club bought and sold many players in the summer transfer window. They broke their own transfer record, paying £6 million for a Spanish midfielder. Would things change?

After only a few weeks of the new season the new manager Harry Redknapp was sacked. Apparently there were management problems behind the scenes. A football club is like any other organisation, there are disagreements and there are internal politics with one person not getting on with another. In a football club, full of alpha males, the disagreements can be nasty. It was said that during Redknapp's brief period in charge there was a bad atmosphere in the dressing room. He had brought with him to the club as an assistant, Kevin Bond (whose father had once been an unsuccessful manager at the Blues). In bringing in Bond this forced out Steve Cotterill, who had been popular with the players. The early season results were not good but Redknapp was only given three games in which to allow the new players to prove themselves. The former director Pavlakis, said he was shocked by the timing of Redknapp's sacking. In July he and his staff had been regarded as heroes and three months later they were thought not to be good enough. In the first few weeks of the season it was said that the players lacked quality, lacked commitment and lacked passion. But Redknapp said in his defence that a number of the new players were not those he wished to purchase and that, behind the scenes, the executive team would not deliver players he wanted.

The new chief executive, Xuandong Ren, claimed that TTA were with the Blues for the long term but that is what one would expect someone in his position to say. He talked about investing more in training facilities and in establishing links with football in China. He had been involved with the development of football in China, in particular the development of training centres and soccer camps. His comment about the sacking of Redknapp was surprising, he said that it had not been a rushed decision and that it was time for the club to move on. He had been involved in the decision to hire Redknapp. The new board did bring to the club executives and advisers with knowledge of Premier League football. Jeff Vetere became Director of Football and Darren Dein became a football advisor. Dein is a lawyer involved in football, he is what is sometimes called a super-agent. He certainly has an impressive football background, his father having been a director at the Arsenal and his wife is the daughter of a former Spurs vice chairman. He was reported to be paid £25,000 a month for his services.

What was happening to the team on the pitch? In 12 months they moved from being promotion candidates to a place in the relegation zone. As at the end of 2017 they had scored less goals than any other club in the top 4 divisions, they were in danger of being relegated to the third tier. Under the leadership of Paul Suen, in 12 months the club had had 4 managers. Those running the football club did not seem to know what they were doing.

New investors were becoming involved with the listed Hong Kong company. By the end of December 2017 TTA only owned 39.87% of BSH shares, Ever Depot owned 21.75%, then came Dragon Villa with 7.45%, and Chigwell Holdings with 5.21%. Not much is known about these new shareholders and because the holdings of any individual has apparently been kept to less than 10% they do not have to satisfy the Football League ownership test.

The football club have been in a bad way financially for a number of years. In the financial accounts of Birmingham Sports Holdings, the Hong Kong listed holding company, for 2016/17 a £17 million loss was shown. The annual staff costs were £22.3 million and their revenue only £16.6 million. Clearly not a situation that could be allowed to continue. On the football side of their business BSH either needed to cut costs or increase revenue – the latter being difficult for a struggling second tier club. It is difficult to be precise about the longer term strength of BSH financial position as it is not easy to read between the lines of the published accounts. This is of course deliberate, it is why companies make use of creative accountanting. In the original figures for the position at the end of June 2016 they reported that the liabilities exceeded the assets, that the business had a capital deficiency, of £5.2 million. They then re-classified the borrowings which resulted in showing a positive equity of £6.3 million. They also re-valued upwards the intangible assets.

The new owners have put more money into the football business. Money loaned to Chigwell Holdings and Dragon Villa has been used to finance the football club. In the latter half of 2017 BSH borrowed somewhere in the region of £20 million from these two shareholders' companies to be used to satisfy the funding needs of the football club. Without this money the club would have been in a mess. Even playing around with figures cannot hide the fact that BSH is not financially in a good position. They need to earn money somewhere and without promotion to the Premier League this will not come from the football club. Relegation to the 3rd tier would be a disaster from a financial point of view. The club will make a financial loss in 2017/18 and will begin to get into trouble with the Financial Fair Play rules, with the Profitability and Sustainability test. Not a promising future.

The future for Blues would depend on decisions being made at holding company level. The chairman of the holding company Zhao Wenqing, visits St Andrews quite often to deal with major issues. The club's CEO, Ren Xuandong and at least two of the other directors of BCFC (all from China), are based permanently in Birmingham. The governance of the club is key to its future success. The fans hope that the decisions made by these executives are better than those that have been made in the past.

An indication of the problems that will be faced by the Blues can be seen from looking at the size of their expected annual revenue. In 2018/19 they will be competing with WBA and the other recently relegated clubs. The Albion will be receiving in the region of £50 million that season as the first instalment of their parachute payment. This one source of income will be more than twice the annual revenue of the Blues. The clubs not receiving parachute payments are at a big disadvantage, the higher revenue means higher wages which normally means better players.

In June 2018 it was announced that the name of the Blues ground would be changed. It would no longer be simply St Andrews. Paul Suen's company Trillion Trophy Asia had purchased the naming rights to the ground. For at least the next three years the ground would be named "St Andrew's Trillion Trophy Stadium". The club's training ground in Wast Hills would be the "Trillion Trophy Training Centre". Large numbers of the fans were not happy with the change but the club did need money. This sponsorship income would help the club satisfy FFP requirements. The Chief Executive referred to the deal as being "a landmark partnership for the club" and though not mentioning what the deal was worth he referred to the amount as significant. Because of TTA's relationship with the Blues, the amount involved would have needed to be at fair market value. The deal did indicate that the owners were prepared to continue to put money into the club.

The ownership position of the club continued to be fluid. As the result of an issue of shares in the summer of 2018, the Investment company Dragon Villa became the second biggest shareholder in the club. Because they owned in the region of 20% of the shares it meant that the Dragon Villa's owner, Lei Sutong, would now need to satisfy the League's Ownership and Directors Test. Little is known about the shareholders of the Blues, it is not known how they have made their money.

Part B: The Early Years

The Blues are another of the football teams that were founded by members of a church (in 1875). A number of cricket enthusiasts who attended the Trinity Church in Bordesley wanted a sport to play in winter months. The football club they formed was first called Small Heath Alliance. They became a professional club in 1885, because the players needed some financial rewards in order to compensate for the loss of income during the time they were travelling or playing football.

Even before the First World War the club had a very up and down existence; the best position they achieved in those days was seventh in Division One (the top division), in both 1904/05 and 1905/06.

During the 1920s and 1930s the Blues had by their own modest standards reasonable success in the League. They were promoted back to Division One in 1921/22 and stayed there until being relegated in 1939 in the last season before the war. The highest positions they achieved during this period was eighth, but there were a number of seasons when they were fighting against relegation. They did however often do well in the FA Cup competition including reaching the final in 1930/31. Despite being favourites to win the Cup they lost to their neighbours WBA, who were in Division Two at the time. In the season they were relegated, in 1938/39 they attracted a record crowd of 67,341 to St Andrews for the cup game against Everton. Their average league attendance that season being 26,434.

At the beginning of the Second World War the district around St Andrews was classified as a "danger-zone" and spectators were banned not only from the ground but also from the area. The ground was in fact surrounded by munitions factories. The area was bombed by the Luftwaffe on more than twenty occasions. The St Andrews ground has often been referred to by Birmingham City supporters as being unlucky; there is a story that a gypsy woman had placed a curse on it. It was certainly unlucky in 1942 when the Main Stand was destroyed by fire, caused by a local fireman mistaking petrol for water, and as a result spraying petrol on what had been a small fire. He could have been an Aston Villa supporter!

In the first season after the war (1946/47) the club were in Division Two – but were promoted to the First in 1947/48. Unfortunately they were relegated again after only two seasons in the top division.

The 1950s began with the Blues in the second tier. In 1954-55 they famously beat Liverpool 9-1, and went on to be promoted. The Liverpool team they beat were a poor team, it was before Shankly became their manager. In the Blues first season back in the top division they finished in 6th place – the highest place achieved in the club's history. In that same year 1955/56 they made only their second appearance in the FA Cup Final. Unfortunately they lost to Manchester City, even though again they had been pre-match favourites. That season was and still is the high point for the club. At the time the directors of the club were ambitious. They entered the team in what was then known as the 'Inter-Cities Fairs Cup' which later became the UEFA Cup. They were enjoying success in the new European competition. In 1959/60 they reached the (two legged) final of the Cup and were beaten by Barcelona. The size of the crowd to watch the first leg of the final in Barcelona was 75,000; the return leg match in Birmingham attracted just over 40,000. The directors of Blues had made decisions that for a time placed Birmingham City amongst the football elite but they could not keep them there. Unfortunately the two clubs who had played each other in that 1960 Final moved in opposite directions over the next 50 years.

In the 1960/61 season they lost in the final to Roma. In the following season the Blues were knocked out in the first round of the competition by R D Espanol. One remarkable aspect of this particular two legged tie, was that in Spain there was a crowd of 60,000 to see Birmingham City play. In the return leg at St Andrews, only 16,874 watched the match. Not encouraging for the future.

The directors of Birmingham City had shown enterprise and foresight by entering European competitions in their early days. In 1955 they became the first English team to participate in a European competition. They can say that at one time in their history they were an elite club. It is a pity they were not rewarded more financially. The background to the Fairs Cup was that cities that held large 'Trade Fairs' were invited to enter a team. Initially, the idea was that the team would not be a club side representing the city, but a team made up of the best players from all the teams in the respective cities. With Aston Villa not showing any interest, Birmingham City became the team representing Birmingham. Those were the early days of European competitions; this new opportunity was taken seriously in other countries.

The directors of the Blues tried to achieve success in the second half of the 1960s by appointing a manager with a proven record. Stan Cullis had been manager of Wolves from 1948 to 1964, a period when they won the top division three times, and the FA Cup twice. He was sacked by Wolves in controversial circumstances. He became manager of Birmingham City from December 1965 to March 1970. He was not able to lead Birmingham City to success. The best achievements during his period as Blues manager were two semi-final appearances in the domestic Cup competitions.

In the 1960s as well as struggling on the football field, they were struggling in the Boardroom. The Board consisted of 3 sets of brothers (the Morrises, the Wisemans and the Dares) plus Neville Bosworth. Each family pulled in a different direction. Board meetings would end with no measure of agreement having been reached on key issues. Throughout the period the Board was seeking to raise additional finance. In 1964 they invited Doug Ellis to become a club director following his unsuccessful attempt to join the Board of Aston Villa. Ellis states in his autobiography that he had "extreme reservations" on whether or not to accept the invitation from the Blues but found it difficult to decline. He was a director at the Blues for three and a half years and his period on the Board made quite an impression on him. He has made clear his opinion on the quality of other directors. He claims that one of his "greatest strengths" when he eventually joined the Villa Board as chairman was that his experience at Blues had taught him "exactly how not to run a football club". He had learned "disharmony and not a lot else … I had learned exactly how not to run a football club while at St Andrews … In any organisation or family, a firm direction has to come from the top with everyone pulling in the same direction. I hadn't seen much of that at Birmingham FC." One wonders why he stayed on the board for over three years if the disharmony made the atmosphere unpleasant.

While the three sets of brothers were squabbling, Clifford Coombs, the owner of a local drapery store, was seeking a place on the Board. He had made a loan to the club of £80,000, (in terms of present day prices, equivalent, to over £1.5 million). But the existing Board members would still not make him a director. He eventually gave the Board an ultimatum, a directorship or give me my money back. They could not afford to pay him back so they then made him a director. Clifford Coombs took over effective control of the club in 1967/68. He later brought his two sons onto the Board (Derek and Keith).

1968-1985 The Coombs Years

The club had been in a bad financial state when the Coombs family took over control. Unfortunately it did not improve very much over the next ten or so years. By 1974 the accumulated deficit was £0.45 million (in terms of today's prices that is £3 million). The current liabilities exceeded the total assets of the club. Clifford Coombs died during the 1974/75 season. His son Keith took over as chairman, and he with his brother became the major shareholders.

The 1960s which had begun quite well turned out to be disappointing, the low point being a final place of 18th in Division Two in the 1969/70 season. They were however an up and down team. They were promoted back to Division One in 1972 and then enjoyed a period of modest success, finishing 11th in that division in 1977/78 before being relegated the following year. Jim Smith had become their manager in March 1978.

Jim Smith commented on the fact that the Coombs family had so much power in terms of shares and money "that nobody else at the club could touch them". Keith Coombs had acted "unilaterally and without consultation with any of his directors" when targeting Smith as the Blues manager. It was not an obvious choice at the time because Smith had no track record in the higher divisions. When Smith moved to the club they were in trouble at the bottom of the First Division with only 12 games left to be played in the season; one manager had already been sacked that season (Willie Bell), and the acting manager (Sir Alf Ramsey) had fallen out with the Coombs brothers.

Jim Smith in fact saved the club from relegation in his first year but they were relegated to the second tier the next season before being promoted again in the next (1979/80). By Blues standard, the club did well in 1980/81 finishing 13th in the top division. The following season again Blues did quite well (they finished 16th) but Smith was sacked during February 1982. Smith had done well whilst with the Blues, the club was desperately short of finance, yet Smith produced an exciting team. The reason he was removed was that a "top" manager became available, and the directors (or rather some of them) were tempted. Smith was dumped. This was not a popular move, both because Smith was liked by the fans and because he was replaced by an ex Aston Villa manager Ron Saunders. Saunders had been successful at the Villa, but had fallen out with the Villa directors. The Blues directors hoped he would bring success to his new club, but he did not.

The manner of Smith's dismissal was clumsy; but was a good illustration of the way industrial relations (human resource management) was handled at the time. Jim Smith had heard rumours that Jack Wiseman, one of the Blues directors, was having talks with Ron Saunders who had just walked out of his job at Aston Villa. Following an away game at West Ham, Smith sat next to Wiseman on the coach journey home. Nothing was said about Smith's position at the time, although Smith later discovered that the decision to remove him had been made before the West Ham game. On the Monday morning following the match, Smith was asked to see the chairman. Then he was told he was no longer needed at the club. Saunders was appointed as manager a few days later. Smith did not blame Saunders, who apparently would only accept the job when he knew that a satisfactory financial arrangement had been made for Jim Smith.

One director who was not happy with what had happened was the well-known comedian Jasper Carrott. Carrott was particularly annoyed because the decision had been made without even talking to him about it. He was sufficiently incensed by the issue to resign as director. Smith refers to his time at the Blues as a "bittersweet" experience "with never a dull moment". Saunders was not successful, he stayed as manager for four years, and the best positions the team obtained under his leadership were 17th in Division One in 1982/83 and 20th in the next season, which meant relegation.

Smith makes the comment that the Coombs family "talked big time but at times they did not act it". The club did not enjoy success on the field during the seventeen years of the Coombs family control. In the period from 1967/68 to 1984/85, they spent six years in the second tier and eleven in the first, but their years in the first division were usually characterised by a fight against relegation.

In the ten year period between 1984 and 1993 the Blues has six managers. Following their relegation to Division Two at the end of the 1985/86 season things went from bad to worse. In their three seasons in that division they finished 19th, 19th and 23rd. In 1989/90 they were in the Third Division. The club had also acquired a reputation for hooliganism. At the final home match of 1984/85 season, Leeds supporters invaded the pitch at St Andrews and police horses were required to intervene before the game could continue. At the match one young man was killed when a wall collapsed on him.

There continued to be a great deal of discontent at Boardroom level. Who were the directors of the club during the 1950s, 60s and

70s period? They were a group of local businessmen who between them ran small plumbing, building and brewing businesses and a law office. The directors knew each other through their work and through the clubs and societies they belonged to. In this respect they were similar to many Boards of Directors at football clubs around the country. They had some wealth, were well connected through local networks and had an interest in football. They were not expecting that their involvement with football would lead to much of a financial gain (or for that matter much of a financial loss). They were not expecting national recognition. Could they work together effectively as a Board? In the case of the Blues the answer was no according to Doug Ellis. This would certainly appear to be the case judging from the decisions made, the performance of the football team, and the financial position of the club.

One director was the well-respected and liked David Wiseman who was a director of the club for nearly 50 years, including being Vice Chairman from 1945 to 1976. He became a director of Birmingham City when he was only 33 years of age. He soon became recognised in football administrative circles at a national level and twice became a member of the Football League Committee (1941/42 and 1949/71). He also served on committees of the Football Association, and was made a life member of both bodies. He has been referred to as "the Grand Old Man of Soccer in general and Birmingham City in particular". He clearly loved the club, and was respected for his knowledge about football. He was awarded the OBE.

Jack Wiseman was the younger brother of David and became a director in 1958, Deputy Chairman in 1975, and later Chairman. When Karren Brady first visited St Andrews in 1992 with a view to a possible purchase of the club by David Sullivan, it was Jack Wiseman who as Chairman welcomed her and helped persuade her that the Blues would be an interesting investment opportunity. He had remained a director of the club through the Coombs family era, the Whelan years, the period with the Kumars in control and into the Sullivan, Gold period.

The second set of brothers were the Dares. Harry Dare was a director of a medium sized successful local building company. He was a director of the Blues for over 30 years, retiring in 1979. His brother Bill Dare was the director of a brewing company. The third set of brothers were Len and Harry Morris whose family business was again in the Building Contracting Industry.

Neville Bosworth was also a member of the Board during part of this period. He was a solicitor and a local politician. He had been Lord Mayor of Birmingham and Leader of the City Council. He clearly was an important figure and the only club director not a director of a small business. All the directors owned shares in the football club, no one was a majority shareholder.

Sir Alf Ramsey became a director of the club in January 1976 but unfortunately resigned from the Board on health grounds two years later. Unfortunately, although he had been successful as the manager of England in 1966, he was not able to halt the slide of Birmingham City.

The directors in 1975 had hardly changed from those in 1965. The major change was the introduction of the Coombs family. Doug Ellis had commented critically on the quality of the Board in 1965, yet it was made up of essentially the same people ten years later. Ellis had complained about disagreements between the different families, there is no reason to believe it was any different 10 years later. Indeed, it could well have been worse, because the Coombs family had become a very powerful faction. There had been attempts to keep Clifford Coombs off the Board but he had been able to force his way into the club and become chairman with the result that the same people who had tried to keep him on the side lines now had to work with him as chairman.

The Finances

The financial position had not improved. By 1974/75 the accumulated deficit of the club had increased to £450,395 (equivalent to over £3.5 million today). In fact 1974/75 was a good year financially. The Chairman was able to state in the

Annual Report and Accounts that "although the principal objective of any football club is not necessarily to make a profit, it gives me great pleasure to record that a profit has been made this year. Although this is only a small profit this is the first (one) for many years."

During the early years of the 1980s the financial position was moving from bad to worse. In the 1981/82 accounts the auditors (Pannell Kerr) in their report drew attention to the fact that the club's liabilities were over £0.5 million greater than their assets. They pointed out that the annual accounts had been prepared on a going concern basis which assumed that "adequate financial facilities will be available to enable the company to continue normal trading operations".

This meant that although the liabilities of the company were well in excess of the assets, it was being assumed by the directors and by the auditors that somebody would pick up the deficit.

The club was operating at a loss as a result of falling revenue and continuing high wage bills. In 1984/85 their income was £1 million and their expenditure £1.4 million. To be fair to the Board of Directors attendances were falling for most clubs (but not all clubs had such high wage bills). In 1984/85 the average home gate was 12,700 – the 24th highest in the leagues. For one game in 1984 they attracted a gate of only 7,043, which resulted in gate receipts of just over £11,000. The gates of nearly all clubs were declining, but relative to other clubs the Blues gate was declining at a faster rate. A major problem was that the directors were not successful at generating income from alternative sources.

The directors decided to issue new equity shares for the public to buy. Unfortunately the supporters were not very interested. Although it can be argued that a football club is of value to a community, in the situation Blues were in the community was not prepared to invest money in the club. The issue of shares was not very successful; they sold just over 50% of the shares on offer. Surprisingly the club reported in their 1984 annual accounts that only "230 supporters became new shareholders". The money raised did not get the club out of financial difficulties. To make financial matters worse the club were relegated at the end of the 1983/84 season.

The directors themselves (at the time of the offer of shares to the public) made loans to the club of £0.524 million – these loans were unsecured and interest free. Whatever one thinks of the ability of the directors to manage and run a football club in the difficult times of the 1970s and early 1980s, there was in the case of BCFC no doubting their commitment to the club. The financial position of the club continued to deteriorate. By December 1985 the club was in a very serious financial position. It now had accumulated deficits of £2.5 million. Its short term liabilities exceeded its assets by £1.6 million.

One can feel some sympathy for the directors of the Blues. They had been struggling to keep the club in the first division. As with directors of other clubs at the time, they had put playing success above the short term profit motive. The directors were Birmingham men who identified with the team. A football team was at that time a 'public good' with strong ties with the local community. The directors at that time were not motivated by personal financial gain. They were prepared to put their own money in the club – for reasons of social prestige and status.

Directors are responsible for the financial position of a business. For one or two years the performance of a business can be influenced by good luck or bad luck, but if you perform badly for over ten years you cannot blame it on luck. From the early 1980s they were desperately trying to find new directors who would bring extra money to the club. The Coombs family had carried the financial burden for a number of years (since the mid-1960s). Keith Coombs had been referred to as "a wonderful benefactor" of the club. He was. By 1985 he had invested about £800,000 of his own money in the club – but he was also a director, responsible for the financial decisions of the club and the appointments made by the club. He was responsible for the financial position of the club.

Early in 1985 Dennis Mortimer at the invitation of Keith Coombs joined the Board of BCFC. There were great hopes at the time that this appointment would strengthen the financial position of the club. Mortimer had been the Chairman of Luton Town at a time when they were a successful Division One club. Unfortunately he resigned in December 1985, less than a year after joining the Board. It had been hoped that he would take over from Keith Coombs as Chairman.

The *Birmingham Mail* reported the resignation as "another shattering blow to a club now surviving on a financial knife edge". The reason Mortimer gave for resigning after such a short period was "business commitments". It is doubtful that he was impressed with the crisis hit club.

The fans were very critical of the Coombs regime. There were however some words of comfort for Keith Coombs from Derek Mortimer. He said "I wonder how much longer the poor man can go on. The directors are a decent bunch of people. If they were a bunch of ratters it would not be so bad. Keith Coombs has been a wonderful benefactor and it is sadness to me that he should have to suffer constant and ill-deserved abuse from a small minority." Although Mortimer was sympathetic, he did not wish to buy the club. Keith Coombs was by 1985 keen to sell his shares in the club. He said he had received several offers to buy the club.

In 1986 the Chairman reported that "the worsening financial state of the company reached a climax in December 1985, precipitating a change in the control and management of the company." Action had to be taken to reduce the mounting losses. This took a "toll on the playing side" the result was the club were relegated at the end of the 1985/86 season. An injection of further capital was still desperately needed. BCFC were seeking other directors. Harry Parkes the ex-Villa director joined Blues Board in 1985 and 1986. He purchased, 10,000 shares, but was not the major backer the club needed.

There had been mismanagement and lack of control, over the 20 year period from the mid-60s to the mid-80s. In the early years of the 1960s the Blues had the highest wage bill of any of the West Midland teams. During this period the team were fighting against relegation from the Division One (first tier). The maximum wage level had ended in 1961.

There had been little investment in the St Andrews ground, it was unattractive and in a rundown state. In the 1965 to 1985 period they had seven managers. By the close of the 1984/85 season the Blues were in dire financial circumstances. The Board, still controlled by the Coombs family, passed a resolution to liquidate the club. The team were near the bottom of Division Two. Their total wage bill was almost the same as that of the Villa (who were in the first division). Astonishingly the Blues wage bill was equal to their total income, therefore all other costs just added to losses.

The total debt/annual revenue ratio clearly illustrates the financial problems of the Blues. At the end of the 1972/73 season the ratio was 1.64, this was whilst Clifford Coombs was in charge. The ratio rose to 2.07, there were doubts as to whether the club was solvent.

1985-1989 The Wheldon Years

A major change in ownership (and in financial policy) did occur on 16 December 1985 when K.E. Wheldon took over control of the club. Wheldon had an impressive record as Chairman of Walsall FC where he had saved that club from near insolvency. He had a reputation for astute and ruthless business deals. He had made his money in the scrap metal business. He had previously tried to buy his way onto the Board of Wolverhampton Wanderers but was unsuccessful.

The financial policy of the club immediately changed. Wage bills were cut. The training ground at Elmdon was sold. The level of debt was reduced. A short term loan was obtained from the Local Council initially repayable in May 1989 and an increase in the Bank overdraft was negotiated, secured by a fixed charge on the clubs ground. Unfortunately at the end of the 1980s at a time when football was taking off in the rest of the country, the Blues were cutting back. At a time when the Premier League was being formed and huge amounts of TV money began to flow to the top clubs, BCFC were taking measures to reduce expenditure.

Ken Wheldon had joined the Board in December 1985. Just over three years later he introduced the Kumar Brothers to the Club and just over a year later, in 1990 he resigned. When Wheldon came to the Blues they were in a disastrous financial state and changes were desperately needed. Ron Saunders was dismissed as manager in January 1986 following a run of 18 matches in which the team failed to win. The club were relegated to Division Two. John Bond was brought in as manager but he was dismissed in May 1987. An ex Blues player, Garry Pendrey, was then brought in as manager. He expressed the opinion that he could "see a little light at the end of what has been a very dark tunnel, thanks to the financial wizardry of the Chairman, Ken Wheldon." Unfortunately there was no light and little wizardry.

The only financial wizardry that was taken by the board under Wheldon's leadership was to reduce costs. The inevitable result was the club were relegated to Division Two at the end of the 1988/89 season. The players in the team were of poor quality. In that season the average home gate was 6,300 which meant there were 46 clubs with higher attendance figures. The board had cut costs but also lost revenue.

In April 1989 Wheldon announced that he wished to sell the club – it was bought by the Kumar brothers for approximately £1.6 million. Pendrey was pushed out of the club, and Dave Mackay a manager with experience at a number of clubs was brought in to replace him. But the new owner and a new manager could not save the club. Bad leadership over many years had resulted in big financial problems and the team were now in the third division. Financially Wheldon and the new Board had had some success; the accumulated deficit had been halved between 1985 and 1989 and by 1989 the assets exceeded the liabilities. Wheldon and his Board failed from a football performance point of view but they had kept the club in existence. When Wheldon took over the debts were in excess of £3 million, and before he became a director the Board had just passed a resolution to appoint a receiver to wind up the club.

Wheldon was able, in his Chairman's report for the year 1987/88, to state "Many shareholders have told me that they have given up hope of ever seeing accounts for BCFC showing a solvent position and a clear auditor's certificate. Therefore I am pleased to send you a copy of the club's audited figures for the year ... showing the situation ... The debt mountain of nearly £3 million that I inherited when I became chairman in December 1985, has been reduced to a little over £1 million." The club had reduced this by the "sale of players and other assets ... We cannot afford a first division team with only a third division income". Several creditors had been good to the club and waved old debts or converted loans into shares, others had taken legal action to secure payment.

Wheldon prevented the collapse of the Blues but he could not turn round the fortunes of the club. By 1990 the wage bill of the club had been considerably reduced. Wages were now only 74% of income. They were one of the few teams to reduce their wage bill between 1985 and 1990. (In fact Aston Villa, Liverpool and Coventry more than doubled their wage bill over this period.)

Unfortunately the Blues were now in the third division. This was the crucial time when football was taking off.

1989-1992 The Kumar Years

In 1989 Wheldon sold his controlling interest in the Blues to BRS Kumar Bros Ltd, the family company of the Kumar brothers. The reported price was £1.6 million. Samesh Kumar became chairman in April of that year and his brother Ramesh Kumar became vice chairman. Jack Wiseman remained on the board.

The Kumar family textile business was based in Manchester, and at the time of the takeover of the Blues, the business was worth about £20 million. The textile company traded through a number of mid to low quality clothing shops. The family had no links with the region. In fact the 102nd AGM of the Blues was held in

Manchester at 9.00 in the morning at the registered office of BRS Kumar Bros. This action resulted in criticism in Birmingham.

Following the many years of bad leadership from one family after another came bad leadership from yet another family – the Kumar brothers.

It was unfortunate that following the problems with the Bhatti brothers at the Wolves the next experience in the West Midlands of Asian businessmen with professional football was also to end up in receivership. BCFC had been acquired by the Kumar family who had little or no experience of running a football club. Unlike the Bhattis the Kumars claimed they would conduct their footballing affairs in a very open fashion, making themselves accessible to the fans. They did not do this. In the three years that they were in control, the club achieved nothing.

As a national clothing supplier Kumar Bros Ltd did start to supply goods to the football club which were sold through the souvenir shop. The sales could not have been very high however because during their period of ownership the club had been relegated from the second tier and spent three years in the third division. The holding club (the textile company) did make loans to the football club, but only for modest amounts of money.

The 1980s saw, at many clubs, the end of the old style directors; those more involved in running a football club than a business. Their involvement was in some cases because of a love of football and in other cases for an ego boost. They had been willing to put some of their own money in the club, and did not expect much of a return, if any. Unfortunately although they had usually been successful in their own careers, they did not have the skills needed in the new environment in which football now operated. The Kumar brothers sold the Blues in 1993, but did come back into football. In 1996 they purchased the controlling interest in Cardiff City, but sold it after a few years.

The Blues were now in the hands of David Sullivan and the Gold brothers.

4

WEST BROMWICH ALBION

The Albion finished the 2016/17 season in tenth place in the Premier League. The financial accounts for 2016/17 showed pre-tax profits of £39 million. The club's revenue for the year was £180 million, a club record. For the sixth season running they were the best team in the West Midlands. At the beginning of the 2017/18 season the question of where did it all go wrong clearly did not apply to them. In the summer transfer window of 2017 the club spent more on buying new players (in the region of £40 million) than they had ever done in the past. The future looked promising, but unfortunately a few months into the new season they were in trouble, with talk of relegation. They had only won two matches in their first twelve games. Surely the bad times were not going to return? They were.

The Albion had been a top team in the 1960s and 1970s, but had had a bad time in the 1980s and 1990s. McOwan has referred to the period from 1982 to 2000 as the wilderness years. In 2000 Bowler and Bains had concluded that as a result of "neglect, small minded parochialism and perhaps even cowardice, WBA had been left standing on the platform watching the Premiership gravy train recede into the distance, not waving but drowning". In the book "Samba at the Smethwick End" the authors argue that as a result of mismanagement and a lack of ambition and of vision at boardroom level the Albion had missed the opportunity to be one of the top clubs. They had their slump in performance at the worst possible moment of time. They were struggling in the 2nd and 3rd tier of English football at the time it was becoming big business. Yet fifteen years later they were the best team in the West Midlands. What changed? In 2000 after a boardroom coup Paul Thompson became chairman. Two years later he was replaced by Jeremy Peace. What did Thompson and Peace do that the leaders of Aston Villa and Birmingham City failed to do?

We will begin the analysis of WBA by looking at recent history, first with the "wilderness years", next through the Peace era leading to the present. In the second part of the chapter we will look at the earlier days, the good times with Jeff Astle, Tony Brown and Cyrille Regis, but also the less good times.

Part A: The Recent History

The Albion started life over 150 years ago as a works team. For most of their life they have needed to be very careful with money. They were known as a penny pinching club but they became, until very recently, the stars of the West Midlands both on and off the field. The question that needs to be asked is what in recent years have the management of the club done that is right? As Jeremy Peace the chairman was proudly able to say in 2015 "we are plugging away trying to compete in the most high profile difficult league in the world, punching above our weight." Yet for a time from the mid-80s the club went into its longest and darkest period. They were relegated from the top division (then Division One) in 1985/86 with the worst record in the club's history. Five years later they were relegated to the 3rd tier for the first time in their history. It was not until 2002 that they were in the Premier League.

The Albion have always needed to be prudent. They have often encountered serious financial problems. In the 1950s the chairman Major Keys, warned that the club needed a gate of 30,000 at matches to be able to pay their way. In the 1960s gates were half that size. Gate receipts accounted for 90% of the club's revenue at that time. Nevertheless the club did have some success.

In 1978/79 they finished in third place in the top tier. The chairman, the respected, but prudent Bert Millichip, commented in the Annual Report that "the name of the Albion really captured the imagination of the football public". What a shame they could not build on this.

The 1980s and 1990s

In the 1980s and 1990s the club were in financial trouble. They were playing for much of this time in Division Two and for five years in Division Three. They were said to suffer from a small town mentality – despite being only 3 miles from Villa Park!

They had been relegated from the top Division at the end of the 1986/87 season. They were then nearly immediately relegated to the third tier finishing in the 20th place (out of 24). They were, however, relegated at the end of the 1990/91 season. They remained at this level for two seasons before returning to the second tier where they remained through the 1990s. So in the year that the Premier League started WBA were playing in the third tier of English football. In 14 years they had nine different managers and six caretaker managers (in one year alone 1997, they had three so called permanent managers and 3 caretaker managers.) The governance of the club was a disaster with bitter infighting at boardroom level.

During this time some of the managers were well known figures. In 1984/85 Johnny Giles was bought back to the club to try to save them. He was told to cut the wage bill. He sold the club's best player Cyrille Regis to Coventry and he made himself unpopular with the fans. Then came Nobby Stiles, but only for 4 months. The experienced Ron Saunders was the next to try to save the club. He set out to cut the wage bill, the "turnover of players was incredible", the good players were not replaced, the crowds stayed away. Ron Atkinson was brought back in 1987. He tells the story that the financial situation was so bad that the club would not pay for overnight accommodation when the team was playing away from home. Ron Atkinson's comment on the chairman, John Silk, was that he was a man not really prepared to invest the necessary sums in the transfer market. Atkinson believed that the board could not resist the temptation to sell any good player when an offer came along and that it led to "the surrender of the Albion as a significant force in football." Atkinson left the club during the 1988/89 season to move to Atlético Madrid in Spain.

The next manager Brian Talbot remained for 3 years. Then came a succession of six managers through to the end of the century. One manager in this time was Ossie Ardiles who had been a highly successful footballer in England and was quite successful as a manager. However he was offered the job of manager of Spurs which he accepted. It was disclosed that the solicitors running the Albion had not given Ardiles an attractive contract. The boardroom over all this time was in disarray. Fans were protesting seeking changes at boardroom level. The club were as always short of funds. Being in the lower leagues they were not benefitting from the large amount of TV money that was coming into the game.

The Chairmen

The struggles of the Albion were due to the lack of ability at the top, at boardroom level. The club lacked clear leadership, it suffered from petty disputes between rather disappointing directors. The chairman from 1974 to 1983 was Bert Millichip. Through most of his time in charge, the Albion were successful and in the top division. He was a local man, educated at Solihull School. He was a solicitor by profession. Atkinson refers to Millichip as a supreme diplomat, "an accomplished tightrope walker in any tricky Boardroom situation". He (like Ellis) was financially very careful, his chairman's statements in annual reports of WBA emphasised "financial security". Atkinson mentions that Millichip stopped improved contracts being offered to certain key players. In the end this worked against WBA, Atkinson took the club's star player Robson to Manchester United when he left the Albion.

Millichip became chairman of the Football Association. But unfortunately the 1980s were difficult times in football. At the FA he became involved in one controversy after another. He was, however, still involved with the FA when he was aged over 80, a 'gentleman' but one many thought should have retired earlier.

Sid Lucas was WBA chairman from 1983 to 1988, his business experience was as the director of a small local firm. Bower and Bains refer to the 1980s as a period where mismanagement was rife across the Midlands, not just in football but in business generally. The West Midlands was referred to as a wasteland, "like the local economy the football club (WBA) were on their knees". Albion like the other clubs were suffering. Tom Silk, a solicitor, a director of a family business with long family connection with the club was the next chairman from 1988 to 1992. The club found one new source of finance without having to bring in new shareholders. The club signed an agreement with Sandwell MBC, in which the council agreed to sponsor the club for 4 years, at £65,000 a year and in return the club and players would help with community relationships. A good deal but too little too late.

The next chairman was Tony Hale, who did begin to help sort out the finances. WBA had been a private company, the directors and major shareholders ran the Albion like a gentleman's club. They were reluctant to bring in outsiders and to lose their power. Tony Hale was the major shareholder in the early 1990s, he was a wealthy Jersey based businessman. He did invest some of his own money in the club. The board decided to restructure the club and to make the Albion a public company. In 1995 the club's shares were listed on the Alternative Investment Market. Other football clubs had followed a similar route, they sold to the public some new equity shares and shares of existing owners. The Albion now had some money to spend. The board took another important step forward when they appointed John Wile as CEO, an ex-Albion player, someone who knew about football.

The directors were, however, still arguing amongst themselves. A new director Paul Thompson joined the board in 1999. He called an EGM to discuss the future of the then chairman, Tony Hale. Hale retained his position through the support of the old established directors. Hale promised Brian Little, the manager at the time, that money would now be made available to buy new players. It was not. Both Little and Hale resigned in 2000.

In the year 2000 the club were, not for the first time, from a corporate governance point of view, in a mess. There were frequent disagreements at board level and frequent clashes between the chairman and the manager. Tony Hale had been chairman for 6 years had decided that it was time for him to go and he was replaced by Paul Thompson who at the time was the club's largest shareholder. Unfortunately the manager was having difficulties working with the new chairman. Thompson in his two and a half years in charge helped to stabilize the club financially. He raised equity funds and helped develop the ground. The construction of an East Stand cost £6 million, it increased the ground capacity to 28,000. It was financed partly by a loan and partly by an equity issue. Thompson wished to become involved with decisions concerning the playing side of the game and this made him unpopular. Megson said in 2002 that the club was not big enough for both of them. After a seven hour board meeting Thompson resigned, but it took another 2 months "and an awful lot of bad blood and a boardroom coup before another chairman Jeremy Peace was appointed". One issue of disagreement at boardroom level was how much freedom should be given to the manager on the recruitment of players. A continuing problem.

The Jeremy Peace Era

Much of the credit for the recent success of the Albion must go to its chairman from 2002. He had been appointed as a non-executive director 2 years earlier. Peace's outside business activities included the media, finance and investment, and property. He was listed in the top ten in the West Midlands Rich List. With this background it was not surprising that he was able to turn the club around financially.

For the first 10 years of the Peace era, however, the club were still known as a yo-yo club. They had been promoted in 2001/2, but over the next 9 seasons were relegated 3 times and promoted 3 times. This could be seen as an improvement as the club had not played at the top level for over 16 years. Peace had a reputation for adopting a cautious approach, but he did in the end turn them around and they became a well-run business. They, with such clubs as Southampton and Stoke were seen as providing a model of how to survive with some success in the Premier League without big resources.

By the 2004/5 season Peace had been able to bring stability to the boardroom. He had ruled out any massive spending spree, he would not spend money to buy big name players. There were rumours of another breakdown in the relationship between the manager and the chairman. Megson who was unhappy with the direction in which the club was moving said he would leave the club at the end of the season. Peace was not willing to wait until the end of the season and so Megson was fired in October 2004. Peace controlled the purse strings. It was said that he wanted Megson to reduce the size of the first team squad by one third. Megson had been popular with the fans; he managed to achieve what no other Albion manager had achieved for many years, namely promotion to the top division.

Finance

One problem for a club such as the Albion is that there is a limit to how much revenue they can earn, relative to other clubs. The club's ground, The Hawthorns, is small, it is not situated in a rich area and with the club lacking glamour they find it hard to generate very much commercial income. During the recent period in which they have been a reasonably successful Premier League club, their match day attendance figures were only in the region of 25,000 and in 2014/15 their match day revenue figure of £7 million was the lowest in the league. Their commercial revenue figure in 2015/16 was £12 million which was also one of the lowest in the league. By comparison that of Aston Villa was £28 million but Manchester United living in a different world, attracted £268 million of commercial income.

The financial wellbeing of the club depends very much on TV broadcasting income. In the Premier League it comprises over 75% of the total revenue. In January 2015 in order to increase their chances of remaining in the Premier League they recruited Tony Pulis as manager who in his 20 plus years of management had never been in charge of a club that had been relegated. In the 2 years before his appointment the club had had 4 different managers.

Those running the Albion appeared to have abandoned their old penny pinching strategies. The chief executive in 2015, Mark Jenkins explained that the club had a few years earlier made a "conscious decision to invest in player wages rather than transfer fees wherever possible". They believed that spending resources in this way translated to better results on the pitch. The club had begun to compete in terms of the wages they would offer. In 2012/13 they spent 77% of their annual revenue on wages, the highest rate of any of the Premier League clubs. In 2015/16 the rate was 74%. In the early years of the Peace era when they were also in the Premier League, the wage revenue ratio was only in the region of 57%. In terms of the actual expenditure the wage bill in 2005/6 was £20 million, in 2008/9 it was £30 million and in 2015/16 it was £74 million. The wage bill had increased by a factor of 2.5 over seven years. In comparison the Villa wage bill in 2008/9 was £71 million and in 2013/14 it was £69 million. A fall over the 5 years, but it did increase to £93 million in its last year in the Premier League.

No wonder Jonas Olsson was pleased. In an interview reported in *The Times* (1 April 2017) he divulged the secret of the Albion's success on and off the field. He moved to the Albion in 2008 when they were a yo-yo club and left in 2017 when they were an established Premier League club. He was proud to be a part of this success story. When he arrived they did not "have the budget, or the will, I don't know – to spend a lot of money but what they did was to reward players with good contracts, they took very good care of players who did well for them." When he arrived the club could only afford – or were only willing to spend sums in the region of £3 million to reward a player. When he left they were willing to spend sums in excess of £10 million on a player.

"We developed a real togetherness at the Albion, us against the opponents, us against the media. It is a family club and I was very close to the players, people working in the club and fans. It is how football used to be. I struggle sometimes with that in England! You're far apart from fans and from reality. The Albion's different. I had my ups and downs but they were very loyal to me, very honest."

The club had had problems with its bonus system. When they were promoted to the Premier League the players were disappointed in that they felt that they were not sufficiently rewarded for their efforts. They fell out with the manager Megson over the issue, not a good start for the first season back in the Premier League.

The club later introduced a wage system in which the performance related element of the players salary was a large proportion of the total. The bonus was partly based on the season's final position. The take home pay included a payment based on appearances and there was a bonus for remaining in the Premier League. Sensibly the contracts containing a clause which allowed for a reduction in salary if the club were relegated.

Net Transfer Expenditure

The club's policy was to reward players well if the club did well but not to spend large sums of money in acquiring new players. The fans would have liked to have seen some big name new players. The chairman explained that the Board was striving "to deliver Premier League football whilst growing the club within our means". The CEO pointed to the fact that "with careful budgeting and tight financial control we have managed to match our revenue to our costs". Doug Ellis had been making the same sort of comments 20 years earlier at the Villa.

In the five seasons from 2009/12 to 2013/14 the average annual net transfer expenditure was only £5.1 million which has been described as frugal. In the following three seasons the net annual expenditure was on average £19 million. These sums are quite small compared to the likes of Manchester United and Chelsea but they are only just below average for the non-elite clubs in the Premier League.

These levels of investment are way behind clubs such a Liverpool who have expectations of qualifying for a place in one of the lucrative European competitions. That club are currently spending on average about £30 million per annum. This is under the ownership of The Fenway Group. Before that, under the notorious leadership of Hicks and Gillett they were spending on average £10 million per annum.

One possible way for a club to increase its cash inflow is from the sale of players. The club will either have had to purchase the players or spend money on their development through an academy. The club can make a profit or loss on the sale; which is measured as the difference between the selling price and the value of the player in the club's accounts. The Albion have been successful in their trading of players but the amounts involved have been quite small, for example in the 9 years to 2014/15 the average annual profit on the sale of players was £6.5 million.

By one measure Albion have been very "efficient" in the transfer market. The cost of transfer fees paid out per point earned in the league in 2016/17 was the lowest of any club. A Sky Sports study showed that the Albion were obtaining the best value for money of any of the clubs. The Albion squad cost £1.5 million per point. A little more expensive than this in terms of cost per point were Burnley and Hull (both of whom were relegated). At the other extreme, not surprisingly were the big spenders Manchester United with a cost of £7.9 million per point. The value of the United squad was estimated to be £497 million, that of the Albion squad £64.5 million. Not exactly a level playing field. Tony Pulis praised the study. It was a measure of financial efficiency but it ignored risk. It indicates a club living on the edge. In 2017/18 the Albion spent more money than usual on new players but they were not the right players. The wage bill went up, the points earned went down and the club were relegated.

Managers

How much of the success of the Albion on the pitch was due to wise financial management and how much to good coaching and the management of players? To be successful the owner of the club and the manager of the team need to have a rapport, there needs to be a like mindedness. What was the position at the Albion? Gary Megson became the manager in 2000. During his four years in that role the club were twice promoted to the Premier League. Unfortunately, they had been relegated once. They were a difficult four years with boardroom disputes and coups. There were two chairman during Megson's time. There was a continuing battle at the club as to who should make the final decision on the purchase of players.

When Megson left in 2004 the next manager was the former Albion player Bryan Robson. He was manager until 2006. The club were in the Premier League during his two seasons in charge but were battling to survive. They were relegated at the end of 2005/6 season. The directors' prudent approach to financial management was not helping. The wages paid being only 57% of turnover. The next manager was Tony Mowbray. He had mixed fortunes, an FA Cup semi-final appearance, a promotion but unfortunately another relegation at the end of 2008/9.

Does the manager really matter? The Albion returned to the Premier League in 2010/11, in the 7 years since they had employed seven different managers. They had made some good appointments but unfortunately also some poor ones, but when in trouble they acted quickly to save the day. It was Roberto Di Matteo who managed the club on their return, but was dismissed in February 2011 following poor results. Roy Hodgson was next, he was very good, very experienced but unfortunately he resigned in May 2012 to become the manager of the English national team. He was replaced by Steve Clarke, who in 2012/13 led Albion to the highest ever final place in the Premier League (8th). He was sacked in December 2013. The next brief appointment was Keith Downing (6 games) Then came Pepe Mel from Spain. The appointment did not last long, during which time the club won only 3 of its 17 matches. He left by mutual consent. The next appointment was Alan Irvine, again only short lived, seven months during which time the club won only 5 of its 22 matches. The club were in danger of losing their Premier League place. This was why in January 2015 Tony Pulis was appointed as manager to save the club from relegation.

Pulis is a respected coach and experienced manager. The Albion were the eighth club he had managed. His most high profile had been at Stoke City where he had been manager for two spells. The first had come to an end when the controversial Icelandic owners sacked him for "failing to exploit the foreign market". He was brought back to Stoke in 2006, he led the club to promotion to the Premier League, they did well under his stewardship qualifying for a place in the UEFA Europa League.

Before moving to the Albion he had managed Crystal Palace. In 2013/14 that club finished in 11th place and he was awarded the title of Premier League "Manager of the Season". He left Crystal Palace in acrimonious circumstances. The club paid him a large sum of money which included a loyalty bonus and a survival bonus. He was paid this before Palace knew he was planning to leave the Palace chairman believed that Pulis had been deceitful and had let the club down. The legal case was argued about in the courts for over three years. Palace won the case and Pulis was ordered to pay back £3.77 million to the club and to pay close to £2 million in legal fees.

Pulis has a reputation for managing clubs that play solid safe football but not exciting football. He has, however, achieved results. To be fair to him he has never had the opportunity to manage a top club. He has never had large amounts of money to spend. He had his critics at Albion, some fans would have liked to have seen more exciting football. In 2016 WBA were sold to Chinese investors. Pulis, in his last season or two at the club had more money to spend on players than any previous Albion manager. He was buying players costing £13 million which was big by Albion's standards. The 2017/18 season did not turn out as expected. After a reasonable start the team could not score goals and could not win games. The fans (and the directors) blamed Pulis. He was sacked. After being a hero at the end of the 2016/17 season (the club finishing in tenth place in the Premier League), five months later he was the villain. As he said at the time "everything is about now, not what you have done in the past".

Tony Pulis was manager at the beginning of the 2017/2018 season but the new players that the club purchased were not a success and were expensive. The players the club obtained on loan were also not a success and their wages were high. There appeared to be a lack of unity in the squad and the fans were not happy. After a poor set of results with the club just above the relegation zone Pulis was sacked. Gary Megson was brought back to the club as temporary manager. Then in November 2017 Alan Pardew was appointed as manager on a two and a half year contract. Pardew was another very experienced manager. He had in the past been named as a Manager of the Season, whilst at Newcastle. Unfortunately at WBA he had problems working with the players. It also came to light that there were governance problems at the club. In February 2018 both the chairman and the chief executive of the club were removed. The relatively new owners were not happy with the decisions that had been made by these executives.

Mark Jenkins was brought back to the club as CEO following fourteen months away, in retirement. He soon let it be known that the club was in a very bad way financially. He expressed surprise at how badly the club had been run over recent months. In April 2018 Alan Pardew was sacked. He had only been able to achieve one win in eighteen matches in charge. There were those who questioned the wisdom of sacking a manager so close to the end of the season. The fans wondered who would come in next as manager. Darren Moore the first team coach was appointed caretaker manager. This was at the time seen as a temporary appointment, but to the surprise of many under Moore's leadership the club nearly avoided relegation. From the last five games of the season the team obtained 11 points. Moore was liked by the fans and liked by the players. What would the owners do? Would they return to the managerial merry-go-round?

They did not. Following a visit to China by Mark Jenkins and Giuliano Terraneo, the clubs new technical consultant to see Lai Guochuan the club's controlling shareholder, a brave decision was made to offer Darren Moore the position of manager. All at the club had been impressed with Moore's leadership qualities shown during the games of the last season. The question was whether he would be able to repeat that success in the Championship and lead the team back to the top level. Moore had his critics who pointed to his lack of experience. A strange point to make when one considers the two very experienced managers the club had employed during the 2017/18 season and where it had got them.

WBA will have problems following their relegation but they will be helped by the income from the very large parachute payments. They will receive in the region of £50 million in their first season in the second tier (that is 55% of a Premier League clubs basic broadcasting revenue). If they are still in the Championship in 2019/20 they will receive in the region of £40 million and if they are still in that League in the following season will receive near £20 million. This will give the club a large comparative advantage over the other Championship clubs.

Leadership

To repeat, much of the credit for the recent success of the Albion must go to Jeremy Peace. He did well for the club but also for himself. There is nothing wrong with this, he invested in the club, spent time running the club and received the rewards resulting from success. This can be contrasted with what happened three miles away in Aston, where Lerner invested very large sums in the club, spent little time watching the club and lost interest in it. His failure lost him in the region of £200 million. Peace's success rewarded him with well over £100 million.

Peace was a highly paid director. In 2010 even before he became chairman, it was explained that he would receive a basic annual salary of £500,000 plus a discretionary bonus. In that year he received £712,000 a very good rate for a director of one of the smaller Premier League clubs.

The highest paid director in 2012/13 which all assumed was Peace received £1,341,000. In the following season he again received over £1 million. In his final year in charge, 2015/16 he received £1.95 million. This was a golden parachute payment. It is not unusual in football for those who had been running the club to receive a large payment when the club is sold. Peace also benefitted from a large capital gain when he sold the club. At that time he held 88% of the shares.

Since returning to the Premier League in 2011 the club had been profitable, the average level of pre-tax profits over the last six years being in the region of £7 million. In 2015 the figure was £4.9 million. This contrasts with the fortunes in the club's yo-yo years. In the six years prior to 2011 the club was more or less breaking even with a loss in some years followed by a modest profit in others.

Peace was an old fashioned type of owner. A local boy who had made good who cared passionately about his team. He had been taken to see his first match at The Hawthorns by his father when he was 7 years old. He attended Shrewsbury School and made his fortune in the City of London. He was professional in his approach to being chairman, studying how clubs were being governed on the continent. He made changes in the way that business was conducted at the Albion. He says that he never got involved in picking or pushing the case of individual players, he left that to the football people who knew what they were doing. Not always how a chairman behaves. Whilst at the Albion he was low key, a modest man who unlike some other chairmen did not seek a high public profile. He believed that he and his executive team needed to keep striving to make things better at the club, "If you stand still you are dead."

The Albion were under his leadership punching above their weight. He believed that as each season went by it got tougher to compete in the Premier League. He commented that "There are huge clubs and the rest of us". In 2014 he talked about the possibility of selling. He said that if there was a big investor who "put more money into the club generally, into local community, it would be great". He appreciated, however, that Albion were not a very fashionable club. To wealthy patrons West Bromwich did not have the appeal of London. When he did sell the club he certainly handed it over in a lot better state than when he found it.

The Future

At the beginning of August 2016 the Albion was sold to a Chinese investment company, Yunyi Guokai Sports Development, for a price widely reported to be close to £150 million and according to some nearer £200 million. This was a sale of a well-liked club that through its 140 year history had modest success. It had been saved from a disastrous period during the 1980s and 1990s to become a mid-table Premier League club. It had once been known for its penny pinching ways, a club run by prudent solicitors. We have seen how this change in its fortune came about. The future now depends on Guochuan Lai the controlling shareholder.

Lai was 42 years old when the investment company he controlled took over the Albion. He had previously managed and built up a company that started life as a regional landscape engineering company and became a very large construction and development company; valued on the Chinese stock exchange at £1.8 billion. The company, Palm, specialises in the design and development of eco-friendly towns.

In 2014 Lai reduced his role in Palm so that he could concentrate on other projects. He is now a director of a number of companies, one of which an investment company, of which he is chairman, acquired the Albion. He is involved in companies engaged in tourism, sport and virtual reality. With Peace leaving the football club, Lai brought into the club a number of new executives including John Williams, formerly an executive at Blackburn Rovers. Lai has said that he did not intend to make any major changes, and that he would maintain the club's stable structure and had no intention of changing the club's ethos. The supporters hoped he meant the ethos of the last 15 years and not the earlier periods.

He purchased a well-run club that has been relatively successful. He did not have to face the difficulties of the new owners of the Villa and Birmingham City. If Lai had hopes of turning the Albion into one of the elite league clubs he would need to invest large amounts of money not just on players but on ground improvements. One of the club's new Chinese directors had said that "the long term policy of the club is to improve the playing squad and its infrastructure year on year". The club were not very active in the transfer market in January 2017, nowhere near as adventurous as the Wolves. The fans were disappointed, they were told to be patient and calm. They had heard that before. However in the summer of 2017 they were very active, spending £42.9 million and only receiving £0.3 million from sales. This made them the seventh highest net spender in the Premier League, higher than Arsenal and the Spurs. Unfortunately the 2017/18 season turned out to be a disaster.

If Lai wishes to cash in on President Xi's plans to make China a top football country he will have to do a lot to increase the appeal of the Albion as a club. As has been shown at the Blues, just being Chinese owned does not mean that football fans in China identify with the club. Would a fan in Shanghai rather be identified with Manchester United or with the Albion? Even though the one is American owned and the other Chinese.

Part B: The Early Years

It is interesting to look at the early years. The Albion have over time on numerous occasions had to struggle because of poor leadership. They were briefly the most exciting team in the country, but missed the opportunity to build on that success.

The club was founded in 1878 by a group of workers from a local factory, the George Salters Works. In 1888 they became one of the founder members of the Football league. They had early success being FA Cup winners in 1892 but their fortunes then on and off the pitch changed over the next 20 years. They were relegated twice and promoted twice. They found themselves in financial difficulties, they were saved in 1899 by the chairman Harry (Henry) Keys. He was chairman from 1899 to 1903 and again from 1905 to 1908. With the club in financial difficulties he and the other directors paid the wages of the players out of their own pockets. In 1909 again Harry had to provide his own money to support the club. The local paper had also done their best to help the club setting up a "Shilling Fund" which raised the total of £401. Aston Villa also helped their poorer neighbours with a donation of £50.

Harry Keys was a local councillor and a "no nonsense business-man", he was also a respected figure in national football circles becoming a member of the Football League Committee in 1905. The Keys family over time have done a lot to help WBA. Harry's son, H. Wilson Keys, was chairman of the club from 1947 to 1963. Unlike the period when his father was in charge, the son was there during the golden years of WBA. He had had a distinguished career in the military, rising to the rank of Major.

The Albion were known as a family club and the Keys were one of the families. In the first season after the First World War, 1919/20, WBA were Division One Champions. Through the remaining Inter War years they were relegated twice and promoted once.

1945-1960

They returned to the First Division in 1949/50 where they remained for 24 years. They were successful. They did win the FA Cup but not the League; although for 3 consecutive seasons 1957/58, 1958/59 and 1959/60 they finished in a top five position in the division. Their style of play made them very popular. In 1954 they had been referred to as the team of the century.

In 1965 in a forward to a book about the Albion the then chairman, J.W. Gaunt wrote "The hard working citizens (of the Black Country) were craftsmen. Their products were made to last and to be appreciated. In their leisure they turned to their football clubs with the same pride ... In this atmosphere rose WBA from its lowly start to become respected from the boundaries of the Soviet Union to the Canadian shores of the Pacific."

Indeed in the 1950s and early 1960s WBA were one of the most respected names in England soccer, they did tour the USA, Canada and Russia (1959) as ambassadors of good English football. They were the first English side to defeat a Russian team in Russia. They were admired for their attractive "push and run" style. They were also the first English team to tour China (in 1977).

Even though they were a "respected" club warning signs were already present. Peter Morris in his introduction to his book on "Soccer in the Black Country 1879-1965" referred to the fact that at the time the chairman's words were being written "shifts and changes in the world of football have taken Albion to the crossroads, as indeed they have so many small town clubs of similar status and traditions." The old days and the old ways are no more. The club have never been really big spenders, they have largely relied on local talent and lately there has been "a regrettable drying up and thinning out of it. Recent seasons have seen a distressing falling off in gate receipts, at times of alarming proportions. A hard core of supporters keep the Albion going but even the staunchest do not really believe they will see their club winning very much, especially not sharing in the European Cup glamour so avidly sought now by clubs who can afford to shun the long arduous business of trying to build winning teams with local youngsters, making do on pinch penny methods."

Morris points out that in the mid-1950s Albion were at the forefront of English soccer, and yet 10 years later they were going nowhere. One reason often given for this is that they are a "small town club". It is true West Bromwich (Smethwick – Sandwell) is small, but it has a population of over 500,000 within ten miles of the ground. Aston Villa are referred to as a big City club, and yet the two grounds are only a few miles apart. The same people who watch the Villa could easily watch the Albion. The small town club story seems an easy excuse.

It has been said many times that "The club has never really been big spenders". This could well be the real reason for the decline. At a time of such changes as the ending of the maximum wage, and changes in the transfer system, it becomes important to spend money to attract the best talent (and to retain it). This charge of "pinch penny methods" by the Board of Directors is one that occurs frequently in the history of the club.

The 1960s

The club were successful in terms of playing performance during the 1950s and early 1960s. Financially, however, in common with other clubs they were less successful. Attendances declined but at the Albion at a faster rate than at most other comparable clubs. With home attendances in the 1958/59 season as a base (100), the attendance index declined to 64 in the 1963/64 season, only to slightly recover to 77 by 1968/69. The index across the top division for comparative years was from 100 to 85 and then 99. WBA suffered more than other clubs.

The club needed an average home gate of 30,000 to pay its way. At that time, in 1957/58 the average gate was 32,357. The attendance figures then fell away. By 1962/63 the gates averaged only 17,282. Income was needed from some other source, particularly as players wages were rising.

There was much criticism at the time of the Board in general and

Major Keys in particular. In 1963 Major Keys resigned as chairman but remained as a director. He was then 70 years old. Gaunt became chairman, he had at that time been a director for 10 years.

Peter Morris refers to WBA in the 1964/65 season as being in the "melting pot". Morris was an optimist. He found "encouraging signs that the club is flexing itself for the possible role of leadership out of the unprecedented depression in which Midlands' football found itself in late 1964 ... Certainly the club have not been afraid to plan for the future boldly and with imagination." In 1962 a development association was found to raise funds for further improvements in The Hawthorns.

Morris writes that "Over the past 2 seasons (1963 and 1964) Albion without ever looking like doing anything big have possibly proved themselves more successful and progressive than any other team in the Birmingham area with the notable exception of Coventry City where young and realistic directors realised what was needed to attract back the crowds."

In 1963 there had been criticism of the Albion's wages policy – believed by many to be uncompetitive with other clubs – and criticism for failing to sign top players who had become available for transfer. When Gaunt became chairman in 1963 he publicly declared "we made a mistake in having a rigid wage policy ... there can be no doubt that it did not pay off in the matter of getting new players. What we saved in wages we lost in gate receipts ... Indeed the Albion had made a mistake in pegging wages when the maximum was removed. They did not, or could not realise that those of their rivals with sufficient business acumen were more than prepared to pay big fees and offer high wages for the star players who would bring them success and attract large crowds ... The Albion whether they liked it or not were moving into an age where there was going to be less and less room for the mediocre or the timorous. Boldness and cash were paying rich dividends, the Albion could not afford to be left behind." In 1960 the wage bill of WBA was only £33,000 one half that of Birmingham City, both were Division One clubs – it was less than that of Coventry who were in the third division. By 1965 the wage bill had doubled, but was still only one half that of Birmingham City, and still less than that of Coventry (who were now in the second division). They were, however, now paying out a much higher percentage of their income as wages (32% in 1960, 53% in 1965 and 57% in 1970). The club was just not attracting the necessary level of income.

The 1970s

Bowler and Bains believe that the decline of West Bromwich Albion was due to bad management at Board level. There has "always been a small time mentality at the club". They quote Bryan Jones who remembered that his father used to say "that Albion were the meanest club in the West Midlands". Bowler and Bains believe that the date the Albion signalled to the world that they "were happy to be a run of the mill First Division club" was the summer of 1979 when they let Laurie Cunningham and Len Cantello leave the club.

Cunningham was one of the footballing "Three Degrees". He was one of charismatic black players that made a major contribution to the success of WBA in the 1970s. In 1979 WBA finished third in Division One and yet were paying Cunningham, perhaps their star player only £120 a week. Johnny Haynes had become the first £100 a week footballer in 1961. WBA were paying their star players only a little more than the top players had been earning nearly 20 years earlier (a period that included many years of hyperinflation.) Cyrille Regis is of the opinion that Cunningham left WBA because of the wages. Regis nearly left WBA himself for the same reason. WBA had been achieving success on the football field despite paying low wages – but although such a policy can succeed in the short run it cannot in the long run. The leadership at the club was woefully lacking in ambition, content merely to exist in the First Division. Once you set your sights that low, if you fail to reach them you leave yourself no margin for error. "Too many good players were allowed to leave too soon, when they didn't want to or could have been kept."

Peter Morris writes that "the men who guide from that cosy little boardroom tucked away in The Hawthorns main stand have had to face up to many problems, not the least of which is attracting back a once healthy local support." Morris refers to the directors as "kindly but typically hard headed Black Country businessmen." What does hard headed mean? Is it a compliment or a criticism? To be soft headed clearly implies that the person does not know what they are doing. Hard headed suggests the person knows what they are doing but that they are stubborn and not likely to throw hard earned money away. The expression is linked to the region in an old saying "Staffordshire born, Staffordshire bred. Strong in arm. Hard in Head".

In 1976 the Vice Chairman, Tom Silk, expressed the opinion that the day of reckoning was coming, "We cannot afford to continue losing money at this rate. We just have to find it from sources outside football." They announced on April 1st 1976 that the club was to build a new sports complex, and that they were to start work on an "ambitious programme of commercial development, aimed to wipe out the losses". The plan was to build luxury private boxes and a luxury restaurant. It was emphasised that the plan was to be financed by the Development Association, and that these commercial developments were not being carried out in preference to strengthening the team.

In the second half of the 1970s the team performed very well under Ron Atkinson's team management. The gate receipts consequently shot up in 1979/80. The team, (with the three degrees – Cunningham, Batson and Regis) won matches and played attractive football. The club made good operating profits from 1976 to 1980. During this four year period it made total profits of £1,231,000 and its net expenditure on new players was £830,000.

The chairman, Bert Millichip, was able to report in the annual accounts for 1978/79 that "the name of WBA really captured the imagination of the footballing public. The brand of exciting and entertaining football played was the envy of many other clubs". It was interesting that he used the word "brand" in connection with the style of football. It was a number of years later before the word was used in connection with the commercial value of a football club's name.

As already mentioned the club benefited financially from the success on the field, the revenue rose as did the wage bill. The chairman drew attention to the difficulties of planning and budgeting in football, and introduced a word of caution by pointing to the need to redevelop the ground, "Very serious consideration will be necessary as to how to finance such an operation". The club did continue, however, to be net spenders in the transfer market.

The 1980s

The 1980s should have been a successful decade for WBA. It certainly turned out to be a crucial decade. Unfortunately it was a decade of failure. At the end of the 1970s they were one of the top teams in the country and the club was financially sound. By the end of the 1980s they were in Division Two and financially weak. This meant they missed the opportunity to be in a position to cash in on the new TV age.

In the 1981/82 Annual Report the chairman pointed to problems in retaining good players. The side that had taken the club into European competitions "were unsettled by mounting pressures", in other words the players wanted to be paid higher wages. Mr Millichip, the chairman, stated "our primary aim must be success on the field but events on the economic side of the football … make it imperative that great care is taken to keep the club on a viable footing."

To be fair to the chairman, 1981/82 was the time when the Wolves were going into liquidation, so one could see why some caution was necessary. However, it was also the time when some businessmen could see a profitable future for football. Scholar was taking over Spurs, Dien was willing to buy a directorship at Arsenal board, and Maxwell was looking for a club to purchase.

WBA from a financial point of view stayed still during the 1980s. In 1981 the total wage bill was £875,000, in 1985 it was £886,000 and in 1989 – £998,000. They were in the top division during the first half of the decade but were not increasing their wage bill! The annual wage bill was more or less the same throughout the 1980-89 period. In 1985 their wage bill was the lowest of the West Midlands clubs. Wage levels determine playing success – they were relegated in 1987. To be fair the revenue was not increasing by very much during this period, and they were making losses. From 1981 to 1987 (except for one season) in the transfer market the cash flowing in from the sale of players exceeded the cash paid out for new players.

In the 1985 chairman's statement Sid Lucas wrote "You may recall in my report to you last year I stated that it was your Board's ongoing strategy to reduce the club's expenditure to an absolute minimum. This we have achieved for the 3rd year running and I am able to report an operating trading loss of only £19,900 (1984 – £166,000) reduced by a net surplus on Transfer Fees of £86,395. Disappointing results – reflected in our gates – an all-time low average of 13,816. One of our priorities must be to arrest this most serious decline."

The Bradford Stadium disaster led to the need for considerable expenditure on ground improvements which, with a ban on sale of alcohol, resulted in a reduction in revenue for most clubs. In the first half of the 80s WBA were very successful in generating revenue from sources other than gate receipts. In 1980/81 the other income figure contributed 25% of total revenue. This other income had by 1985/86 more than doubled and was contributing over 50% of total revenue. One source of income were the new executive boxes. The chairman in the 1981/82 accounts reported that the development of the Halford Lane Stand was now virtually complete and the stand was in full use.

The chairman reported that the directors had "introduced a stringent system of budgeting control to prevent any further drain on the clubs very limited cash resources". However, when by

Christmas 1987 the club realised that they were faced with the prospect of relegation to the third tier, the Board did make available to the manager a sum in excess of £200,000 for the acquisition of new players ... And also "to sanction the appropriate" additional payroll costs.

What did the word "appropriate" mean, was it suggesting that before the release of this additional money the payroll costs were not appropriate? In drawing attention to low payroll costs and the need for new players the directors were recognising that the penny pinching policies had harmed the club. This was at the time when a Premier League was being formed, and TV money was transforming the finances of big clubs. The directors in the 1987/88 annual report commented on another weakness of the club – the lack of long term finance. The chairman (Sid Lucas) wrote "Many money raising ideas are being pursued and contrary to some views, consideration is being given to a possible rights issue to shareholders."

The club escaped relegation to the third division by a whisker. The average home gate was only 10,078. A new commercial director had been appointed in 1987/88 but he could not work wonders. In the 1988/89 report, reference is made to another disappointing season. The commercial department was thanked for its untiring efforts. In fact gate receipts did rise, and the deficit was reduced.

New directors were appointed during 1987 and 1988 and John Silk became chairman, but again they were businessmen from small, modest businesses, such as local display and shop fitting companies. The directors did not seem to have realised that football was becoming a big business and that new talents and abilities were required. Bowler and Bains referred to the "small time mentality at the club". The capital structure of the club indicated a small time mentality, with a small group of shareholders anxious to maintain control.

Millichip was not of course the only 'conservative' director at the club. The Board's attitude towards directing the club did mean that they avoided the financial problems of the Wolves and the Blues, but it also meant the decline of one of the leading football teams in the country. The success of the 1950s and the promise of the late 1970s resulted in very little. Opportunities were missed.

Slowly the situation began to change. First with Paul Thompson as chairman, then with Jeremy Peace, the club benefited from good governance.

5

WOLVES

In the 1950s Wolverhampton Wanderers were the best team in the UK. They were at that time one of the truly great names in football. In Division One in the nine years from 1952/3 through to 1960/61 they were champions on three occasions, runners up twice and third on three occasions. The manager during this period was Stan Cullis a highly respected figure in football. The club led English teams into Europe with high profile, floodlit matches against top European teams (with home crowds of more than 50,000). The club attracted great attention when they beat a leading Hungarian club, Honvéd, whose team included players that had recently played for the Hungarian national team who had embarrassed England twice. At that time Wolves were being called "Champions of the World". In 1955 they visited the Soviet Union.

What went wrong? They have been in administration twice and have spent most of the last 25 years in the Championship. They were ruined by decisions made by a series of poor chairmen and directors. It was not being too prudent that ruined them in the 1980s, it was being over ambitious. Having been at the top they tried to keep pace with the other leading clubs, like Liverpool, in spite of the fact that in the 1970s the Wolves team was not good enough, their star players were no longer with them, and the club was short of money.

They were saved by a local fan who had sufficient wealth to be a sugar daddy (he called himself the golden tit). Sir Jack Hayward pumped money into the club and after a number of disappointments the club did get into the Premier League in 2003. But the club did not have access to enough finance to be able to maintain the top tier status. Wolves had become one of the clubs with a successful past that had not been able to maintain this position. Fortunately in 2016 they were purchased by a very wealthy Chinese owner (said to be four times richer than the Villa's new owner) and the future looked much more promising.

A headline in the *New York Times* on August 4th 2016 read "The owner brought the money, the agent provided the players: now what?" The Wolves were by far the best club in the Championship in 2017/18. They finished top of the League with 99 points, the second club Cardiff City finished the season with 90 points. The Wolves were respected, they played with style and won 30 of their 46 games. The club had owners with money who seemed to know what they were doing. They had a good manager with different ideas.

Part A: The Recent History

The Jack Hayward Era

Sir Jack had purchased the club in 1990. Despite his investment it took 13 years to achieve Premier League status ending a 19 year absence from the top tier. Unfortunately they were relegated after one season at the top. Sir Jack bought control of the club from a building company Gallaghers. He promised a huge injection of money into the club. He did what he promised and in the summer of 1991 ground improvements began. In September 1992 the club regained control of Molineux. The Molineux ground is one of the best medium sized grounds in the country. Unfortunately Wolves could not quite achieve promotion to the Premier League. Sir Jack provided funds so that the club could buy new players. But their investment in players was not successful. The players they bought were said to be "inadequate and underperforming". They were also highly paid.

Billy Wright was appointed a director of the club because of his football knowledge and loyalty to the Wolves. The club now had a very wealthy benefactor and one who had been a life-long supporter. From 1992 Sir Jack's son, Jonathan Hayward took over the chairmanship. Graham Turner was manager from 1986 to 1994. Over this period he was manager for 355 games. This managerial spell ranked as one of the longest for managers over the last 30 years. Wolves were clearly not engaged in swapping managers quickly. Turner's win ratio was good, being 0.567. A higher ratio than that of Brian Clough at Nottingham Forest and Ron Saunders at Aston Villa.

Wolves had the financial resources but were still in the second tier. Mark McGhee was brought in as manager in December 1995. He failed in three seasons to obtain promotion and so was sacked in November 1998. McGhee had spent quite heavily in the transfer market. Colin Lee was then brought in as manager, but he did not achieve promotion and so was removed in 2001.

Wolves invested heavily, they were gambling to achieve Premier League status. They could only do this because the club's owner was willing to subsidise heavy losses. It has been estimated that by the year 2000, Sir Jack Hayward had invested £27 million in Wolverhampton Wanderers. Not far behind the £30.9 million Sir Jack Walker had invested in Blackburn Rovers.

Sir Jack agreed to spend £10 million in the summer of 2001. In 2002/03, Wolves (with Manchester City) at last obtained promotion to the Premier League. These were the two teams from the second tier that had spent the most money and had the most experienced playing squad. They also had two managers of Premier League experience. Unfortunately the Wolves were relegated at the end of the 2003/04 season. They then remained in the Championship until 2009.

The Steve Morgan Era

Morgan was a football fan from Liverpool. He had made his money in the construction business and was chairman of a large public company. He had made a number of attempts to purchase Liverpool F.C but had been rejected by the owners at the time who did not feel he was offering to pay enough. Hicks and Gillett acquired Liverpool in 2007. Morgan then turned his attention to the Wolves, who he would refer to as his second club. In 2007 he bought the club from Sir Jack for £10 on condition that he invested £30 million in the club. Morgan became chairman of the Wolves. In May 2009 they were promoted back to the Premier League but went down to the Championship in 2012. Unfortunately they were then relegated to the third tier before returning back to the Championship in 2014; another higgledy piggledy club. They had not made the most of the opportunities arising from the big money coming into the game, they had not made good use of the Parachute payments they were receiving following their stay in the Premier League. They went into what their Chief Executive called a 'tailspin'.

The club had become prudent and made some strange managerial appointments. The club did not borrow, they paid relatively low wages and made profits. The club was planning for financial stability. Morgan said "we have tried to manage this as a proper business and I wish other clubs would do the same" (similar comments to Ellis at Villa). Unfortunately a number of other clubs were not being prudent and were winning. To be fair Wolves had in the recent past seen where financial risk taking could lead. They had seen the club fall from the then Division One to Division Four, they had twice been in administration.

The club had made some strange managerial moves. The successful Mick McCarthy had been removed and replaced by his assistant Terry Connor who had limited experience. The club then hired a Norwegian with little English experience, following poor results he resigned after six months. Then came Dean Saunders. The club were relegated to the third tier. In May 2013 the experienced Kenny Jackett became manager, he was quite successful but was removed in 2016 by the then new owners. In 2015 Steve Morgan had resigned from the board and put the club up for sale. It was purchased in July 2016 by a Chinese company, Fosun International, for £30 million.

The Present

The new Chinese owners were at first predictable, they immediately sacked the existing manager Kenny Jackett. This was not popular with fans, Jackett was liked, he had led the club out of League One. The owners brought to the club as manager a former Italian international player Walter Zenga. He had little relevant experience and was sacked after only five months in charge, 14 games. Paul Lambert formerly of the Villa was brought in as the new manager. Governance at the club was not good. The new Chinese owners were taking advice from one of the global "Super agents", Jorge Mendes (agent of Ronaldo and Mourinho). Not only did Mendes advise the new owners during the acquisition process, he continued to advise the owners after the acquisition. During Zenga's brief period in charge, the club made 12 new signings, some of which were arranged by Mendes. As an agent there was always the danger of a conflict of interest; obtaining rewards from both the purchasing club and from the players they represented. Lambert was not happy with the outside interference. The owners backed the agent and not the manager. In 2016/17 the club finished 15th in the Championship and Lambert after ten months in charge resigned because of the outside interference. The soap opera continued.

The new owners appointed an outsider, the ex-Porto manager Nuno Espirito Santo. This turned out to be a success. During the summer of 2017, the new owners still with the guidance of Mendes, invested heavily in the transfer market. Fosun were behaving in a manner which showed they wished to see the club in the Premier League as soon as possible. They signed over 10 new players in the summer, some of whom had already played at International level. One young international from Portugal cost in the region of £16 million. In the first 12 months of ownership they had spent over £47 million on over 25 new players. This was big spending for a Championship club. Perhaps at last the Wolves were going somewhere! The club were at the top of the Championship, playing quality football and were the bookmakers favourite for promotion. They were attracting home crowds equal in size to those who watched them over 30 years earlier. The manager, the head coach, impressed the fans and the pundits.

The club were now involved once again with one of the major characters in the football world. Jorge Mendes has been referred to as the world's most successful agent with "probably the greatest sense of recklessness when it comes to complex financial arrangements to avoid tax". (Buschmann and Wulzinger)

There was a possible governance problem the club would face when it entered the Premier League. The club's owners also owned a 20% stake in Gestifute, Mendes' agency. This could be seen to be against the third party ownership rules. Certainly a link between the owners of a club and an agency could lead to a conflict of interest when negotiating contracts for players. Gestifute is in fact not just an agency it is the leading agency. In the summer of 2017 it had been involved in six high value transfers. There were rules seeking to ensure that an agent did not engage in behaviour that would be normally be undertaken by a football club's director. After an investigation Wolves were cleared, it was decided that Mendes did not have too much influence.

Wolves were also in danger of getting into trouble with the Profit and Sustainability regulations. In 2016/17 they spent £28.2 million on players wages (a 50% increase on the previous season) which was more than the club's annual revenue of £23.7 million. Not surprisingly they showed a big loss, a loss of over £20 million. In the Premier League they will be allowed to show a total deficit of £39 million over three years. The financial results for 2017/18 would therefore be important in determining whether or not sanctions would be introduced against the club.

Part B: The Early Years

It helps to understand the club's present position by looking at its history. The Wolves were founder members of the Football League in 1888. They moved from one home ground to another, before becoming settled at the Molineux. Initially they rented the ground from a brewery for £50 per annum; yet again a link between a brewery and a football club. At the club and the adjacent hotel no doubt large quantities of the brewer's product were sold. In 1922 the club purchased the freehold of Molineux from the brewery for £5,607. The ground nearly ruined the club in the 1980s or to be more exact the directors nearly ruined the club. This was partly the result of over ambitious plans and partly the result of years of neglect of the ground.

In 1959/60, the club finished second in Division One and in the following year, third but unfortunately things then began to go wrong. In 1961/62 they finished 18th and in 1964/65 they were relegated to Division Two. Billy Wright in his autobiography written in 1961 said that he did not think that despite the recent bad results Stan Cullis, the manager, would need to worry about his future; that he would not get the sack. Cullis has stated that all successful teams go through bad periods. Cullis was a controversial figure. He was a hard disciplinarian, and he liked to run the club in his own way. He did not want interference from members of the Board of Directors. He had a reputation for being dictatorial. He worked well with the chairman, Joe Baker, for many years but Joe Baker resigned on health grounds in 1962. Cullis clashed with the new chairman, John Ireland, who demanded more say in the control of the club. Ireland was a second-hand car dealer from Wolverhampton. Football in the 1960s was equivalent in size to a small business. It was run as a small business by directors of other small businesses.

By the mid-1960s the club had lost its glamour. To try to rectify the position the club spent money on buying new players. This did not help. They had become an "ordinary side playing ordinary football". In 1964/65 they were relegated. The average home crowd was now little more than 21,000. In 1965 the Board said they no longer had confidence in Cullis. He had been with the club over 30 years and was the most successful manager in the club's history.

Ronnie Allen was appointed as the new manager. The performance of the club improved. They were promoted (with Coventry City) in 1966/67. The potential of the club can be judged from the fact that for the promotion battle with Coventry City they attracted a crowd of 51,000. Jimmy Hill, manager of Coventry City, marketed the game as the "Midlands Match of the Century". The club was back in the top division and appeared to be on the way back to being a leading team. They brought to the club new stars, including Derek Dougan. In 1968/69 they signed Alun Evans from Liverpool for £100,000 – he was at that time the most expensive teenager in the country. In 1970 they entered the new Anglo-Italian Cup tournament. The improved performance of the team led to an increase in support. The future looked quite promising.

The 1970s

The club were successful in the first half of the 1970s. They finished 4th in the First Division in 1970/71, and 5th in 1972/73. They won the league cup in 1973/74. The club were ambitious and willing to spend money. In the "Anglo-Italian Cup" they attracted crowds of over 40,000, which showed the potential. Derek Dougan was the most colourful personality in the team. He was a national personality and was made chairman of the Professional Footballers Association during the 1973/74 season. In 1970s Wolverhampton Wanderers invested heavily. The money was used to improve the stadium and to buy quality players. The club was clearly ambitious. The directors cannot be criticised for this. Unfortunately there were many problems with the ground development project and the team's performance began to decline; gates were falling dramatically. The result was a financial crisis; the club had overstretched itself. Bowler and Bains criticise the directors referring to dismal planning and over-reaching ambition. To be fair to the directors a certain amount of capital expenditure needed to be undertaken. The Molineux ground was in need of improvement. There had been little change in the stadium since 1932. Funds generated in the successful 1950s and 1960s had not been reinvested in the ground. The Bradford stadium fire tragedy led to a new Act on the Safety of Sports Grounds (1978). The Molineux Street stand failed to meet the standards now required by law. In order to improve the stand the club purchased terraced houses in Molineux Street. The club had become involved in property development. In 1977/78 plans for a new much improved stadium were announced.

The Board were ahead of their time. The proposed stadium was just what a Premier League club would want fifteen years later. The Wolves crowds of the late 1970s were only averaging 22,000 and in 1981/82 only 15,000. Being wise after the event, the 1970s and early 1980s were not the times to build and develop big new stadiums. Chelsea and some other clubs made the same mistake. Wolves could not afford the new stands being proposed. As Bowler and Bains state "by looking to the future, the club had lost sight of the present". This is clearly a case of bad leadership, of poor planning, of poor corporate governance.

Unfortunately at the time the club was spending money on the ground, the team was performing badly on the pitch. The team were relegated to the second tier in 1975/76. Matthews refers to the team in that year as one lacking 'real personalities' (Dougan had retired in 1974/75) and to the fact that a vital spark was missing. The team did immediately bounce back by winning Division Two in 1976/77.

There were, however, still problems and these became apparent in the season 1978/79. The club spent big money buying players (but also received big money selling players). It became known that there were disagreements at Board level. The club did win the League Cup in 1979/80 but this was to be their last real achievement for some time. The club had mixed fortunes from a playing point of view in the 1970s; but financially it was on a knife edge. Decisions had been made that would ruin the club. Large amounts of short term bank borrowing had been accumulated with high interest costs. This could only be justified if gate receipts did not fall. A high risk strategy for a team that was on the margins of Division One survival.

The 1980s

In 1980/81 the team finished 18th in Division One. In 1981/82 they were relegated. In 1982/83 they were promoted back to the first tier. In 1983/84 they were relegated to the Second Division, in 1984/85 relegated to the Third Division and in 1985/86 relegated to the Fourth Division. A team could not have had a more disastrous period. Not surprisingly the average gates declined; from 21,551 in 1980/81 to 4,020 in 1985/86.

The dismal performance on the pitch was mirrored by events off the field. During the 1970s the club made a surplus on trading players. Even the expensive acquisition of Andy Gray in 1979/80 (a British transfer record at that time) was matched by the funds earned from selling players. Surprisingly "uncharacteristically" the club spent more than it received from sales of players in the 1981/82 season. This was the season in which they were fighting against relegation. They knew that relegation would mean lower gate receipts, and so they invested (gambled) on spending cash now in order to earn cash in future. This, might be argued, was a brave but a risky policy.

Where the Board can be criticised is in the approach they adopted to finance their new ground developments. The first stage cost £2.8 million. It was a long term investment but it was financed mainly with funds obtained from short term bank borrowing. One of the 'rules', 'guidelines', of business finance is to match maturities – long term assets financed with long term funds – short term assets with short term funds. The directors of Wolves ignored this. The equity capital of Wolves was very low. There was only £9,000 of issued equity capital in Wolves (plus reserves). This means that the few people who controlled the club had invested very little of their own money. The club had a very high level of gearing – they were relying on bank loans to undertake high risk projects.

The new stand was completed in summer 1979, it provided 42 executive boxes. This was the first phase of what was seen as a completely new modern stadium that would cost in total; £10 million, which it was planned would be completed by 1984. But financial problems became apparent in the 1980/81 season – the annual accounts revealed current liabilities five times greater than current assets. They were financing the new stand with short term bank borrowing.

The initial plans for the new stadium provided for a 50,000 seater stadium, but the plans were modified in 1978 to a 40,000 capacity, of which 30,000 would be seated. Unfortunately the timing was wrong. The 1980s was a disastrous time for soccer in general and Wolves in particular. The first plans had been drawn up in 1977 just when the club had been promoted back to Division One. By 1978/79 the club was in a mess. There were problems at Board level. The team was performing badly and the fans were showing their disapproval by staying away from the ground.

In 1981/82 season the supporters were unhappy. A supporters 'Action Group' was formed. The manager, John Barnwell, resigned. Alex Ferguson, then at Aberdeen was approached to see if he would be the new manager, but he turned the job down. "He sensed the club had deep rooted problems". Graham Hawkins was appointed manager.

Where had the club gone wrong? Bowler and Bains state that the problems were due to "a combination of dismal planning and over-reaching ambition". Larry Canning believes that West Midlands clubs in general have been a "magnet for poor business practice … We attract abysmal chairmen".

Sir Kenneth Cork, a famous liquidator (of the accounting kind) summarised the lessons he had learnt from the type of work in which he was engaged. One lesson was that a business should not undertake an investment (in fixed assets or in an acquisition of another business) which is so big that if it fails it leads to the financial disaster of the business undertaking the investment. This is what Wolves did. On 6 June 1982 the club announced they were £2.6 million in debt. Ten days later the chairman, Harry Marshall resigned.

On July 2nd 1982 it was announced that the official receiver was to be brought in. The options open to the receiver were to find a buyer for the club (company) or to close it down and sell the assets. Surprisingly the receiver brought in Doug Ellis as the new chairman. Ellis who up until this point had shown little interest in Wolves (he had already been on the boards of Aston Villa and Birmingham City). He angered everyone by recommending that the club should go into liquidation. The club was in fact put up for sale. At this time it was uncertain if the club would be able to compete in the 1982/83 season.

Ellis had been invited to become involved with the Wolves by a representative of Lloyds Bank and a senior partner in a leading firm of solicitors. The club were in desperate need of directors with experience of football who were prepared to invest in the club. Wolves "were in a state bordering on bankruptcy and their affairs were in the hands of the bank". It was possible that Ellis following his "financial rescue" act at Villa in 1968 could do the same with Wolves. There was a danger that the Bank would bring in the receivers who would close the club down.

Ellis agreed to become chairman on the condition that Malcolm Finlayson was also brought in as a director. Finlayson had been a successful player for the Wolves, was a friend of Ellis, and had become a successful businessman in The Black Country. Ellis also wished to bring in his own accountants. His conditions were met and he became chairman in 1982. The analysis of the club by Ellis' accountant revealed that the club was "hopelessly bankrupt". The debts were said to be £2.5 million, at least £0.5 million more than Ellis had believed.

Ellis' period as chairman only lasted 10 days. He was the person the fans criticised for taking the club into receivership, for nearly bringing to an end the life of this once famous football club. It is not surprising he was the one being criticised. He was associated with Aston Villa not Wolves. Conspiracy theorists could see it was a move by a Villa man to eliminate a rival club. Ten days is a very short time to try to save a business. Ellis of course had not been responsible for building up the debts. Ellis could claim that his experiences at the badly run Blues and the out of control Wolves helped teach him "about the necessity of keeping a football club's finances in good order".

A successful bid to purchase the club was received only three minutes before the deadline set by the receiver. If a bid had not been submitted or if it had been submitted and found to be unacceptable, the club would have gone into liquidation. The receiver accepted the bid. The club were saved, they competed in the 1982/83 season, finished second in the second tier and were therefore promoted back to Division One. This was their first season under new owners. Who were the new owners?

At first it appeared that a consortium had taken over the club, led by Derek Dougan and the property developer, Douglas Hope. Later it was revealed that the immediate owners of Wolves were in fact a company called Allied Properties, which had a registered office in London. But the owner of Allied Properties was a company registered in Jersey named 'API Group Holdings'. The Jersey company was owned by the little known Bhatti brothers who were now in control of the football club. The ultimate holding company had agreed to provide financial support for three years; they would ensure the club could meet its liabilities. This of course did not mean it would provide finance to enable the club to grow.

Unfortunately the club's troubles were far from over. In 1983/84, they were relegated again to the second tier; they had a very poor squad of players. What were the motives of the new owners in buying the club? The directors of the club in the 1970s were old style directors. They may have made mistakes but they loved Wolves football club, trying to restore the glories of the past. The directors who took over in 1982 (with the exception of Derek Dougan) were property developers with no record of having been interested in football. They saw a business opportunity. By the time they sold the club in 1986 the Wolves were in a disastrous state – they were on their way to Division Four. The objectives of the new owners were far from clear – what they said was one thing what they did was another.

The company that became Wolverhampton Wanderers Football Club (1982) Ltd started life in 1979 as a shell company Sempson Mfg Co., with a paid up share capital of only £2. The name of the company was changed to Wolverhampton Wanderers Football Club (1982) in July 1982. In July 1982, a few days after the new owners acquired the assets and liabilities of the club the properties which became known as the 'Molineux Estate' (which included the Molineux Hotel and properties in Molineux Street) were mortgaged to Lloyds Bank. These were the major assets of the club.

Dougan was a character – much loved by supporters. He was a talented player, scored goals, got into trouble with referees and generally livened up a game. When he stopped playing he moved into 'union' work. In a way it was surprising that he later became associated with the Bhatti brothers fiasco – but he had football management ambitions and had lots of modern ideas that he wanted to put into practice. If the owners Allied Property had been able to (or really wanted to) "restore the financial viability of the club", Dougan may have been able to show what he could achieve. He was not given that chance and resigned from the Board.

Dougan was respected for the work he did with the PFA. He was elected chairman in 1970. The rival candidate for the post was Bobby Charlton. The early 1970s were a time when there was considerable "disillusionment with the state of the game on and off the field". The financial health of the clubs depended upon efficient and skilful management. The Chester Report pointed to the lack of commercial expertise in managing clubs. "The PFA was taking on a responsibility for the game in general that the industry's management had barely considered". Dougan was at the forefront of discussions on the proposed changes, "Dougan would serve the Union well".

There was of course criticism of Dougan whilst he was chairman of the PFA. Eamon Dunphy expressed the opinion that "Since Jimmy Hill no one else had emerged with the character to unite the Union behind any of its demands". Some of the developments in the game were not liked. *Foul*, a football magazine, criticised the "greed, vested interests and phoney glamour" that increasingly seemed to characterise the British game – if they complained in the 1970s what would they think of the position 40 years later?

Dougan was a reformer but for various reasons did not have great success. In 1974 an article in *Foul* referred to the PFA as "Pretty Feeble Altogether" and described Dougan as "smug" suggesting that his real aim in life was to secure a comfortable managers job. The article expressed the view that chairmen of the PFA used their position to "advertise their conformity and responsibility".

In 1974 Dougan did reveal that he was interested in running a football club, he attempted to take over Walsall F.C. He failed, but a year later he became chief executive of Kettering Town F.C, a non-league club in financial difficulties. Dougan was an enthusiastic supporter of the ideas contained in the Chester Report, there were many aspects of the game he wished to change. Unfortunately he ran into problems with the many reactionary people running the game at the time. He proposed that Kettering should be able to show a sponsor's logo on the front of the players shirts. He ran into problems with the authorities in Kettering when he proposed that a 'sports complex' be developed with the football ground as its centre. He was ahead of his time. He left Kettering Town in 1978 having not been able to overcome the financial problems at the club. He tried to become manager of Wolves in 1978 but was unsuccessful. He then went into public relations before coming back to the Wolves in 1982 as a result of the Bhatti brothers takeover.

Strange things were happening at the club from a financial point of view. Money came into the club from a bank overdraft (Lloyds) of £1.5 million, a loan from the holding company of £0.45 million and from the purchase of equity shares by the holding company. The overdraft was secured by a charge on the assets of the club together with a guarantee given by a third party. These are the type of transactions one would expect to see in a company in Wolverhampton Wanders' situation.

It was the second stage of the financing exercise that was unusual. As the football club's 1984 accounts explain "The Company's beneficial interest in the freehold Land and Buildings known as the Molineux Complex was acquired by the Company's immediate holding company". These assets were acquired by the holding company for £1.6 million. But the holding company mysteriously did not pay cash to the football company – they owed the company the money. In the accounts for the period to June 1983 this debt owing to the club is clearly shown in the club's balance sheet as "due from holding company" £1.8 million. The holding company, Allied Properties, owed the football club money.

The 1986 Crisis

Unfortunately in 1983/84, their first season back in the top Division, did not begin well. Public meetings were organised at which fans criticised the Board for the lack of money being made available to spend on quality players. The Board did not respond. The manager, Hawkins, was sacked to be replaced by the high profile manager Tommy Docherty. No money was, however, made available for Docherty to purchase new players.

When the company had been taken over there was talk of a £22 million redevelopment plan. This was forgotten. The annual losses of the club increased. In 1983/84 the team were relegated back to the Second Division, in 1984/85 they were relegated to the Third Division. The average home attendance dropped in two years from 16,000 to 8,000. Derek Dougan had resigned as a Director early in 1985.

1985/86 was another disaster season. The team were relegated to the Fourth Division. The average attendance halved again to 4,000 (the lowest in the club's history). Because of the concern with ground safety (following the Bradford fire) two of the stands at the ground had to be closed down.

Just under four years after the Bhatti brothers became involved with the club, Lloyds Bank appointed a receiver and manager to take over the property of Wolverhampton Wanderers (1982) Ltd.

The club had defaulted on the mortgage debenture and Lloyds Bank had a charge over all the "assets, undertaking and property of the company both past and present". In July 1986 the owners, Allied Properties were taken to court for non-payment of debts – the judge ordered that Wolverhampton Wanders be wound up. The owners announced that they would take steps to inject new cash into the business. The crisis was temporarily averted and the club was able to continue in existence.

In the summer of 1986 new owners were found for the club, and a financial deal was arranged that gave the company security and an opportunity to build a successful team. Unfortunately the deal came too late to give the club the opportunity to be a leading club at the time when the 'haves' and 'have nots' began to emerge. They had not restructured and refinanced themselves in time to find a place in the Premier League.

The club were saved because of what would now be called a joint public private finance initiative. The local Council purchased the ground and adjoining land, and property developers, together with a supermarket chain, agreed to pay off the club's debts. The developers, Gallaghers, and the supermarket chain, Asda, were prepared to help save the club in exchange for permission to build a supermarket behind one of the stands. The Council protected Wolverhampton Wanderers as a football team by a covenant which included the clause that the ground itself could only be used for sporting and recreational purposes.

The person who arranged this deal was John Bird, who at the time was leader of Wolverhampton Council – he was a keen supporter of Wolves. John Bird, together with Sir Jack Hayward (from 1990) saved the club and allowed it to continue into more prosperous times. Unfortunately the quality of the directors in the late 1970s and most of the 1980s meant that Wolverhampton Wanderers were not in a position to be major beneficiaries from the football boom that came in the 1990s. But perhaps with better leadership, good times lay ahead.

6

COVENTRY CITY AND WALSALL

The Coventry City club started as a works team in 1883. They were elected into the football league in 1919. They played in the Third Division (South) until 1936 when they were promoted to Division Two. They were relegated down to the Third in 1954 and then to Division Four in 1959. This might have been thought of as the end of the club but in fact it turned out to be a new beginning.

In the 1960s they had outstanding leadership. An innovative manager, Jimmy Hill, and a dynamic chairman, Derrick Robins backed by a supportive board of directors. Hill had been chairman of the Professional Football Association, and had been very instrumental in ending the maximum wage system. He introduced change into the way the club was run, and introduced many of the new marketing ideas coming into sport from the US.

Starting from the fourth tier they proceeded to move upwards through the divisions until in 1967/68 they were in Division One. This was the first time in their history that they had played at the top level. They then enjoyed remarkable success. They remained in the top tier for 34 years. Only three other teams have had a longer tenure at that level; the three being Liverpool, Everton and Arsenal. The highest position Coventry achieved in this period was sixth, in 1970. They qualified for the European Fairs Cup but were eliminated in the second round. They had on a number of occasions narrowly escaped being relegated from the top tier, finishing 19th in 1973, 1983, 1984 and 1992. But just to survive was quite an achievement. They are a club from a medium size town, they are some distance from the main centres of population in the West Midlands, and they only have in the region of 160,000 people living within 10 miles of the ground whereas the Villa, Blues and Albion have a population of over 500,000 living that far from their grounds.

Unfortunately in the 1990s things began to go badly for the club. The directors decided that the club needed a bigger stadium. They club were in the Premier League and they expected to remain there. The directors had decided to sell their existing ground Highfield Road for housing development and to move into a new 45,000 seater modern stadium at the edge of the City. But following relegation, the plans were modified. It was now to be a 32,000 seater but still one of high quality. There were construction delays, with the result the club did not play its first game in the stadium until 2005. Once they moved to their new stadium, the Ricoh Arena, their financial problems increased.

They were having difficulties on the pitch as well as off it. In fact clubs across the Midlands were having difficulties with managerial appointments at that time. By the half way stage of the 2004/5 season eight big Midlands clubs had removed their managers, they had either been sacked or resigned by mutual agreement. Not a sign of a successful season. Peter Reid had left Coventry, Joe Kinnear had departed from Nottingham Forest, Micky Adams from Leicester City, Dave Jones from Wolves and Gary Megson from West Bromwich Albion.

For Peter Reid it was his fourth departure from the position of manager of a club. In 1993 he was required to leave Manchester City, in 2002 Sunderland, 2003 Leeds United and 2005 Coventry City. The last two appointments were from his point of view far from ideal, he was expected to save the clubs involved without any money to spend. When he left Coventry they were in twentieth place in the Championship, the lowest position they had been in for 41 years. As is well-known, managers take the blame for failure, although the chairman of Coventry, Bryan Richardson, was kind enough to say that "We as a club were underachieving, but don't put all the blame on Peter Reid. The players have to be accountable as well". He should have added: so do the directors.

In December 2005, the directors of Coventry City appointed Micky Adams as their new manager, their fourth manager in 18 months (Adams was sacked in January 2007). The club were £20 million in debt, and were only 3 points clear of the relegation zone. Adams said, "We are in a precarious position, and the players' fate plus that of the club this season rests in their own hands". The decline in the fortunes of the club over a six-year period, was the result of decisions made by the club's directors.

In 2007 the club narrowly avoided moving into administration. They were saved by the actions of SISU Capital, a London based hedge fund. Such funds invest the money of wealthy clients and money that the fund have borrowed. SISU was incorporated at the end of the 1990s with a small number of partners, all very experienced in the Investment banking business, but not in sport. The founder and CEO is Joy Seppala. The directors of the fund decided they wished to buy a football club. They were interested in a club that had potential but one that was having problems and so could be purchased cheaply. They hoped to be able to solve the club's problems to sell and make a profit. In 2007 SISU offered to purchase 55% of the shares of Southampton, that club was experiencing financial problems, it went into administration. Fortunately for Southampton but unfortunately for Coventry their offer was not accepted. SISU Capital purchased Coventry in 2007. The club had been in danger of moving into administration. They were playing in the second tier at the time and had debts of £60 million. The move to the Ricoh Stadium had made their financial situation worse.

The new Ricoh stadium had been financed by Coventry City Council and the Higgs Charitable Trust. The original plan had been for the car company Jaguar to purchase the naming rights to the stadium but in the end that did not happen. The original plans had been for the football club to acquire a financial stake in the stadium but when the time came to pay they could not afford it. The club had hopes of being able to one day buy the 50% holding of the Higgs Trust but they have not been able to afford this. They became just a club having to pay rent to use a stadium.

The operators of the stadium are ACL (Arena Coventry Ltd.) It was at first agreed that the club would pay £1.2 million as the annual rental. But the club were short of money and said that they could not pay this amount. This meant that the operating company ACL were themselves short of funds. ACL were saved by a £14 million loan from the Coventry Council. SISU made themselves even more unpopular when they claimed that the loan to ACL from the Council was illegal. They claimed that it was an illegal use of state funds.

In 2012 ACL took the club (SISU) to Court over unpaid rent bills. The club had been trying to have its rent payments reduced. Throughout 2013 squabbling between ACL and the club continued over a new lease agreement. In the end the club moved all of its staff out of the Ricoh Stadium. The club began to play their home matches in Northampton, having entered into a ground share agreement with the local football club. This move meant that fans had to make a 70 mile round trip to see home games.

In 2013 the club were deducted 10 points for going into administration. The club were deducted a further 10 points following a failure by the parties involved to agree to a company voluntary arrangement proposed by the administrator. As a result of a financial engineering exercise the club came out of administration. The parent company of the football club Coventry City Football Club (Holdings) (that was itself owned by SISU) owned four subsidiary companies. It was one of these subsidiaries, Coventry City Football Club Limited (CCFC) that was placed in liquidation. The Administrator said that this subsidiary had debts of over £70 million, most of which was money owed to SISU related activities, with some being owed to ACL for unpaid rent. The Administrator, who was trying to sell the subsidiary accepted a bid for CCFC Ltd from a business named Otium Entertainment

Group. They were the highest bidders. But Otium were related to SISU, they were not independent. It is true that there were three former Coventry players involved with Otium, but basically from a governance point of view little had changed. The football club continued with more or less the same ownership and had walked away from some of their debts. The owners knew little about football but they did know about the world of finance. The fans were not happy, but did that matter?

In 2014 the Ricoh Arena was sold to the company that owned the Wasps Rugby Club. Coventry football club returned to the stadium in 2014 with an agreement to allow them to play there for two seasons with an option to play for another two seasons. This would mean that the tenancy expired at the latest in August 2018. The move back to the Ricoh resulted in the football club having to pay compensation to Northampton Town football club because they had not remained as tenants for as long as they had originally agreed.

The football club was not surprisingly operating at a loss. The accounts for Otium for 2013/14 revealed that £61 million of the club's loan debt to SISU had been converted into equity shares, a debt for equity swap. SISU converted the debt as part of an agreement with the Football League that allowed the club to maintain its league membership.

As with all badly run clubs, Coventry frequently changed managers. In the first ten years of SISU ownership they had ten managers and eight caretaker managers. They only, however, had three chairmen over this period, the first of whom was Ray Ranson (2007/2011) who had been involved with the negotiations for purchase of the club by the hedge fund. One of the managers was Tony Mowbray who had been appointed in 2015 but who resigned after 18 months in charge. He had managed four clubs before Coventry and at one time had been chosen as a Manager of the Year. He had had a successful time as manager of WBA, having led them back into the Premier League and to the semi-final of the FA Cup.

When Mowbray resigned from Coventry they were struggling to survive in the third tier. He said that it was embarrassing to manage a club who went ten games without a win. He said that you cannot build a club around loan players, you have to invest in footballers who you can keep and build a team around them. He understood, however, that the club had little money. Coventry had been relegated from the Championship at the end of the 2011/12 season. They then spent five seasons in the third tier before being relegated to the fourth tier for the 2017/18 season.

SISU had talked for some time about building a new stadium in Coventry but nothing happened. There was also talk about the club entering a ground share agreement with the local rugby club (not the Wasps). The drama off the field continued with SISU again suing the local council, this time for selling their 50% share in ACL to the Wasps. There were doubts as to whether or not the football club would be allowed to continue to play at the Ricoh beyond 2018. The Wasps, landlords at the Arena, said that they were fed up with the "distraction" of legal action by the football club owners SISU over ownership of the Ricoh.

On the pitch the team were doing badly, they did however have one moment of glory. In 1987 they had been FA Cup winners beating the Spurs 3-2 at Wembley stadium. In 2017 they returned to Wembley to win another cup. Unfortunately it was a cup with slightly less prestige, namely the Checkatrade Trophy. A lot had happened to the club in the 30 years between their two Wembley appearances. In the 1980s the club were probably at their best and in the early 2000s probably their worst. In 2017 they were relegated to the fourth tier. Their appearance at Wembley did however show one thing. They could still attract the fans, 40,000 people went to Wembley to support Coventry. This was to see the Final of a competition for teams from the third and fourth tier and for teams of under 23 years of age players from certain top clubs.

In 2017 SISU were voted the second worst owners of any club in England. Under their 10 years of leadership the club had moved from the second tier to the fourth tier. In 2016/17 they were the worst team in the third tier and were relegated. SISU clearly mishandled the club. They upset everyone, fans, the local council, and the community. Again an example of owners not knowing what they were doing. There have been many rumours about a takeover of CCFC. Those said to have been interested include wealthy Russians, wealthy Saudis and even wealthy local businessmen. But nothing happened.

Leicester City

Coventry's problems began with the decision of directors to move to a new stadium. They were not the only club to suffer at that time from making such a decision. One other club that built a large stadium was Leicester City but the fortunes of that club and Coventry following their investment decisions were so different. Leicester City progressed to be the Premier League champions and Coventry City finished up playing in the fourth tier.

Leicester City and Coventry City were both playing in the second tier when they moved into their new stadiums. Both suffered from a fall in expected revenue, both clubs went into administration. The Leicester move into administration caused a great deal of ill feeling in the football world, and led to changes in the rules relating to clubs in administration. Leicester City had built themselves a new stadium. In doing so they had built up debts of over £50 million but as a result of going into administration they were able to walk away from many of these debts. To rub salt in the wound, they were promoted back to the Premier League in the season in which they went into administration; (2002/03). Clubs who only spent what they earned were not promoted but a club that spent more than it could afford was promoted.

Leicester had in fact faced serious financial problems for a number of years. The directors had in the late 1990s decided that one way to raise finance to help overcome their liquidity problem and to help finance a new stadium was to issue equity shares in the stock market. The timing was wrong. The public float in October 1997 was not a success; it was right at the end of the period in which the financial institutions were interested in football club shares. The prospectus offering shares to the public referred to the directors' confidence in the fact that "the club would continue to grow". The directors did correctly point out to potential investors that there were dangers. Whilst in the Premier League the club had been receiving a share of the large amount of money received from the sale of television rights. The prospectus did point out that if the club were to be relegated to the Championship this "may have a significant negative impact upon sources of the club's income." It did.

Work on the new Walkers Stadium started in 2001. It would cost in the region of £35 million. They were in the Second Division in 2002. The club entered administration in October 2002, which led to four months of uncertainty. The administrators were able to arrange a deal with the club's creditors, and it was this deal which upset other clubs who were managing their finances more carefully. Leicester had an outstanding tax bill of £6 million and to the surprise of many the Inland Revenue agreed to settle for one tenth of this amount, (or one fifth if and when the club were promoted back to the Premiership). The adverse reaction to Leicester's financial behaviour led the Football League (and later the Premier League) to introduce a points penalty system for clubs that move into administration.

Leicester City had something to show for their debts that they had accumulated, namely a new stadium. Coventry City had built up debts of £60 million and finished up not owning a stadium. Coventry were effectively saved by the intervention of the Local Authority, Leicester City were saved by being able to walk away from their debts.

The members of the consortium that purchased Leicester City out of administration included Gary Lineker, his agent, the chairman of the plc that owned the club prior to it going into administration, Greg Clarke, and the football club chairman Martin George. All of these and other members of the consortium were Leicester City supporters. A spokesman said that the club "had always been a nice club run by groups of local people rather than a dictatorial chairman." In February 2007 another consortium led by the ex-Portsmouth chairman Milan Mandarić purchased Leicester. Mandarić's time at Portsmouth had been very controversial.

Leicester were relegated to the third tier for the 2008/09 season but they only remained there for one year. In August 2010 the club were purchased by a consortium of investors from Thailand, led by the respected and well connected head of the duty free retailers 'King Power Group', namely Vichai Srivaddhanaprabha. The investment group was named 'Asian Football Investment'. Mandarić continued to be involved with the club until 2010 when he moved to Sheffield Wednesday. Leicester initially had problems, but the new owners continued to invest in them, demonstrating their long term commitment by converting £103 million of loans that they had made to the club into equity. The club were promoted. The objective became Premier League survival, but it was a struggle.

In the 2014/15 season they were battling against relegation which they only avoided by winning seven of their final nine games. The manager at the time was the popular Nigel Pearson. Unfortunately he said things that upset the Thai owners and some of his players behaved disrespectfully whilst in Thailand. Pearson was sacked during the close season and the experienced and well liked Claudio Ranieri was brought in as manager. Here again was a case of foreign owners turning to an "elite" foreign manager. In this case it worked well – for a while. Most of the players and coaching staff remained at the club and only a small number of new players were purchased. Ranieri, who had a reputation for tinkering, did not change things very much at the club. To the surprise of most Leicester City were winners of the Premier League in the 2015/16 season. Leicester City had a Thai investment group as owners. Coventry City had SISU, fund managers based in London as owners. The objectives of the owners were so different, one long term the other short term.

In December 2016 Ranieri was named Coach of the Year and Leicester named Team of the Year. Unfortunately Leicester had problems in 2016/17. In February 2017 Ranieri was sacked, with the club only one place above the relegation zone. This illustrates the random nature of a manager's life, hero one moment, villain the next. There were stories about a dressing room revolt. The next manager appointed was Craig Shakespeare who had been a coach at the club for some while. He only remained as manager for a few months, he was sacked in October 2017 with the club in 18th place in the League.

The owners then turned to another foreign manager, Claude Puel, who had recently enjoyed some success at Southampton. Before that he had led Monaco to be Champions in France, and had taken Lyon to the semi-finals of the UEFA Champions League. He was given a two and a half years contract by Leicester and promised £30 million to spend in the January transfer window. The owners described him as "the perfect fit" for their long term vision. The supporters hoped this was correct, the club had changed the manager 3 times in 8 months.

The sagas of Coventry and Leicester illustrate the importance of ownership to success. The Leicester owners wealthy, willing to invest, with a long term objective. The Coventry owners in contrast, petty. There is also an element of luck in success – Leicester walked away from their debts!

The Present

Fortunately in 2017/18 things began to get better for Coventry. The team's performance on the pitch began to improve. They finished the season in 6th place in the fourth tier. This might not seem very much but it did mean that they qualified for a place in the play-off games and it was the club's highest place finish in any league for 47 years. In 1970 they had finished in 6th place in Division One, the top tier, but this was a long time ago.

The club during the SISU ownership frequently changed managers. In March 2017 they appointed Mark Robins as manager, he was returning to the club after a successful period in charge in 2012/13. He was the eleventh managerial appointment since SISU had taken over the club in 2007. He replaced the unfortunate Russell Slade who was sacked after 16 games in charge with the club at the bottom of the third tier. Robins was not able to save the club from relegation in 2017 but in the next season he was successful. In June 2018 they beat Exeter 3-1 in the final of the play-off games and so were promoted back to the third tier. After a number of disastrous years it looked as if the club's fortunes were improving. The club had a good manager and a good young team. The club still had a good fan base 37,000 followed them to Wembley for the play-off final, and agreement had been reached about an academy and training ground for the club. Progress was even being made in discussions on the use of the Ricoh Stadium.

The City of Coventry received a boost when it was announced that it would be the UK City of Culture in 2021. It was also announced that the Ricoh Arena would be the venue for the netball competition at the 2022 Commonwealth Games. Both of these events would be good for Coventry, but whether or not they would benefit the football club would depend upon the owners of the club.

Walsall

There is another team in the West Midlands that plays in the Football League, namely Walsall FC. They are a club that have never hit the high spots but are locally a much admired community team. The highest position they have ever achieved was 14th in the second tier (Division Two) in 1961/62. They played at Wembley in 2015 for the first time in their history in the League Trophy Final, but they lost. In 1984 they nearly qualified for entry into a European wide competition. They had defeated Arsenal, at Highbury, in the League Cup and advanced to the semi-final stage. Unfortunately they lost to Liverpool in the semi-final. If they had got to the final they would have qualified for Europe and been able to enjoy a moment of fame. They have twice been champions of the old Division Four.

It is a surprise to many to know that Walsall were in 1892 founder members of the Second Division of the football league. They were, however, relegated from that division in 1895, they were back in, in 1896 but out again in 1901. They became founder members of Third Division North in 1921 and in 1958 they became founder members of the new Division Four.

They have never played at the top level and clearly there is now little chance of them doing so. They are, however a very valuable part of the Walsall community. The club are successful in attracting commercial income, they make a modest profit each year, and they offer free season tickets to under 18 year olds. Most of those involved in running the club have local connections, with almost half of their players having come through their academy system. A good local club.

7

THE CITY OF BIRMINGHAM

One hundred years ago Birmingham had a genuine claim to be called the Second City. It was home to some of the great British companies, to leading politicians and to good football clubs. It was the "Workshop of the World".

In the 18th century Birmingham was a place for a man to make a fortune. Even in the 1870s a local saying held that "Any fool can make a fortune in Birmingham". Industrialists, scientists and bankers came to live in or near the city and did well for themselves and the community around them. "A city of makers and traders. Its citizens boasted of its industry, its independence, its bustle and its power." In reality Birmingham was noisy, dirty and chaotic, but it was exuberant, individual and inventive. The manufacturers and traders were global in outlook, they saw their market as not just national, but also as the countries on the continent and in the empire.[1]

In 1851 Birmingham was the fourth largest town in the UK. Joseph Chamberlain had moved from London to Birmingham to help run the family business. He increasingly became involved in local politics. He became mayor in 1873. He helped transform the city and became known as the father of modern Birmingham. He was proud to be able to claim that Birmingham was the 'Second City of the Empire'. It was, however, not until the boundary changes in 1911 (the Greater Birmingham Act) that it became the second city in the UK in terms of population size.

Birmingham in the late 1800s was an important city from a political as well as an industrial point of view. The Chamberlain family were leading national politicians, while Quaker industrialists such as the Cadbury family were demonstrating new ways of providing welfare for workers and the local authority were pioneering new ways to improve the quality of life for people living in a city. Two of the banks that had been established in the region, Lloyds and the Midland, were leading national financial institutions.

In 1870 the City Council decided to take the responsibility for the supply of gas and water out of private hands. They decided that the supply of these utilities was so important to the health and safety of citizens that they could not be left in private hands. This has been referred to as municipal socialism. With Joseph Chamberlain as leader the municipal finances were transformed and became a model for local growth, a model which it was said would last for more than a century. It did not.

At a national level the city of Birmingham has been of importance. It was very significant in the movement for social reform. Meetings of the Political Union Party in Birmingham in 1831 and 1832 attracted crowds of more than 200,000 people. Threats of a revolution led to the 1832 Reform Act. Lord Durham who drafted the Act said "the country owed reform to Birmingham". The City was also involved in the pressure leading to the second Reform Act of 1867. This was the act that gave for the first time voting rights to the working class (men) of the big cities. Industrialists and the Local Authority were pioneering new ways to improve the quality of life for the working classes in the city. Out of this came an interest in organising sport for the masses to keep them healthy and to keep them out of trouble. Aston Villa were, at the beginning of the 20th century the top team in the country, their name known all over the world. Birmingham was leading the country.

As far back as the 1760 to 1850 period Birmingham businesses registered three times as many patents as businesses from any other city. The success was based on its entrepreneurs, many who came from outside the region and on the range of skilled trades employing innovative skilled workers. The region has had a long and proud manufacturing history. By the end of the 16th century it was already known for its metal working, and for its iron wares. It had become a centre, not just for gun manufacturing, but also for the manufacture of toys and other metal goods. In the 18th century it was known at the 'Toyship of Europe'. The word toys at that time had a wider meaning than it does now. It was the first manufacturing town in the world.

In the 1950s and 60s, Birmingham was still a prosperous city. Chris Upton in his 'History of Birmingham' has a chapter entitled 'What went wrong with tomorrow'.[2] He refers to the confidence that existed in the city well into the 1960s. Until the 1970s it was the most rapidly growing city outside London. In 1969 Jacobs noted that "today, only two cities in all of Britain remain economically vigorous and prosperous. One is London. The second is Birmingham".[3] Much of its dynamism was concentrated around the car industry. The working man, as well as enjoying his prosperity, was also able to enjoy watching the successful football teams WBA and the Wolves, two of the elite teams of the 1950s and early 1960s.

The city had a Labour controlled council, with plenty of money to spend and the councillors were keen to invest. But they made some bad decisions. Unfortunately the city is still living with the results of some of these decisions. In particular, poor quality high rise flats, and new roads destroying the inner city and creating a concrete collar. To be fair the city did build more houses than any other single authority in the UK but they were of poor quality. Much of the blame for this waste must lie with Herbert Manzoni, the city engineer and surveyor. He destroyed many worthy old buildings. He believed that the life span of the new modern buildings being constructed should be no more than 20 years.

Birmingham was successful into the 1970s, the car industry was still booming. Surprisingly at that time the average household income in the city was similar to that of London and the South East. Unfortunately being a prosperous city in the 1960s and 1970s turned out not to be a good thing. Expansion plans were controlled, by central government. The 1945 Distribution of Industry Act aimed to redistribute industry around the country. The recession in the manufacturing sector in the 1980s hit the West Midlands badly, partly because they had not been allowed to diversify.

The Decline

Up until the 1970s the manufacturing sector in Birmingham was still doing well but then came a collapse, particularly in the production of motor cars, motor cycles and machine tools. There were a number of reasons for the decline in the fortunes of these industries. One was increasing competition from foreign manufacturers but the other was the use of out of date manufacturing techniques. There was a history of under investment in the new technologies. This lack of investment by overcautious management was the story in many sectors. The companies were being prudent. This combined with bad labour relations, ruined companies such as BSA, British Leyland, Lucas and Metro Cammell. The annual production of motor vehicles was 1.9 million in the 1970s but it fell to 1 million in the 1980s. The collapse of the automotive industry saw Birmingham suffer significantly more than other manufacturing centres in the country. What had been a high employment, high wage city moved into an underemployed and deprived city. This decline in the manufacturing sector continued. Between the 1960s and 2000 the number of people employed in manufacturing halved. Many big name firms disappeared, and the jobs went with them. The unemployment rate in 1966 was 2%, by 1981 it was 21%. Wage levels fell, those working in the car industry had once been relatively very well paid but now they were out of work.

Ironically, it was at this time that football in the region enjoyed its greatest success for many decades. Aston Villa were champions of Division One (the top tier) in the 1980/81 season and European champions in 1982. It did not do them a great deal of good, it did not do the region any good. TV at the time was not selling the game all over the world. The club's directors talked of the Villa being a global brand but did little to exploit it.

Reinvention

In Birmingham the public sector became increasingly important in trying to stabilise the economy, in trying to create jobs. They came up with new ideas, with new initiatives. Prestige projects were started, designed to make the city a more attractive place, to make it a centre for international business, a centre to attract visitors. Canalside developments took place, a National Exhibition Centre was built, as was an International Convention Centre, a Symphony Hall and the National Indoor Arena. These projects would create jobs in the service sector. Not much financial assistance came from Westminster. In the late 1970s and 1980s the European Community did provide support. One noticeable project at the time was in the International Convention Centre – officially opened by the Queen in June 1991 but more quietly opened by Jacques Delors a number of months earlier. It was funded jointly by Birmingham and the European Regional Development Fund.

The city had been trying for over 30 years to recreate itself as a city for sport and a city of culture. It has had mixed success. The Council developed "a thirst for staging international sport".[4] Unfortunately they had not, until the announcement about the 2022 Commonwealth Games been particularly successful in bringing high profile events to the city.

They bid for the 1982 Commonwealth Games, but withdrew the bid. In 1986 they were selected ahead of London and Manchester to be the UK city to bid for the 1992 Olympics – but they failed at the international selection round. They were beaten by Manchester in the choice of the UK city to bid for the 1996 Olympics, Manchester failed with the Olympics bid but did attract the 2002 Commonwealth Games. These games boosted that city's profile, as well as resulting in them finishing up with a number of modern sports facilities. To its credit Birmingham kept trying and in the end were successful, they are to host the 2022 Commonwealth Games.

Unfortunately Birmingham has been awarded the Commonwealth Games just at the time when many people are questioning the Games relevance. Two questions were being asked, one being the relevance of the Commonwealth in the 21st century, and the other whether or not these Games mattered as a sporting contest. The moral justification for the old Empire has been discredited, and the economic relevance of the Commonwealth is unclear. With the UK's planned departure from the EU would the old links between the Commonwealth countries become important once again? All Birmingham could do was go ahead as planned and hope for the best.

Birmingham would like to be seen as a city of culture, it has had mixed success. It has achieved international recognition and respect as home of the CBSO and the Birmingham Royal Ballet. It attracted a lot of attention with the opening of a new library (although of it has had difficulty in finding enough money to keep the library open). The city has, however, had its disappointments. It lost to Liverpool in its attempt to be the 2003 European City of Culture. It lost again to Londonderry in 2013 in its attempt to be named as the UK City of Culture. The council had estimated that had it been named as the UK City it would have benefited the local economy by £200 million. It did not bid to become the 2017 UK City of Culture; that went to Hull. As with many other attempts the city has failed to obtain support at a national level. It has been overlooked, bypassed.

The case for being a city of culture was not helped when the BBC closed down their Birmingham production facilities. The BBC is a national broadcaster but only 1.7% of its programmes are made in the Midlands compared with 23.1% being made in the North. This is a redistribution of income, the licence fees being paid in the Midlands and the money spent elsewhere.

Problems

In the thirty or so years since Birmingham ceased to become a city for manufacturing there have been some changes for the good but also some problems have emerged. One problem has been a failure at local government level. In 2015 the Kerslake Report highlighted many weaknesses in the way the city was now being run.[5] Reference was made to local government decay, to the lack of good leadership. It was found that there had, for some time, been resistance to change within the authority and there was what was referred to as organisational disobedience. Serious mistakes were made, a major one being a reluctance to pay women council workers equal rates of pay to men and then not to appreciate the pension implications of paying women equally. Key departments in the council such as education, children's services and social services had been underfunded and mismanaged for a number of years. There is an argument that the Council is too big to function properly. The report concluded that the Council was holding the city back in relation to other major UK cities. The local council has experienced huge financial problems resulting in major cuts in it expenditure. The leadership did not get any better. In 2017 the Leader of the Council had to resign over his mishandling of the strike of the dustmen. Refuse had not been collected for many weeks, he promised the dustmen a deal which he was not able to deliver. His party colleagues on the Council were not willing to back him. The contrast between the good governance in Manchester and the poor governance in Birmingham is striking.

One other problem that the city now faces is a skills gap. Birmingham, once the workshop of the world, now finds itself with 15.6% of its working age population with no qualifications. The national average is 8.8%. The youth unemployment rate in the city is 31%, that for England is 21%. This is particularly important because Birmingham has a young population with 40% of the population being aged under 25, and 25% aged under 18, it is the most youthful city in Europe. Unfortunately it has the lowest percentage of adults with high level qualifications and the highest percentage of adults with no qualifications. So much for skills.

It has a high immigrant community with 22% of the population born outside the UK (14% is the figure for England). If one looks at the younger age group, 60% of children in Birmingham are from minority ethnic groups (with a national average of 26%). There is a need for improved social integration. Unfortunately there is a high level of unemployment (19.2%) amongst black, asian and minority ethnic groups. The unemployment amongst the white population is 10.2%. The income inequality is the highest of the major cities. Perhaps surprisingly 40% of the population are living in areas classified as being the 10% most deprived parts of England. To repeat, Birmingham has one of the worst educated populations in the country. Only 28% of the working age population has a higher level qualification (in Manchester the figure is 38%). The labour productivity in the West Midlands in 2013 was 10% below the national average. Birmingham is creating jobs but there is still increasing unemployment, the jobs are being created in areas where skills are not available.

The Centre for Cities pointed out in 2015, that Birmingham had performed relatively well in terms of private sector job creation. This may seem encouraging but it has to be remembered that London had for a long time been sucking talent from the rest of the country. Since 2010 London have created 10 times more private sector jobs than any other city. The economic gap in the country is widening, but this is a different issue. It is doubtful whether talk of regional powerhouses and a high speed rail network will prevent this gap increasing.

Perceptions

One of Birmingham's biggest problems is its image, the way in which it is perceived. For a time a region that once had something to be proud about lost its way. Its fortunes had declined as had that of other large manufacturing cities. It struggled. The local accent was mocked. In many people's minds, including some employers, the accent was associated with being less intelligent.[6] This was just a perception, it was a prejudice. But the city has made big efforts to re-invent itself. It has tried to become known as a city of sport, as a city of culture, as a city for tourism and as a city for commerce, a city for shopping. A major problem has been getting its message across.

For example, it still has a reputation for being dour, a city of motorways but it is in fact one of the greenest cities in the UK with green space covering 15.6% of the area which compares favourably with the national average for cities, of 6.8%. Only a small number of boroughs in London are greener than Birmingham. The problem again is perception. The centre of the city is not attractive, it does lack green space, the large parks and golf courses tend to be two to three miles from the city centre. But the city has done well in exploiting its canal network. Even Bill Bryson, the well-known travel writer, admitted on his second visit to the city that it was making great strides in "restoring itself to agreeableness".[7]

The local media and those responsible for promoting the city like to refer to Birmingham as the UK's second city. This might be a good marketing tool that can be justified on the basis of the size of its population. Whether or not being the second largest city is of any value is debatable. The governance of the City of Birmingham is now a mess and its administration has been called dysfunctional. The problems are partly a result of its size. There is a danger that the city will be divided up. The governance in Westminster had threatened to send in outside experts to run the city.

Most people in Britain do not in fact recognise Birmingham as the second city. A 2017 study by BMG revealed that 38% of people thought that Manchester was number two with only 36% believing it was Birmingham.[8] Of significance is the difference in belief by different age groups with younger people choosing Manchester as the second city and older people choosing Birmingham. Perhaps it was football and the BBC that helped Manchester create its new image. Another poll, by the BBC, found that 48% of people thought that Manchester was the UK's second city whereas only 45% believed Birmingham to be the second city.[9] This study also showed that in the younger age group (16-25) 58% believed that Manchester was second (only 38% said Birmingham). If such surveys were undertaken of opinions of people outside the UK, Manchester would win by a much greater margin.

When Birmingham does these days hit the national headlines; unfortunately it is for the wrong reasons. It has recently been labelled the "benefits capital of Britain". In parts of the city one adult in 10 in the so called active population is on welfare.[10] The proportion of active people claiming benefits nationally was 2.6%. Not surprisingly the local paper, the *Birmingham Post* goes out of its way to encourage people to feel good about the city. It does, however, also draw attention to the downsides. In September 2016 an article was entitled "Identity crisis could see the rest of the world bypass us".[10] The article was referring to the fact that the new regional authority was to be known as the WMCA not as Greater Birmingham. It was thought by the Councils coming into the new grouping, that is Walsall, Wolverhampton, Dudley, Smethwick, Coventry and Solihull that the name Greater Birmingham would fail to have appeal around the world. So much for brand value. They believed that the title "West Midlands Combined Authority" would have more appeal.

This may not be surprising, the city has for a number of years been attracting such headlines as "Second City, Second class". That was the title of an article in the *Economist* in 2012 where the failings of the city were seen to be the result of over centralisation and poor management.[11] Another headline is *The Daily Telegraph* in 2016 was "Birmingham? You couldn't pay me to go there".[12] These were comments being made by some HSBC employees when being told that they were to move from London to a new bank development 100 miles to the North. Yet another headline was "Our Second City is third rate and its children are paying the price".[13] This article was drawing attention to the fact that the education standards in Birmingham were very poor and the skill level in the city was very low. Fraser Nelson pointed out that there were more than 120 politicians on the City Council which was more than in the Scottish Parliament and more than in the US Senate.

When Bill Bryson first came to Birmingham in the 1990s he had some interesting comments to make. He said that he had never seen a city that was so ugly on purpose.[14] He also believed the culprit was Sir Herbert Manzoni. The city's best buildings, Bryson believed, had been demolished. But when he returned to the city in 2015 he found that it had much improved. Indeed much has improved but there are critics of some of what is happening. It is said that the city still lacks taste, that it is a hotchpotch of different building styles.

The Recovery

Birmingham is certainly now a city for visitors, for tourism. In the 2015 travel book "Rough Guide" they placed Birmingham as "one of the top ten cities in the world to visit" (this might be going over the top).[15] In 2013 the *New York* magazine had advised its readers to go to "Birmingham instead of London" they describe the city as "big shouldered, friendly and fun".[16] Unfortunately it still cannot attract tourists by claiming it is a city to visit for sport.

The city is again becoming known for its entrepreneurial spirit. It was named by Start Up Britain as the most enterprising city outside London, based on the number of new businesses established.[17] Not all new businesses of course succeed and the future with Brexit is more uncertain than ever. But if you do not start you cannot succeed. Start-up indicates the presence of a talented and risk taking business community, some of it based on the first generation of immigrants, all backed up by the required support services. The West Midlands has been successful in securing foreign investments with a record number of projects being recorded in 2016, one half of these were in manufacturing with strong growth also in the financial and commercial sectors. Jaguar/Land Rover have invested heavily in the region which benefits much of the engineering sector. HSBC are bringing jobs from London to Birmingham, as are HMRC. With the work and jobs the promised HS2 will bring to the region it is fair to say that Birmingham is again a city for business, for commerce.

Unfortunately for how long this will continue depends upon developments at the national level. With the UK's planned exit from the European Union the motor industry is threatened. A House of Commons report says that with the wrong exit deal hundreds of thousands of jobs are threatened and millions of pounds of investment will be missed.[18.] This would particularly harm Greater Birmingham with its dependence on the motor industry.

Unfortunately there is still not widespread respect for the city. There are those who live in Birmingham or nearby who know it is not such a bad place. Indeed it could be said to be a good place in which to live and work. But the image of the city and the region is still poor. It lacks an identity, indeed the city council have needed to host a conference on the subject of what is a Brummie. Not many people within the city, and that is not just those in the more recent immigrant groups, want to be known as a Brummie. At a national level, the city and the region is easily overlooked. Success in football would have helped. Carl Chinn, a Brummie and well-respected Birmingham historian, points out that his city is "dynamic, exciting and innovative". He believes that the city can look forward to a promising future, "Thanks to the entrepreneurial, skilfulness, adaptability, vitality and ingenuity of its people".[19.] It is to be hoped that what happens at the national level does not harm that future.

8

A TALE OF TWO CITIES

I n this chapter we will compare the fortunes of two cities, Birmingham and Manchester. Both have claims to be the UK's second city. The cities have much in common, both were key cities during the years of the industrial revolution, a period of which saw rapid growth in the population of the cities with wealth for some and a difficult life for others. In more recent times both have suffered from the decline in manufacturing industry. For a long time they have been centres of immigration. Both have, in recent years tried to re-invent themselves, with one possibly enjoying more success than the other.

Why has Manchester been more successful than Birmingham? Has it been the result of local decision making? Has it been the result of national decision making? Has it been the result of globalisation? The chapter will briefly look at the history of Manchester. It will look at differences in the political scene. The fate of the football clubs from Birmingham has been covered in earlier chapters, to provide a contrast we will briefly look at the football clubs from Manchester.

The Past

It has been claimed that Manchester was the first industrial city in the world. This was based on developments that had taken place in the city between 1760 and 1830, in the cotton, chemical and general manufacturing industries. The peak time for cotton mills in the city was 1853. With the completion of the ship canal in

1894 the city became a port, it became the third largest port in the UK. The golden age for the city is said to be 1895 to 1900. Disraeli said "What Manchester does today the rest of the world does tomorrow".[1]

The city has been the centre of much political activity. In 1819 the Peterloo massacre took place when rioters who were protesting about the lack of representation in Westminster were shot. The industrial revolution brought much wealth to the city but also much poverty. It was the subject of a book published in 1846 'The Condition of the Working Class in England' written by Friedrich Engels. Karl Marx visited the city. The city was a cradle for the growth of the Labour Party, the Co-operative movement and left wing politics.

The peak of British cotton cloth production was 1913. After the First World War the industry began a rapid decline, it was ruined partly because of bad leadership, by a failure to invest and to improve production processes. It could not compete with cheaper overseas products. In the 1920s there were those asking the question "what was the future for Manchester? … The men are spent, the machine is broken, the glory is forever departed". The real victims of the decline were the working classes "Clogs to clogs in 3 generations". The decline was evident in the 1950s. The city lost 150,000 manufacturing jobs between 1978 and 1984. At that time it was one of the poorest cities in Britain, 50% of neighbourhoods were in the most deprived 10% in the country.

Birmingham was the first manufacturing town in the world. It was a town of small workshops, with skilled metal workers producing guns and jewellery amongst its 55 metal trades. It relied on micro inventions, its industry being granted 90 patents in the year 1800 as compared to 27 awarded to Manchester. However, over the next 50 years it lost its position as a top industrial city. Manchester's success was based on a few major inventions. The success of any city depends on one or more of a number of factors. The large cities of the North and Midlands owe their success to a mixture of geography and social and political attitudes. The damp climate benefited the growth of the cotton industry in Manchester, the presence of iron ore and coal helped the West Midlands. The politicians governing the two cities did not discourage the movement of people into their regions; skilled and knowledgeable immigrants were welcomed as were the unskilled to provide a labour force.

In the interwar years Manchester suffered from the Great Depression and from foreign competition, in particular the decline in the textile industry. In the 1960s and 70s heavy industry suffered, as in the rest of the country. Since then Manchester has worked hard to make itself an attractive city. In Manchester as in Birmingham the service sector has grown, in particular financial and professional services. Manchester has done particularly well as a centre for research and development and from the growth of science based industries.

The Present

The population of Birmingham is now close to 1.1 million, that of Manchester 0.5 million. But the size of the population of the conurbations of which the two cities are centres is much closer. Both Greater Manchester and Greater Birmingham have populations in the region of 2.5 million.

The new Mayor of the WMCA (of Greater Birmingham?) refers to the friendly competition between the two cities. Birmingham was extremely disappointed when President Xi Jinping of China decided on his 4 day visit to the UK in 2015 to visit Manchester rather than Birmingham. The local political and business leaders regarded this as a snub; they had been lobbying hard to bring the President to Birmingham. This was his only visit outside London. Whilst he was in Manchester he visited the University, the Town Hall, the National Football Museum, the City's football ground and the new football academy. Manchester hope to benefit financially from the promised inward investment in infrastructure and research projects as well as the publicity surrounding his visit. Was it the President's love of football that lured him north? Was it George Osborne's talk of a Northern Powerhouse? Was it just the Midlands again being overlooked?

Those responsible for promoting a city choose the news items, the data and the research studies that show their city in the best possible light. Both Birmingham and Manchester have grand plans. Manchester is said to be looking forward to its future as the centre of the Northern Powerhouse. Birmingham is said to be looking forward to its future as the hub for HS2. What about the recent past? What Manchester can refer to is a study which came out in 2016 showing that they had secured £8.2 billion of commercial property investment in the city in the past decade, which put it ahead of Birmingham, (with only £6.5 billion).[2] Of particular interest were the factors that were considered key to this success in attracting inward investment. The factors were civic leadership, quality of life, infrastructure, talent in growth sectors and political support from central government. Birmingham could certainly not boast about its civic leadership nor its government support. But Birmingham could point to a different study which came out in 2015 which named Birmingham as the top city in the UK in which to invest. This was based on a survey by ULI and their advisers PWC.[3] The city was named as the 6th best in Western Europe in which to invest with London only 10th and Manchester not even in the top 25. This assessment was based on the significance in the global economy of certain key business sectors. Birmingham was found to be important in eight of these sectors, Manchester in only one.

There is again confusion with regard to prosperity and quality of life. In a recent study Birmingham was ranked as only 142 out of 170 regional areas in a prosperity index. Manchester was ranked 152 and Liverpool 167.[4] Not surprisingly the most prosperous areas were in the south of England with 4 being around the centre of London. The least prosperous area was unfortunately Wolverhampton with Sandwell only one place better. Again confusion. Recent research by Barclays Bank showed Birmingham as the nation's fourth most prosperous city.[5] Yet another study, puts the quality of life in Birmingham ahead of that in places like Rome and Los Angeles. It was the highest ranked English city outside London. Edinburgh was higher, Birmingham was equal to Glasgow. The study evaluated living conditions, the political cultural and social environment, education, health, recreation and housing.[6] All very confusing, but useful material for those promoting the cities.

Manchester sells itself as a city of football, of science and of culture. It is a city of science. In 2016 it received a grant of £235 million to set up an Institute for Advanced Materials Research, a subject in which it now leads the world. It has come a long way since cotton! It has recently received a £78 million grant for a theatre and arts centre. The total investment, in what will be known as "the Factory", will be £110 million. The leader of the council said it will "make Manchester a genuine counter balance to London". It will be a permanent home for the very successful Manchester International Festival. Birmingham has failed in its attempt to be recognised as "the city of culture". In the 1980s it did very well supporting and promoting the CBSO, the Birmingham Royal Ballet and the Welsh National Opera. Those running the city had high hopes of being recognised officially but unfortunately that title has eluded them. A big blow to Birmingham as a centre for culture was when the BBC decided to run down investment in the city and to invest in a new media centre in Greater Manchester.

City Governance

One startling contrast between the governance of the two cities is the continuity and stability in the leadership in Manchester and the discontinuity and uncertainty in the leadership in Birmingham. In the last 32 years Manchester has only had two 'Leaders of the Council'. Graham Stringer from 1984 to 1996 and Sir Richard Leese from 1996 to the present. They only had one CEO between 1998 and April 2017, Howard Bernstein. This means that for nearly 20 years Leese and Bernstein worked together to run the city. In any successful organisation, continuity is needed, as is a good working relationship between those at the top. Unfortunately the City Council in Birmingham is an example of political infighting, of change and uncertainty. It has recently been described as dysfunctional; this has not come about overnight. In the 1980s when Birmingham was doing well in recreating itself Dick Knowles (Labour) was leader of the council. He worked well with the Chief Executive. They must be given a great deal of credit for helping to transform the city, for the ICC, for the Symphony Hall and for canal side developments.

In 2004 there was a change in political leadership in Birmingham. A conservative liberal coalition took over running the city. Policies changed, budgets were cut. A Tory think-tank chaired by the ex-Prime Minister Ian Duncan Smith, said that the council needed to tackle the crushing poverty and unemployment in Birmingham. One of the hobby horses of the leader of the council at that time was a new City of Birmingham Library. It cost over £190 million; at first it was thought that private money would be willing to finance the building. It did not. The city became responsible for obtaining the funds, mainly through borrowing. The Library's high interest costs, nearly £1 million per month has meant that it is short of funds for books and management.

The city of Birmingham once had political influence at Westminster. The Chamberlain family being of particular significance. In the 1930s Birmingham supplied five cabinet ministers, each with local patriotism. Since the end of the Second World War politicians from Birmingham have had very little influence. Roy Jenkins represented a Birmingham constituency from 1950 to 1977 during which time he held the office of Home Secretary. One of the comments he made was that "Birmingham is not a city which easily clutches at the heart strings". Michel Heseltine said that "it was a city that had lost its way". One local politician that did have a national impact was Enoch Powell, unfortunately for the wrong reasons. It is a long time since Birmingham had a powerful spokesperson in Westminster. Manchester has had much more influence in the corridors of power.

In Manchester a new confidence began to develop in the 1980s and 1990s. It had very good civil leadership. Those running the city co-operated with central government. Manchester had a Labour controlled council with an outstanding Chief Executive. The City decided to play by the rules set by Margaret Thatcher, not to fight her. They obtained funds for Urban Regeneration Projects. They were successful in bringing the Commonwealth Games to the city. In 2009 they were the first city to utilize the new Local Democracy Act. They were willing to embrace the concept of Greater Manchester and to take what was being offered by Westminster. They received £30 million per annum from the government for investment in transport which they used to further develop the Metro Link. Birmingham has not been good at winning political allies.

Football

The success in promoting Manchester as an exciting city, as a base for an economic powerhouse, is due in no small part to the success of the local football clubs. It has been called a symbiotic relationship. The success of the football clubs is partly due to the co-operation of those running the city. The success of the football clubs has helped sell the city. The same could not be said for Birmingham.

One example of this success is the development of the two impressive football stadiums in the city, one seating 75,000 and the other 45,000. Old Trafford is the largest club stadium in the UK. United, however, are not yet satisfied. They have plans to extend the stadium to a capacity close to 95,000 – over twice the capacity of Villa Park. Those running 'United' have always been prepared to take risks. When they moved to Old Trafford in 1910 the plan was to have a capacity of a 100,000. The directors have always been ambitious. In 1995 work began on new stands costing nearly £19 million. This raised the capacity to 55,000 but still not enough. Further work was undertaken in the late 1990s and early in the 2000s raising the capacity to 68,000. Later work brought it to its present capacity.

It has been said that "Mancunians walk with a swagger, Brummies are always head down". If this was the case, one possible reason for it could be the divergence in the fortunes of the football clubs. The two Manchester clubs are amongst the elite, this is the result of good governance at one of the clubs, good luck at the other and to wise local political leadership. The Birmingham clubs have missed out on all three factors.

It must not be assumed that the relative status of football in the two cities has always been as it is now. It has not, there have been times when the Manchester clubs were in the doldrums and the Birmingham teams were on top. One hundred years ago Villa were the leading team in the country, more recently in 1980/81 Villa were Champions of the old Division One (in that year there were five West Midlands clubs in the top tier). In 1982 Villa were European Champions. In the first year of the premiership Villa finished in second-place. Manchester City has not always been at the top. Far from it, in the 1990s they were a good example of how not to run a club, there were bitter boardroom disputes. Manchester United were a poor team in the inter war years and more recently they have spent sometime in the second tier.

In earlier chapters we have looked at what has happened to the clubs from the Greater Birmingham area. Now we will look at the fortunes of the two Manchester clubs. It is illuminating in that it shows how good leadership has always been important for success, at some times more than others and it shows that now access to money is a necessary condition for success. It would have been very difficult over recent years for the Birmingham clubs to have kept up with Manchester United who from the 1950s generally made the right decisions in terms of investments in people and property. They have only made a few mistakes. Manchester City's success could be put down to luck, but in fact it was due to more than luck. When Sheikh Mansour purchased the club in 2008 he gave as his reasons for buying that particular club the fact that they already had the use of a large modern stadium and they had the name Manchester which all around the world was associated with football success. The club also had an owner who needed to sell at the time the Sheikh and his associates were interested in buying.

It is often assumed that Manchester United have a long and distinguished history and that Manchester City have always been the 'junior' team in that city. This is not the case. In the inter-war period, City were far more successful than United. In the 20 seasons between 1919 and 1939, Manchester United finished the season in a higher place in the league than Manchester City on only 3 occasions. In fact United spent nine of these seasons in Division Two. In one season, 1936-1937, Manchester City were Division One champions and in other seasons they finished second, third, fourth and fifth. The highest position Manchester United achieved during this time was ninth in Division One. Clearly Manchester City during this period were the top team in the city and Manchester United were a below average team.

In terms of the support from fans Manchester City were also more successful. In most seasons in the interwar period City attracted a larger average gate than United. Remarkably, in 1938-39, a season when City were in the Second Division, they had higher average attendance figures that United, who were in the First Division. It should be appreciated that at that time neither of the Manchester teams were attracting the largest crowds in the country. In the years just before the Second World War it was Arsenal and Aston Villa that attracted the largest gates. Manchester was not a leading football centre.

Manchester City

The club were successful in the late 1960s and in the early 1970s. They went into decline, they were relegated from Division One in 1983 and 1987. They had seven different managers in the 1980s. They had some success following their promotion in 1989 finishing fifth in Division One in both 1991 and 1992. In 1996 they were relegated from the top tier and continued downwards into the third tier. They were promoted back to the Premier League in 2002.[7]

Despite the move into their new home at the City of Manchester Stadium in 2003, the club's finances were in a mess. They were taken over in 2007 by the ex-Prime Minister of Thailand. He was a controversial figure, had made many enemies and he was being sued for corruption. The Thai Government froze his assets. In 2008 the Abu Dhabi United Group, some members of whom controlled the vast wealth of Abu Dhabi decided they would purchase an English Premier League club. One of the major reasons for doing so was to increase the global visibility of their county, hopefully to win friends which might help their security in times of trouble. It was like taking out an insurance policy, necessary in the geo political world of the Middle East. It was a move to demonstrate their "soft power". Sheikh Mansour and his advisers had looked at other clubs but it was Manchester City they chose to buy.

The way they achieved success for the club was by spending vast sums of money and employing the best managers. They not surprisingly were soon in trouble with the Financial Fair Play regulations (they were fined £16 million in 2014). In 2011 they had incurred the highest ever loss in a season by an English club (£197 million). In 2010/11 their wage bill was £133 million and their revenue only £125 million. In the following season it was even worse with wages of £174 million which was 114% of the revenue. In their first year of ownership by the Abu Dhabi group the net spending on new players was £113 million. In their first three years at the club the average net spending was £109 million. A very different world to that of the West Midlands clubs.

The chairman had expressed the opinion that "sporting success and commercial sustainability must go hand in hand". Nobody would disagree with this, it was the Doug Ellis and Randy Lerner argument to justify prudency. The crucial question is how much can one afford to gamble to buy success? As the Sheikh said "success on the pitch delivers both in terms of immediate financial rewards but also by building the brand. This makes the sport attractive to potential sponsors (and indeed players)".

The earlier history of Manchester City is unremarkable, no better, no worse than the West Midlands clubs. But for them their fortunes changed. First when the politicians and leaders in Manchester attracted the Commonwealth Games to the city and then, the second stroke of good fortune was when the owners of a very wealthy country decided that they need to promote themselves on the world stage. What better way of doing this than owning a successful football club.

Since the acquisition the club they have been Premier League champions three times. The owners are very ambitious, in 2015/16 they finished in fourth place in the Premier League which the chairman described as disappointing "below our expectations". The manager, Pellegrini, was removed despite the fact that the club had just won a domestic cup competition and had reached the semi-final of the UEFA Champions League. In 2016/17 the club appointed Pep Guardiola as manager and finished in third place in the Premier League, presumably below the owners expectations. They were champions the next season.

The Bad Old Days

In the 1880s a group of enthusiasts formed a team that became Manchester City. They built up a good team and they won the FA Cup. Unfortunately, in 1906 all the players, some of the club's directors and the club secretary, were banned from football after the FA found that certain players had been receiving illegal payments. The specific game that caused the problems was the final match of the 1904/05 season. If Manchester City had won at Aston Villa they would have been Division One champions. Aston Villa won 3-2. Rumours circulated that Aston Villa players had been offered money to throw the game. Meredith, the City's best player, was suspended – he denied the accusation – but later changed his story. He admitted to offering an Aston Villa player £10, but he claimed to only do this on instructions from his manager. An investigation found that in addition to paying player bonuses, the directors had also paid senior players above the agreed maximum weekly wage and that they had paid 'amateurs' a wage. Money was important in the sport even at that time. Manchester City were not the only team to make such payments but they were the first club who were caught. Not an auspicious beginning.

The club moved to Maine Road in 1923 to what was one of the first really big provincial football grounds. In 1934 they attracted a record crowd of over 84,000 to their cup-tie against Stoke City. They were a wealthy club and signed a number of top players. Unfortunately for them, they were relegated at the end of the 1937-38 season, and so started the first season after the 1939-45 War in the Second Division. They became known as an 'up and down' club. They also became known for their bitter boardroom disputes.

They did have, however, periods of success; they won the FA Cup in 1956 and 1969, and were Division One champions in 1967/68 (with Manchester United in second place). In 1976/77 they finished second in the Division One and fourth the following season. The success City did enjoy in the late 1960s was based on a very successful partnership at manager level, the flamboyant Malcolm Allison and the reliable Joe Mercer. They had a board of directors that supported them.

During the 1971/72 season, Allison and Mercer fell out. The board were divided. When Peter Swales joined the board he acted as arbitrator between the two battling groups and shortly afterwards became chairman, with Allison the sole manager. But Allison soon left, fed up with politics at board level. Swales appointed a new manager, Ron Saunders (later of Aston Villa and Birmingham City). Peter Swales now controlled the club.

Manchester City went through a period in which they were "badly run by a succession of boards, more concerned with feuding and sacking managers than winning football matches". They continued to under-perform and to adopt the standard solution to overcome this problem; change managers.

When Francis Lee, once a star player at the City, ended his football career he became a very successful businessman with wealthy friends. In 1993 he launched a take-over bid for control of the club. Swales was defeated, but not before a nasty and wasteful battle. Lee became chairman and the largest shareholder. The club were relegated in 1995/96. In 1998 the power at the club changed once again when John Wardle and David Melkin became major shareholders. Francis Lee was replaced as chairman by David Bernstein, who had been the club's financial advisor. The club were promoted back to the Premiership in 1999-2000 but relegated again the following year. They then appointed Kevin Keegan as manager, and in the 2001/02 season were promoted back to the Premiership.

In 2003 Bernstein resigned as chairman following a dispute with the manager and with other key directors. Keegan thought that Bernstein was too conservative, that he would not spend enough in the transfer market, and that he was not ambitious enough. This despite the fact that the club had spent £46 million to purchase 17 players in the short period between the time Keegan became manager and Bernstein's resignation. The annual wage bill rose from £24 million to £35 million.

With the club moving to an impressive new stadium (built for the Commonwealth Games) in 2003/04, once again many supporters believed the dark days were now at last over, but unfortunately they were not. Keegan spent a lot of money on new players, but the club were still not successful.

The quotes from some of those involved in the boardroom squabbles throughout the 1990s give a feeling of the depth of the emotions of those involved, and of the problems of the club. "I've played in the World Cup, sweated out multi-million pound business deals. I've trained some good horses and I am a father. Yet 90 minutes at Maine Road can make me feel like an old dish-rag." (Francis Lee, on being chairman of Manchester City, 1997). Frank Clarke expressed stronger views just before he resigned as manager in 1998, "It will take a very long time to sort things out. It's a rat infested place." In such a business situation it is not surprising the club were underachievers. With Stuart Pearce as the new manager, with a new ground, and with some stability at boardroom level,

2005/06 looked promising, but unfortunately once again the club underachieved. 2006/07 was another disappointing season, at the end of which Pearce was sacked.

The Stadium

The 'story' of the City of Manchester Stadium is notable in itself. It shows how a local authority using public sector money can work in partnership with its local football club to the benefit of both parties. It is a story familiar in the USA. When in 2002 the Commonwealth Games were held in Manchester a new sports stadium suitable for athletics was built. It was paid for entirely with public money, the largest contribution towards the cost being £77 million of lottery money that was made available through Sport England. The city council initially claimed that if allowed to host the Commonwealth Games they would break even financially, but they failed to achieve this goal. The Games were not a financial success and the organisers needed to be bailed out with an additional £100 million of public money. The City Council put in £50 million of this additional money, Sport England another £30 million and the UK Government £20 million.

There was always a question as to what would happen to the new stadium after the event? Manchester City Council approached Manchester City FC to see if they were prepared to make use of it; the club said that they were, subject to certain quite demanding conditions. They wanted the stadium to be adapted so that it would be suitable for football, they wanted it to be recognised as the permanent home for the club, and they made it clear that they were only prepared to pay a comparatively small amount of money for its use. The club argued that they already had a perfectly good ground at Maine Road that seated 34,000, and that if they stayed at their present home all the revenue they generated belonging to them. The 'Commonwealth Stadium' had a capacity of 48,000 and so they argued it was only the additional net income resulting from the extra 14,000 seats that should be shared with Sports England

and the City Council. They were arguing that they should pay no rent at all for the use of the new ground until crowds were above the Maine Road capacity. Sports England and the City Council were in a weak bargaining position with no other tenants for the new stadium and so they agreed the terms. Therefore Manchester City moved into a large new stadium paid for with lottery and public sector money.

A number of other football clubs moved into new stadiums at about the same time as Manchester City, but none of these other clubs received such large amounts of public money. These other clubs were required to spend their own money to finance their developments. Only Manchester City received what is in effect a huge public subsidy.

Manchester United

The club's success since the Second World War can be said to be due to a combination of factors. Good leadership, good managerial appointments, an imaginative youth policy and bold brave decisions on stadium developments. The word prudence does not appear in the history of United.

They have developed a large fan base around the world (it is estimated to be over 600 million) which has meant that even in their less successful years they have been able to pay high wages and been able to purchase the best players. When the Glazer family purchased the club in 2005 the acquisition was not popular amongst the fans. It was seen to be dangerous. It was a high risk leveraged takeover. The Glazer family had to borrow large sums of money in order to purchase the club, they needed the cash generated by the club to pay the interest on the debt, which meant the money being earned from football was being paid to banks and was not available to build up the team. There were many people who thought, (who hoped) that this cowboy capitalism approach would fail. It did not.

In 2008/9 interest charges paid by the club were £117 million which was 42% of the club's revenue that year. As a result of a number of refinancing deals, the debt was reduced and the interest charge fell. As a result of successful commercial operations and success on the pitch revenues rose with the result that by 2015/16, the interest payments which were now only £20 million, were only 4% of the year's revenue (£515 million). The Glazer model was working. Commercial revenue had increased from £42.5 million in 2004/5 to £189 million in 2013/14. Big companies from all over the world wanted to become 'Business Partners'. Since the takeover United had been Premier League Champions 5 times, won the FA Cup once and the League Cup 4 times; and been UEFA Champions twice. Not bad.

The club have however, by their own standards had problems. They finished in only 4th place in the Premier League in 2014/15, in 2015/16 in 5th place and in 2016/17 6th place. In 2015 they failed to qualify for a place in a European competition, the first time since 1990. What were the club doing wrong? The Glazers reacted like all the other unhappy owners, sacking managers. Following Ferguson's retirement in 2013, they had as managers, David Moyes (10 months), then Louis Van Gaal (2 years). They then appointed the present manager Jose Mourinho in May 2016. In 2017/18 they finished the season in a lower place than their City rivals.

Life is never dull around Manchester United. Each month there is a new drama, just right to keep people following the soap opera. In the summer of 2017 there were stories about a mysterious Chinese tycoon who was interested in buying a stake in the club or taking it over. There were also stories about disagreements in the Glazer family with two or three of the siblings wishing to sell. What next?

The Past

So much has been written about the Manchester United story that there is little more that needs to be said.[8] They have, however, by their standards had bad times as well as good. We will concentrate on the bad times.

The club were not founder members of the football league. In the early 1900s the club was known as Newton Heath, they were nearly bankrupt. An autocratic businessman J.H. Davies saved them. He changed the name of the club. In 1909 he and his fellow directors decided to move to Old Trafford and to construct a large stadium. The decision was brave and risky as the club were not successful. The club were in debt, had been served with a winding up order and were in the Second Division. With Davies' backing, the fortunes of the club changed. They became Division One champions in 1908. The new ground was impressive and an FA Cup Final was played there in 1911. The club had already become known as "Moneybags United".

In the 1919-1939 period, the club were relegated to the second tier on three occasions, and in 1934 nearly relegated to the Third Division. Manchester United were for a long time a second rate club.

In October 1930, over 3,000 fans held a meeting and passed a motion of no confidence in the board of the club. In 1931, with the team floundering in the Second Division, the club's bank refused to advance them money so that they could pay the players' wages. The club had debts of £30,000 (a comparatively large sum at the time). This is not the distinguished history one would expect of the club that became the 'biggest' in the world. In 1931, for a second time, a local businessman saved them. This time it was James Gibson who was the director of a local clothing firm. He paid the wages that were due to the players, arranged for new shares to be issued and initiated a public appeal for money. In fact Manchester City helped raise funds to save Manchester United. James Gibson became chairman and helped build up a solid base for United.

What turned United into a cult team? During the 1919-1939 period they were a poor team both from a playing and financial point of view. By 1938, however, they had benevolent owners, and a farsighted management team. Helpful ingredients for success in any industry. They established a junior football club in 1938 in order to produce good young players. This turned out to be an extremely significant decision in helping them produce outstanding teams. But perhaps most important of all, the directors appointed an outstanding manager.

The Busby era, which began when he was appointed manager in 1945, turned out to be remarkable. With Matt Busby in charge Manchester United immediately began to win trophies. Busby had inherited a number of good players, but he also purchased wisely and soon had begun to develop his own young 'Babes'. The club were champions of Division One in 1951-52, 1955-56 and in 1956-57. In 1957 at a time when the average age of the team was only 22, they took part in the then new European Cup competition (now the UEFA Champions League) against the wishes of the English football establishment. The Division One champions of the previous season, had been instructed by the FA not to take part in the European competition.

Manchester United was one of the few clubs in England to realise the opportunities offered by European football. When they played their first match in the European Cup, in September 1956, they played on the Manchester City ground; their own ground did not have floodlights. There were many who did not think that the game would attract much attention, but 43,635 people attended. For their next match in the tournament, again taking place at Maine Road, the attendance was 75,598. Manchester United lost in the semi-finals of the Cup to Real Madrid, who were the dominant team in Europe at the time.

The club were again involved in European competition in 1958 but this time tragedy struck. The plane in which they were returning home from a fixture in the former Yugoslavia, crashed in Munich. This disaster destroyed the so-called 'Busby Babes'. Eight of the team were killed and Matt Busby was badly injured. Busby recovered. The sympathies of the nation were with Manchester United after the crash. The tragedy in Munich affected United in many ways. If the 'Busby Babes' had been able to stay together as a team they would probably have dominated

English football, and possibly Europe, for a decade. Partly because of the deaths of so many talented players the club did not dominate, but the disaster did have an unexpected consequence. As Mihir Bose points out, "Manchester United were a well-respected club before Munich, but the air crash elevated them on to a different level." Bose was referring, in particular to United's international reputation, which has meant so much to the value of their brand.

It is true that Manchester United became known around the world, but in order to maintain and build on that recognition it was necessary for the club to be well managed and to take advantage of any opportunities that arose. To maintain the value of the brand name it was necessary to have continuing success. In 1964-65 and again in 1966-67, the club were Division One champions, and in 1968 they won the European Cup – the first English club to do so. This brought the Busby era to a glorious end.

Busby was clearly an outstanding manager, but to be successful he needed the support of the directors of the club. Immediately after the Munich crash, a new director, Louis Edwards, joined the board. He would have a profound influence on the future of the club. It is sometimes suggested that Edwards built up his successful business using unfair and underhand practices. It is claimed, for instance, that he bribed Manchester City Councillors in order to obtain contracts to supply meat to local schools and other Council controlled outlets. Having a brother, Douglas Edwards, as a City Councillor – later to become Lord Mayor – could have helped him obtain Council contracts. The meat supplied to schools was, it is said, not always good quality. This earned him a reputation for supplying second-class meat at first-class prices.

Louis built up his shareholding in the football club, some of the methods he used to do this have been criticised. He also set about looking after the financial affairs of the club. In the 1960s Manchester United were not particularly profitable, they desperately needed money for ground improvements and to buy new players. Gates were falling across the country – football matches were only just beginning to be shown on television – and the difficult years of the 1970s and 1980s were still to come. In the 1960s buying shares in a football club did not seem to be (to most people) an attractive investment opportunity.

The club during Louis Edwards' time as chairman were successful. Whether or not the leading person behind the achievements was Louis Edwards or Matt Busby does not really matter. They needed each other – that is what good corporate governance is about. Unfortunately, by the end of Busby's period as manager the two had fallen out. Eamon Dunphy now a respected journalist, but once a Manchester United player, speaks well of Edwards. He refers to Louis Edwards as generous; he always "bought the lads a drink, and he wasn't a snob". This, he said was different to the previous chairman.

Louis Edwards died in 1980 and his son Martin took over the running of the club. He was unpopular amongst supporters. The club went through troubled times in the 1970s and 1980s. They had won Division One in 1966-67 and the European Cup in 1968 but then there were 20 years in which their performance was relatively poor. They were relegated to Division Two for the 1974-75 season. In his autobiography Martin Edwards refers to the difficult times in the 1980s when he took over the club. "I won't say we ever nearly went bust, but we weren't profitable We had to watch how we spent our money".[9] Some people at the time thought that he was only involved with the club for the money he could make out of it and that he was lucky in inheriting the shares. He emphasises that it was not easy, that he took risks. His personal debt in the early 1990s was nearly £1 million and that his bank had his house as security. He took risks. He became a Life President of the club.

One remarkable fact about these troubled years for the club was the loyalty shown by their fans. The club's lowest average home crowd was 33,490 in 1961-62, a season in which they finished fifteenth in the First Division. In the year they were relegated, 1973-74, the average was 43,000.

In 1983 Martin Edwards nearly sold control of Manchester United, and as much as the supporters disliked him, they disliked the possible alternative owner even more. Football was at a low point, and Martin Edwards was told that someone wanted to buy the club for £10 million. The interested purchaser was Robert Maxwell. Martin Edwards decided to turn the offer down, a popular decision. Robert Maxwell was a rough businessman.

Busby had retired in 1969, and between that time and Alex Ferguson's appointment in November 1986, the club had five managers All had individually achieved success elsewhere, but they could not bring the success United thought they were entitled to. The managers found it hard to work with the chairmen and all the others who still lived in the glory of the past.

In 1989 Martin Edwards told Alex Ferguson; "I'm going to sell the club, if you know anyone prepared to pay £10 million for my shares and spend another £10 million on the Stretford End." Edwards was prepared to sell because he felt he had tried to revive the club, but that he could not win over the fans. Alex Ferguson felt sorry for him, and appreciated the patience he had shown, "The chairman provided good backing without ever interfering with the running of the team."

The club was up for sale. There were a few offers. The club needed money and so the directors decided to float the company in the Stock Market. Other clubs were doing the same thing. At the time of its launch the equity in the club was valued at £42 million. This was a time before the very lucrative TV broadcasting contracts came into existence.

Martin Edwards made gains by selling shares at the time of the flotation, but he would have done a lot better if he had hung on to the shares for a few more years. Opinions on Martin Edwards differ. He had helped turn the club from one that was struggling in the early 1980s to one that, 15 years later, was one of the top 3 or 4 in Europe. As Alex Ferguson explained, Edwards carefully looks after the finances of his business, "Conversations with Martin Edwards are usually straightforward and pleasant until you ask him for more money. Then you have a problem." The club in fact spent large sums of money buying top international players, "No manager could have had better treatment than I have had from my chairman when it comes to running the playing side of the club. He has never interfered in the slightest with my decisions about players".[10]

A major problem (or opportunity) arose in 1998 when BSkyB decided that they wanted to buy the most successful club in the country. By this time institutional shareholders owned over 60% of the shares in the plc. The directors of the football club agreed to recommend acceptance of the BSkyB offer. The supporters of the club fought a brilliant battle to save the club from the TV company. Fortunately for the fans the Monopolies and Mergers Commission decided that the takeover would not be good for the game of football in England.

The Present

Manchester United were now a public company. They had Alex Ferguson as manager guiding them through a remarkable period of success. The manager himself was an astute businessman, both in looking after his own financial interests as well as those of the club. He had a well-known interest in horse racing. Through this hobby he met the two very successful Irish racehorse owners, John Magnier and J.P. McManus. Ferguson invested in racehorses. In 2001 the two Irishmen, through a specially created company, Cubic Expression, began investing heavily in the shares of Manchester United.

Surprisingly, early in 2004, Alex Ferguson fell out with the, by then, two major Manchester United shareholders over the division of the breeding rights to a racehorse in which Ferguson had an interest. Alex Ferguson threatened to issue a writ against John Magnier. The two unhappy racehorse owners used their power as major shareholders in Manchester United to ask a number of embarrassing questions about the governance of the club. They would not agree to Manchester United offering a new contract to

Sir Alex until these questions were answered to their satisfaction. The two shareholders won the dispute, Ferguson did not receive the income from the breeding rights that he thought he was entitled to, but his contract at the club was renewed. The club did improve its level of financial disclosure as the two shareholders wanted, including giving details of the amount paid as agent fees, a controversial issue.

Manchester United have been well run for a number of years. Old Trafford has been developed to be the best and largest ground in the country. There have been disagreements but compared to most other clubs there has been stability both at board level and in the chairman's relationship with the manager. Martin Edwards recognised he needed marketing and financial expertise on the board and brought in respected figures in these areas. A necessary condition for success is a stable board – so many teams have failed to achieve their potential because of boardroom squabbles. Martin Edwards supported Ferguson, even though in Ferguson's first four years in charge there was little success and some fans wanted him removed. Louis and Martin Edwards brought onto the board quality directors when they were needed. They recognised the need to run the football club as a business despite this leading to their unpopularity with fans. The directors made some decisions which in retrospect were wrong; this is of course the case with all businesses.

In 2005 Malcolm Glazer, a wealthy American, appeared on the scene. With his family they were the owners of an American football club, they knew nothing about soccer but did know about making money. His other business interests included owning trailer parks and shopping centres. The directors of Manchester United were against the take-over, one reason being that it would burden the club with having to service a high level of debt. Glazer needed to borrow in the region of £600 million to buy the club, and the cost of servicing the debt would be very high.

Alex Ferguson was manager before the Glazers came to the club, and continued in that role afterwards. He, to the surprise of many supporters of the club, spoke with enthusiasm about the new owners, describing Malcom Glazer as excellent for Manchester United: "I can only speak from my own perspective and I've been more than happy with the new owners. They've supported me 100% and there has never been one bit of a problem. They've given me the money I wanted to buy new players so what am I supposed to do? Tell lies?"

The Glazers purchased the club for £790 million. They listed the shares of the club on the NYSE in 2012, selling 10% of their holding. They received £150 million, a bit less than they expected. Following Ferguson's retirement the club had a difficult time on the pitch but off the pitch it was having a huge commercial success. In 2016 they were the world's richest football club. Forbes valued them as being worth £2.8 billion, over five times the annual revenue of £515 million. When Malcolm Glazer died in 2014 the control of the club passed to his six children, not surprisingly they have disagreements.

In 2017 it was said that there were investors interested in buying a stake in United. The shares are very tightly controlled with few available to buy on the stock market. The Glazer family between them control about 80% of the shares, either through a company, Red Football, that they own or through the personal investment trusts of the Glazer family members. Other shares are held by hedge funds and investment companies. But not all the club's shares are equal, the class B shares have greater voting rights than the other classes and it is the class B shares that the family own. It would be very difficult for an investor to be able to purchase a significant number of United shares. That is unless the Glazers, or one or two members of the family decide that they have had enough of football.

The drama continues.

9

REGIONAL DIFFERENCES

In the previous chapter the decisions being made in Birmingham at the local council level and at the football club level were compared with those being made by the council and clubs in Manchester. The civic administration in Birmingham does not come out well in terms of leadership when compared with its counterpart in Manchester nor do the leaders of the football teams. In this chapter we consider certain other factors to see how they, if at all, have contributed to the contrast in the development of the regions. The first issue considered will be the North-South divide in England. The second issue will be concerned with any differences in the character of the people in the two regions. Finally the impact of fans will be considered.

The North-South Divide

The Midlands is often overlooked. Too many discussions, whether on the economy, or politics, or sport revolve around a discussion on the North versus the South. There is a huge area of land in between. There are millions of people who do not identify, who do not want to identify, with either the North or the South. There are no clear boundaries. Writers from the south of England see the North as somewhere up the M1 beyond Watford. Writers from the North see the South as somewhere beyond Sheffield. Large areas of the country, large cities, are classified as North for some purposes and South for others. Cities such as Derby, Stoke, Birmingham, Leicester and Oxford are just pushed into inappropriate boxes.

We can use football to illustrate the problem. A too simple classification could be seen in a recent article in *The Economist* (13th August 2016).[1] The article was entitled "A Country of Two Halves". The article was seeking to make the point that outside of Manchester and Liverpool, northern football clubs were on the decline. It stated that the most successful northern club in 2015/16 outside the two big Lancashire cities was Sunderland who finished in 17th place in the Premier League. There was, according to the analysis, only one other northern club in the top league namely Newcastle who finished in 18th place. There are two things wrong with this, one being that the Premier League Champions that year were Leicester City. Stoke City finished the season in 9th place and the WBA in 14th place. These three clubs were being classified as from the south. The Midlands did not exist. A second criticism of the article was why ignore Manchester and Liverpool? It is like saying if you ignore London the south is not doing very well. In fact in the top eight places in the Premier League in 2015/16 three were from London, three were from the north, one was from the Midlands, and one was from the south. This is "Southern" based journalism. There is more to England than the North-South divide. To be fair to the argument in the article, clubs such as Southampton, Bournemouth and now Brighton have done remarkably well and a number of the northern clubs have done badly, for example Blackburn, Bolton and Sunderland. But the south has also had its failures, Portsmouth and QPR.

It is true that the Midlands is a region without a strong sense of identity. In the book "Sport and identity in the North of England" the difficulty of deciding on a boundary for a North-South divide is discussed.[2] The authors regard the Midlands as the North. As Tony Mason points out, football as a game, was not invented in the North but he concludes "football as a spectator sport was". He refers to the grip of the North on the elite end of the game being assured in 1888 by the organisation of the twelve clubs into the Football League. But six of these clubs were in fact from the

Midlands, not from the North. Mason states that "Professional football was a Northern innovation at which Northerners were top dogs. Not only did they play it better than Southerners, they also watched it with more knowledge and intensity". The Midlands was again being included in the North.

Over time, as Mason believes regional differences in terms of passion, intensity and knowledge began to disappear and by the 1930s with Arsenal the top club, loyalties and passions did not depend on geography, "The North is an imagined territory with no fixed boundaries and the range of qualities which have been seen as characteristics of Northerners are so diverse as to defy neat definitions".

But regional differences do exist. The disposable income per head of population is almost double in the South to that in the North and the Midlands. Regional inequality in Britain is greater than in almost all other major European nations. This is not really surprising; nearly all the important political decisions have been made in London. The media is concentrated there. The North and Midland regions have in fact done very well out of the European Union. Regional development funds have helped in the past but what will happen to this after Brexit is unclear.

The UK is a highly centralised country, it suffers from the London-centric decision making. More funds are spent in some regions than in others. One clear example of this is the amount spent on transport in London compared with the rest of the country. Up to 10 times more money is spent on transport in London than in parts of northern England. Nearly £2,000 per head will be spent each year on road and rail projects in London over the next 5 years compared to £190 per head in Yorkshire and Humber. Almost £2 billion more was spent on Crossrail in London than all of the northern transport projects put together. There is talk of the new HS2 and HS3 but little action. It is estimated that in the next five years more than half of the total national transport expenditure will be in the London region. Already there is talk of another Crossrail line. Even with HS2 from London to Birmingham it has been estimated that the biggest beneficiary will be London.

London and the South East are clearly major attractions to foreigners whether they be investors, football players or players' spouses. London is clearly a glamorous, global, rich city. It is the home to many large multinational companies and to a large financial community most of whom are willing to spend money on corporate hospitality. The stadiums of the major clubs in London are already large or are being enlarged partly to provide increased hospitality facilities. Spurs are moving to a bigger ground, West Ham United have moved to the Olympic Stadium. Such moves will increase the revenue of these clubs.

London and the South is attractive to wealthy foreigners. Headlines appear in the press such as 'Saudi billionaires targeting London clubs for takeovers'. What lay behind this particular story was that Saudi Arabia plans to develop its own professional league. The plan of the investors would be to use the English clubs as a "Tie-In" with sides they own in the domestic league. Similar to the plans of Chinese investors and similar to what has happened at Manchester City, where the club owns associate clubs in the USA and Australia.

One explanation for the lack of success in the Birmingham region is that offered by Bobby Gould, who played for Coventry and West Bromwich Albion. He argued that the Midlands lacks glamour.[3] Bowler and Bains quote Bobby Gould: "It's not a glamorous area, there is apathy there and the Midlands clubs never took off like Liverpool did, or United have done recently. We didn't have the flamboyancy as an area, when players reach a certain level, they outgrow the area. It's unfortunate, but it's a fact of life".

One would have to agree with Gould in respect of comparing Birmingham as a city with London, but is glamour an expression one can use when describing Liverpool and Manchester. Perhaps the top players avoid the Midland clubs because they want success, they want to play in winning teams, they want to play on the

European stage. Birmingham has recreated itself over the last 20 years, but it cannot offer success in football. Newcastle, Sunderland and Middlesbrough are also finding it harder to attract the top players. They are no more glamorous than Birmingham, and they also are not home to winning teams.

The People

It has been said that the people of Birmingham and the Midlands should love the region more than they do. It is also said the citizens of Birmingham are self-deprecating. Part of this problem is, as explained, that the region suffers from the North-South polarisation. Whichever category Birmingham is placed in it is usually to its disadvantage. It is often said that Birmingham does not have a strong 'self-image'. It is true that compared to cities such as Liverpool it does not appear to have as much character. It has in recent time been seen by many as the centre of a large sprawling conurbation dominated by motorways and cars. In the 1970s it was run down, but then so at the time were Liverpool, Manchester and Newcastle.

The traditional 'Brummie' and the man from 'The Black Country' was known for pragmatism, inhibition, hard headedness and a 'dull' accent. He was not known for his passion, sense of humour or cockiness. But some things have changed. Birmingham and the Black Country has become a region of canals, exhibition centres and Balti food. It has also become an entertainment centre. But unfortunately one thing has not changed, the term Brummie has negative connotations.

In popular folklore, Brummies have a bad accent, they are associated with old style metal bashing industries and they live in or around a city with educational, social and racial problems. As mentioned in an earlier chapter the accent is often associated with being less bright. Research in 2011 found that people with a Brummie accent (as those with a Glaswegian accent) were regularly rated low in terms of traits like competence, leadership and creativity.[4] Such stereotyping does harm the image of the city. It makes it harder for the city to recreate itself.

There is a problem in Birmingham with identification. Birmingham is now ethnically diverse. A study by the local council found that nearly all the 200 or so different ethnic groups in the city, felt themselves detached from any sense of civic belonging, "It is an emotional cartography of anonymity dislocation and the anodyne".[5] It has been said for some time that West Midlands people should have more self-belief and more pride. Owen Hatherley contrasts Birmingham with certain other cities. He writes "Manchester, Liverpool, and Glasgow notwithstanding recent decline, exhibit the overwhelming pride and scale of a metropolis. Birmingham does not … it keeps itself to itself. It is fundamentally modest".[6]

The mayor of Greater Manchester Andy Burnham, was able to say after the terrorist bombings of May 2017 that "there is a self-belief, confidence in who we are, what we are, what we stand for. This is Manchester. We do things differently. There is solidarity and we look after each other … The Manchester thing is about equality and togetherness. It is deep rooted and it goes back a long way. There is a Mancunian pride in that. This is one city".[7] Burnham was making an emotional speech to help people to recover from the outrage and to continue with their everyday lives. It is doubtful, however, whether in similar circumstances a lord mayor of Birmingham (or a mayor of the WMCA) would have been able to use words like pride and solidarity in a speech. A Manchester poet, Tony Walsh, referred to Manchester as a gritty city, born out of adversity, a working class city looking for a route forward through the arts, sport and education. The same could be said about Birmingham, but the people of Birmingham do not seem to be working together in the same way as those of Manchester.

Liverpool is a city self-conscious of its own importance, of its own exceptional identity. This is based perhaps on history, on hardships, on characteristics such as humour, aggression and music, and probably on a mixture of all these factors. A dean of history at Liverpool University has said "There's a Liverpool thing, in a way I don't think there's a Leicester thing, or a Birmingham thing".[8] He is probably right. Nobody would ever say that Liverpudlians suffer from low self-esteem. However, if Merseysiders love themselves because of their perceived characteristics, they are loved in far off places because of their football. In China young people know of Liverpool because of the football team.[9]

One reason why football in Birmingham has not developed as an asset for the city is that the community no longer has a common identity. It does not have a common heritage. One problem is that even those that can be identified as a Brummie do not want to be known as one. They are not proud of being identified with the city.

Fans

Significant changes have taken place in respect of an individual's identification with a club. At one time the vast majority of those who followed football became fans of the local team. They would support the team whether or not it was successful – they had little choice, this was the only team they could watch on a regular basis. The players in that team were the only ones they could identify with. But some teams were more successful than others. And with the increase in the marketing of the game, and the increased exposure of teams through the media, some clubs developed a 'brand' name that was respected nationally. They developed a national image. Young people now have a choice, they do not need to support the local team; through TV and media coverage they can easily follow the fortunes of a club with a glamorous image, a team that are capable of being champions. Over half the people who watch Liverpool and Manchester United home games travel over 50 miles to be there, so it is not the passions of a region that are important.

Another change that has come about is that in many places the people living near a ground do not want to watch the local team. Much of the inner city, where the grounds are based is populated by comparatively recent immigrants and their families, particularly those from Asia and East Africa. Birmingham (as is Manchester) is a multi-racial city. British Asians have not taken to football. There was only one British Asian that played football in the Premier League in 2016/17. Like it or not football crowds can be racial in their behaviour, not perhaps in the hospitality areas or where journalists sit, but on what used to be called the terraces. Why should a Brummie with an Asian background place himself in an environment which can turn out to be hostile?

It was argued in the Introduction that as a result of new technology, globalisation and weak regulation that the Holy Trinity in football is now "the players, the TV companies and the owners. Supporters do not matter, they are only there to be exploited". Not all would agree with this cynical view. One respected sports writer, Matthew Syed, has argued that at "at the epicentre of the global phenomenon today and for evermore will be the fan".[10] The phenomenon he is writing about is the Premier League. He claims that the game is about community, drama and narrative, "It is the common fan that provides football with its mystique, it is their passion that creates the atmosphere that makes the game so watchable … A club becomes a totem for a community and the symbol of its civic and industrial pride". This is a somewhat romantic view of the game, it might be the case for a fan living in Manchester, Liverpool or north London, but it is not the case for a fan of say Wigan, Hull or Birmingham City.

The inequality in the game, the lack of competitiveness of the game means that many of the traditional type of fan is being starved of success. The fans are losing their pride in their club and do not experience many moments of passion. A rather sickly advertisement of Barclays Bank appeared on the TV screens in the 2016/17 season. The message was "to the millions of fans who make the Premier League what it is – we thank you". If the fans are so important for the atmosphere why are they just treated as consumers?

It is sometimes claimed that people in the Midlands are not as passionate about their sport as, say, those in the North East or North West regions of England. This is an easy statement to make, but one that is difficult to prove (or disprove). There was certainly a 'passion' about football in the Midlands in the early days of the League and Cup. In the 1882-83 season, when West Bromwich Albion played

Aston Villa in Birmingham it was reported that the rival group of supporters were throwing sods of turf and stones at each other. In 1892 when Aston Villa lost to West Bromwich Albion in the FA Cup Final, the Aston Villa fans blamed their own goalkeeper for the defeat and proceeded to smash the windows of his pub. The strong local rivalries in football in the Birmingham area has a long history, as does crowd trouble. But those were the old days.

One problem is that supporters of football clubs in the Midlands have in recent years had little to be passionate about. Given something to become excited about they could offer a level of support as good, if not better, than supporters in any other part of the country. This has been proven in cricket. The England cricket players are full of praise for the support they receive at Edgbaston. Reference has been made to the 'raucous patriotism of Edgbaston' that brings out the best in the English players. Freddie Flintoff, referred to the great atmosphere at the cricket ground in Birmingham, with the crowd 'being like a twelfth man'. Edgbaston is apparently the favourite ground of the English cricket team. There is no reason why a similar level of emotion would not exist at the West Midlands' football grounds if the owners, the directors of the clubs provided the supporters with teams worth getting excited about.

The Scottish footballer Gary McAllister who after leaving Liverpool played for Coventry for a number of years commented that "Coventry isn't a great crowd; none of them in the Midlands (are), except maybe Wolves. It's not really a football area. Football is most popular in economically depressed areas, in the North and in Scotland. It cheers up people's lives and lets them feel like winners for once. They really identify with their teams, and get behind them".[11] He expressed this opinion when writing about the advantage a team obtains from having a good home crowd – how such a crowd benefits the team. He believes such a crowd "intimidates opponents and puts an extra yard on you".

McAllister argues that football is more popular in economically depressed areas. A similar point was made many years ago by the famous old footballer and sports journalist Charles Buchan, "Up in the North East the crowd takes its football very seriously … I think they know more about the game than Southern crowds." But this again was the old days. There is a belief by some in the game that fans in the North of England are more loyal to their team than fans in other parts of the country. It is certainly true that Sunderland and Newcastle attract home crowds of 30,000 to 40,000 even when the teams are playing badly. This does not happen in the West Midlands. The Birmingham and West Midlands clubs have not been well supported. In the 2016/17 season for most matches the Villa and the Blues were only half filling their grounds.

There are now different types of fan that a club can appeal to. The majority of the fans of some clubs now watch the game on a screen. They can be in the UK or overseas. They can be as passionate about their club as the locals who attend matches. In fact watching a game in the open air, outside a bar in say Hong Kong or Singapore can be more enjoyable than sitting in the cold rain in a dull stadium. Even modern fans who watch the games in their home can now communicate with each other through social media. They are enjoying companionship. These fans are important to the club. They pay to watch TV and the TV companies pay the clubs. The fans buy club merchandise. Fans in say India or Africa can be just as serious about 'their' club as those from the home town. Again unfortunately the West Midlands clubs do not attract many of these football followers.

There is yet another type of football fan, those who are happy to watch a good game and to watch a local club when it is doing well. They are more passive fans. It was estimated a few years ago that 45% of British adult men expressed an interest in football but that the average weekly attendance was only 3% of the population. This of course varies region by region but it does indicate that for a club playing attractive football with top players and a comfortable ground the demand can be high.

10

GLOBALISATION AND INEQUALITY

Globalisation has not been good for the West Midlands football clubs or to express it in a different way the local clubs have not benefitted from the possible gains from globalisation. Clubs are now exploitable brands to be sold around the world and the local clubs have not succeeded in selling their product to a larger market. They have not attracted rich benefactors, they have not attracted a sovereign wealth fund or owners with sufficient football knowledge and financial resources. They have not attracted top international players. Globalisation does not have to result in increased inequality, but it has done. This is the result of the values of those with power and of weak regulations. This applies to football as to many other aspects of life.

Ownership

An important part of the globalisation of the world's markets has been the movement of capital from one country to another. Restrictions of the movement of funds have been relaxed. Technological developments have meant money can flow very quickly between countries. With some countries not worrying very much about secrecy it is not always clear where the money has come from.

In the past the motives for owning a football club included an interesting hobby and a means of boosting ones status in the community, a trophy asset. As big money came into the game there were international investors attracted to ownership. Some of them saw it as a way of making money; this group would include the Glazer family. Others who were attracted were individuals and sovereign funds who were seeking worldwide recognition and respect, a means of promoting their name, a political insurance policy. A group who were seeking what has been called "soft power". This group would include the present owners of Manchester City, of Chelsea and of Paris Saint-Germain.

At one time the game was local, the Birmingham and the West Midlands clubs could attract owners who were wealthy enough to be able to support competitive teams. Times have changed. The West Midlands is no longer a region that attracts the world's wealthy. To be fair Villa did attract Randy Lerner but his motives for ownership were not clear. When he bought the club there was a good chance they would be successful and profitable. The Blues did attract Carson Yeung but he was not as rich as the fans were led to believe. As Ivery and Giles point out "once a rich benefactor loses his desire or the means problems come to a head quickly".[1] The Blues had a benefactor whose means (money) came to an end quickly and Villa had a benefactor whose desire came to an end.

In a way the Blues were unlucky they had an owner who knew about football and who seemed to be a fan of the club. He is not the only owner of a football club in England to be involved in money laundering, but he was one that was caught. It turned out he did not have access to as much money, clean or dirty, as he thought.

Over one third of the wealth in the world is in secret hands. London, is one of the money laundering centres. Respectable banks such as HSBC and Barclays have been fined large sums for assisting in money laundering. Most of the expensive apartments in London are owned by companies registered in tax havens (or secrecy havens). It is often dirty money that has been deposited in these tax havens. Over one half of the top clubs in England are owned by companies registered in tax havens. Football has attracted global finance.

Clubs were once seen as an asset of the local community. The community identified with the club, it was something they could be proud of, it gave a sense of belonging. The football club was in turn dependent on the community, for its support and for finance from spectators and the local business community. Most people in England would support the view that it is important to preserve the country's heritage and culture. Football is a part of the country's heritage and culture, yet only a few voices are raised in protest at the sale of our football clubs to a strange mix of foreign investors. Amongst those purchasing the clubs or acquiring substantial shareholdings is a person who has spent time in prison, a person who has been found guilty of financial crimes and given a suspended sentence, a person accused of corruption in his own country, and more than one person who has been closely associated with money launderers. In addition there are club owners from overseas who know little about the so called beautiful game but who do know how to borrow money from banks.

The danger is that with over half the Premier League clubs already owned by foreigners and with the strong possibility of other clubs going the same way that in future the most important decision affecting the Premier League will be made with the global interests of the owners in mind rather than in the best interests of English football. It is the owners of the Premier League clubs that have the real power; they control the money. The new owners are, not surprisingly, not emotionally attached to the game in this country. There is the danger that the country will lose control of the football industry, as it has lost control of many other industries. With football the country will also have lost control of an important part of English popular culture.

As Foer points out in his book entitled "How soccer explains the World" football was once part of a community's fabric, a repository of traditions.[2] Soccer clubs would help glue together small cities and towns. This no longer applies. There is still a need amongst fans for local identity but those running clubs are more interested in selling a super brand around the world.

Winners and Losers

Those who have governed the game of football over the last twenty or so years, have by their values been very successful. It is the most popular sport in the world, it gives pleasure to many millions, but not all those involved with the game have benefited. What has happened in football mirrors what has happened in the rest of society. An increase in inequality has been experienced in all walks of life; from people's day to day existence through to their interests in sport.

In football the market share (that is the share of the total revenue of all the clubs in the Premier League and Football League), of the largest 5 clubs is currently 55%. Ten years earlier it was only 38%. At the other end the bottom 50% of the clubs now only receive 6% of the revenue, ten years earlier it was 16%. This should not come as a surprise. In 1997 David Conn warned in his book on the Football Business that "The future of football will follow the course of every industry which has been subjected to the divisive effect of market forces ... Every decision will be made solely on the basis of whether it will make money for the already rich".[3] The power in football as in the rest of society is with those who control the money. Many leading economists are now worried about the rapidly increasing inequality. There are problems that can result when wealth captures policy making. The elite produce a framework which benefits them at the expense of the rest.

"The most important problem we are facing today is rising inequality".[4] This is the view of Robert Shiller a Nobel Prize winning economist. He was referring to the growing inequality in income and wealth distribution in the major economies of the world, but the problem he identified, widening inequality, applied equally in sport. It is endangering the future of football, cricket, rugby, golf and motor racing. Should we be worried about what is happening in football and other sports, or should we just sit back in our armchairs, drink Heineken beer, bet online and place the winnings in Barclays Bank?

In a society obsessed with wealth, money can buy anything. Qatar and China are providing evidence of this. It has been argued by another of the world's leading economists that when wealth captures policy making the rules bend to favour the rich often to the detriment of everyone else. Stiglitz argues that those with wealth, with power, are able to write the rules and to write them in ways which enhance their prospect of winning.[5] He is in fact discussing what happens at the level of the national economy but his words are applicable to football. If one looks behind the hype of the Premier League it is obvious that something is wrong with the game. The lack of success of the England national team, the financial struggles of smaller teams and the lack of support for grassroots football all point to serious problems. Basically what is happening is that the rich are getting richer and the rest are struggling.

One problem is propaganda and misinformation. Those with power inform stakeholders that what is happening is for the best and that in time benefits will trickle down to all. Football fans in England are continually told that they are lucky to live in a country that is home to the richest league in the world. A league in fact in which the majority of the owners, the majority of the players, the majority of the managers and the vast majority of the armchair fans are not from England. A league in which there is talk about playing some of the regular season games overseas.

Nearly 30 years ago we were told when the Premier League was formed that it would help build up a successful national team. It has not. We are told that if we sell the national stadium it will benefit all. We were told that the money from the top would trickle down to the grassroots. It has not. The propaganda process, in which those running the system justify what they are doing, is known as system justification. The need for such justification is greater the more extreme the inequality. Overselling and manipulation is what one would expect. Perceptions are what matter; as Stiglitz pointed out perceptions and beliefs are malleable. In politics (and in football) the powerful seek to shape beliefs in ways that serve their interests.

To move away from sport there is concern by some at the direction in which society in general is moving. A group of rich and powerful politicians, businessmen and opinion formers meet every year at the Davos World Economic Forum in Switzerland. In 2014 they perhaps surprisingly decided that the most pressing threat to the global economy was inequality. The risk being that capitalism in its present form could not survive if income and wealth become concentrated in too few hands. There are of course those that disagree, who argue that if globalisation is allowed to continue that inequality will disappear. But a recent study by Milanovic shows that this is not the case, that unless there is change inequality will increase.[6] Is there a lesson here for football?

The globalisation of the English game is of course good for many. It is good for football in China, in South East Asia and in the Middle East. It is good for the large multinational companies that use football to help sell their products around the world, it is good for the gambling industry, and it is good for the administrators of the game and for the owners and the players at the top clubs. It can even be argued that it is good for the supporters in England of the few elite clubs. It is however, bad for the supporters of the 'also ran' clubs, it is financially dangerous for these clubs as they struggle to compete and it is bad for those who want to see sport as balanced competition.

To bring the argument closer to home, on the last day of the 2016/17 season Birmingham City managed to hold on to a 1-0 victory at Bristol City. If Bristol had equalised the Blues would have been relegated. At the start of these final day matches it was one of three teams that would be relegated, Blackburn, the Blues or Nottingham Forest. All of these clubs had enjoyed better days, two in fact had not so long ago been winners of the top division. *The Times* newspaper, a day before these matches were played had a headline "Incompetent owners have poisoned great clubs".[7] It was the Venky family from India that had ruined Blackburn, it was Fawaz Al-Hasawi at the Forest and investors from Hong Kong at the Blues. The Venkys clearly knew about the chicken business in India but did not know about football. They had taken Blackburn Rovers from a mid-table position in the Premier League in 2012 to the third tier. Nottingham Forest had eight managers in the five year ownership by the investors from Kuwait. *The Times* article pointed to other examples of failed leadership at clubs that had once enjoyed success (including Leeds United).

Inequality

Investment by foreign owners, together with official sponsors and commercial income have become key factors in accounting for the wealth of clubs. The inequality in the revenue of clubs is dramatic. One source of income, the commercial income of Premier League clubs in 2015/16 ranged from £268 million at Manchester United to £122 million at Chelsea, £12 million at WBA to £5 million at Bournemouth. Manchester United have 35 official sponsors and their new deal with Chevrolet was worth £59 million per season and that with Adidas £73 million per season. The income from just one such sponsor is approximately equal to the total annual revenue of Stoke City. How can such teams compete on equal terms? The reason for this inequality is obvious, sponsors are interested only in clubs that have global appeal.

There are those who would argue that there is nothing wrong with this. We have inequality throughout nature. We should not expect life to be fair. That is correct, but there are steps that those running the game could take, if they wanted to, that would make it a fairer game, would reduce inequality, would reduce risk.

Deloittes frequently point out in their financial surveys that the financial position of many of the third and fourth tier clubs is challenging and that without correction it will inevitably lead to sporadic insolvency cases.[8] The situation is even worse among the Non-League clubs. With smaller clubs disappearing and fewer clubs winning anything there is a danger that the demand to watch the game, to support the game, will change. Fans, particularly the young fans, like to think the club they support has a chance of winning something.

There are alternative approaches to those at present being followed that could be adopted by the football establishment. It is true that one of the reasons for the Premier League's success is that the income from the sale of TV rights is divided quite equitably. It is this pattern of distribution that has enabled the smaller Premier League to provide exciting competition. But we could be looking at additional ways of achieving competitive balance. The financial fair play rules are a joke, just helping maintain the status quo. There is, in fact, a danger that the establishment will take steps that will increase inequality. The big clubs are demanding a bigger share of the money received from selling overseas broadcasting rights.

A study by Pawlowski found that 70% of fans did care about competitive balance. The researchers concluded that some football competitions might be at the risk of moving into territory where fans' interest will fall off in the future.[9] The demand to watch sporting contests depends partly on the uncertainty of the outcome. Once the result of a match becomes easily predictable football loses its appeal to many potential spectators. This means that it is necessary to regulate competition in order to ensure that no one team achieves too much market power. It is not sufficient to have uncertainty over the outcome of an individual match, it is also necessary to have uncertainly over who will be champions in an individual season. Balanced competition clearly results in more interest. So how does this fit in with the fact that in the 26 years of the Premier League, Manchester United have won the league 13 times, Chelsea 5 times, Arsenal 3 times and Manchester City 3 times.

The number of clubs with the resources to enable them to be champions is declining. In the 1960s seven different teams were winners of the top English League. In the 1970s five teams, in the 80s four teams, in the 90s four teams and in the 2000s four. Money does buy success. As mentioned in earlier chapters the amount spent each year on wages is a good predictor of the clubs final league position, a better predictor than the amount spent on transfer fees. This is partly because some of the big money transfers finish up as spectacular failures. Wages and final league position are closely related. Over the period 1995 to 2013 on a season by season basis in the Premier League the total wages paid by a club explains approximately 80% of the club's final league position. Looking at a more recent period 2003 to 2012, again in the Premier League, an individual club's wage bill, relative to the average wage in the league, explains about 90% of its final league position.

The best players understandably want the best wages. In 2015/16 Manchester United could afford to pay an average wage to its players of just over £6 million. Chelsea, Arsenal, Liverpool and Manchester City were also paying in excess of £5 million. The teams lower in the League were paying an average of nearer to £2 million per player. It must not be thought that all footballers are well paid, wage levels drop dramatically as one moves down the leagues. It is believed that in the fourth tier of English football the average wage is in the region of £50,000 per annum.

Not all agree on how important competitive balance is for the success of football. Being able to predict final league placings is one thing but that is different from being able to predict the outcome of a particular match. On its day a smaller club can beat a bigger club. Stefan Szymanski and Andrew Zimbalist raise the question of whether the lack of competitive balance really matters to a fan.[10] They point out that football is currently the world's most popular sport even though competitive balance has been on the decline for a decade or two. Jonathan Michie and Christine Oughton have shown that over the period 1974-2004 there has been a decline in competitive balance in English football.[11] The rate of decline has been more marked since the introduction of the Premier League, and it is getting worse. They find that the decline is associated with the widening gap in wage expenditure, the unequal distribution of broadcasting revenue and the widening revenue gap between the Premier League and the Championship.

The Regulators

There are numerous calls for a change in the way football in England is being run. But unfortunately the demand is not coming from those who can bring about change. A recent debate in the House of Commons called for steps to be taken to ensure that no clubs could be ruined again by mysterious foreign owners. The vast majority of football fans in England would probably agree with this view, but not many of the owners of Premier League clubs, nor the overseas fans of English clubs, nor unfortunately the so called governing bodies.

No single body controls football. Organisations such as FIFA, UEFA, the FA, the Football League and the Premier League each have limited power and they each have their own agendas. They are in competition with each other, the leagues and the cups they organise compete for sports space and they compete for the money consumers can spend. They also compete for the time and skills of the top players. FIFA claim that they need to maximise the benefit that football can offer to society as a whole. They have tried to claim the moral high ground, although the recent bribery scandals involving some of the officials has not helped their case. They claim they see football primarily as about sport, but some of them act as if it is about money.

The international competitions often lead UEFA into conflict with the top clubs who wish to control the use of the top players. Last time this happened the top clubs formed the G14 group and UEFA gave way. The clubs are more powerful than the organisers of competitions.

When in the 19th century the Football League broke away from the FA, William McGregor the founder of the league explained that "they must be a selfish body whose interests are wholly bound up in the welfare of the affiliated clubs". The Premier League clubs expressed similar sentiments when they broke away from the Football League. The Premier League is a company owned by its 20 clubs with the FA as a special shareholder. The primary objective of any company is to look after its own shareholders' interests. It is not their prime responsibility to look after the interests of the national team or of grassroots football. The FA do have these responsibilities. But they cannot control the financial matters and the ownership issues of Premier League clubs. They do not seem to be doing a very good job with the grassroots; they seem more concerned with covering the costs of the expensive Wembley stadium.

FIFA regard themselves as the international governing body. But they have been shown to be a power base for a small elite. This becomes more evident each year. One scandal follows another, the latest being the award of the 2022 World Cup to Qatar, a country that has little to offer but money. To be fair to FIFA their values have not declined – we have known about corruption at their level for over 30 years. Match fixing exists in some countries of the world. It is ironic that whilst the players are expected to behave as role models, others higher up in the game set a poor example and get away with it.

Football is a huge success as a business but if it is to be more than a business those running the game should look as what is happening. The governance of the game is weak. Some owners should not be allowed to be involved in the game. The increasing inequality means many clubs become just 'also rans' with their fans and local communities having to settle for second best. This is the problem for the Midlands clubs and the signs are that things are not getting better.

Even though we are living through an era of globalisation we should not think it will go on forever. We can see signs that those who have missed out, who are discontented are beginning to look for change. The Brexit vote in the UK and the vote for Trump in the USA are signs that many people would like to return to a more nationalist agenda, a more local regional agenda. There have been eras of globalisation in the past and they have come to an end. One interesting such era was that of the Silk Road which, together with its seafaring, turned China into a global powerhouse. In the 15th century, China turned in on itself, it became inward looking. The example is interesting because now China are turning to their version of market based capitalism; their President's vision is to turn China into a world football super power by 2050. The acquisition of European clubs is a small part of this plan.

Globalisation has meant the free (or freer) movement of labour and of capital. From a football point of view it has meant that many of the best players in the world have played in England in the richest league in the world. This has been good for the followers of football in England. Unfortunately hardly any of them have played for the clubs from Birmingham and the region. Local fans have had to be content watching them play for the opposition.

What about the movement of capital? Clearly some fans do not mind foreign ownership. The fans of the two Manchester clubs, of Liverpool, of Chelsea and of Arsenal are happy (although some at United are still not convinced.) However the fans at the Villa, Blues, Notts Forest, Blackburn, Reading and others are less so. The list of clubs that have been let down by foreign owners is much longer than the list where the ownership has been a success. However, it is the few high profile clubs that hit the headlines. Indeed it is now 14 years (2003/4) since the Premier League has been won by a club with UK owners.

11

THE FUTURE

What of the future for the football teams from Birmingham and the rest of the West Midlands, will one of them, one day, be good enough to qualify for the top European competitions? We can never know what will happen in the future but one thing is certain that unless something unpredictable happens the answer to the question is "no". It is accepted that "there are things that we know and things that we know we don't know but, there are things we do not know we don't know". Unless something unexpected happens, local West Midlands fans will have to continue to support their modest teams. Either that or they can behave like most football fans around the world and support a team, wherever it is based, and be identified with that club. The success of their adopted club hopefully giving them satisfaction.

We will look at what is happening in football today and at what might happen. We will look at the good things and the bad things to see how they might affect the local clubs. We have already looked at globalisation and the increasing inequality. In this chapter we will return to foreign ownership of clubs. We will look at dangers to the game from activities such as betting, the gambling industry and from the activities of some agents. We will then look at Birmingham as a city and at the surrounding region to see what the future is for them, with or without success in football.

The football bandwagon will continue to roll forward, with any problems being pushed aside. It is true that viewing figures for those watching Premier League matches on Sky have fallen (from an average of 1.5 million per match in 2011/12 to 1 million in 2016/17), but other ways for fans to watch matches are becoming available. In addition to BT Sports there are the big internet companies that are becoming interested, with the likes of Google considering bidding for the rights to show the top matches. The Premier League are to make more live matches available to TV, increasing the number from 168 to 200, with 8 matches to be played and shown live on TV at prime time on Saturday night. Attendance figures at matches are also increasing, partly as a result of the new larger stadiums. During one weekend in November 2017, there were five Premier League matches with crowds of over 50,000 watching them (Liverpool, Man United, Newcastle, Spurs and West Ham).

The media love football. The TV, the press, the radio, the publishers and the internet all love the matches and the soap opera that surrounds the players, the managers and coaches, the owners and the fans. Between matches there is always some off field drama, whether it be racial problems, sexual harassment, bullying, drink problems, cheating, a clash of egos or contested decisions. There is plenty to keep the fans, the consumers interested.

The World Cup in Moscow in 2018 was a great success from a football point of view. It was also a success financially for some and politically for Russia. The global audience for the games was estimated to be 10.8 billion, up 14% from the previous World Cup held in Brazil. But in 2018 there were signs that some things were beginning to change. Many of the younger generation who watch football were switching from TV to streaming. It is said that the younger audience would rather watch the matches on their mobiles, on their smart phones, than to sit in front of a television for 90 minutes. It means for them that they can combine watching the football with chatting on social media, with gaming and with betting on line. If this trend continues it will affect the amount TV companies are prepared to pay for broadcasting rights for the games. It will change the way in which advertisers use the media. There were already signs of change with Amazon in 2018 purchasing the rights to show 20 Premier League matches per season for three years. These are changes happening to the business of football that we know about now.

Those with power, with financial interests in the game, have so much to gain from the world wide popularity of the game. The media, the players, the managers, the executives, the regulators, the advertisers, the owners of clubs, the sponsors and of course the fans (but not all of them) benefit from the increased popularity of the sport. FIFA have increased the number of countries competing in the World Cup Finals from 32 to 48. UEFA have increased the number of clubs that take part in their Champions League. Money paid for TV rights to Premier League games increased from £3,018 billion for the rights to the three seasons from 2013/14 to £5,136 billion for the three seasons from 2016/17 – a 71% increase. Players' wages increased. Transfer fees reach record levels. The world's largest companies compete to be business partners of the elite clubs. Richer and richer owners come into the game. There are problems affecting the game but they are cleverly pushed aside.

The combined value of Europe's 32 richest clubs increased by 14% between the end of the 2016 season and the end of the 2017 season. Not a bad rate of growth. This was due in part to increased broadcasting revenue and in part due to the increased profitability of the clubs following the implementation of the Financial Fair Play rules.[1] These rules have helped the top clubs to maintain the status quo. Manchester United were in 2017 (according to *Forbes*) the most highly valued football club (£2.73 billion) followed by Barcelona (£2.69 billion). There are six other English clubs amongst the ten most valuable in Europe. Unfortunately none of these are West Midlands clubs. The gap is great, Tottenham, the 10th highest is valued at (only) £782 million.

There are problems in football but none of them seem big enough to suggest that the future path of football is not one of continuing growth. Even proven corruption amongst the top level of administrators in the game does little to affect demand for the game.

Political interference

There is nothing new about a political involvement in sport. Many years ago, at the time of a Communist government, China used success in sport to demonstrate the superiority of their system. Now the new government have turned to football. This interest is driven partly by a love of the game but also by political and economic considerations. The Government is willing to invest large sums of money to promote the game at grass roots level and to develop the national team to be one of the best in the world in a few years' time. The country is promoting its domestic Super League. The clubs are offering high salaries to the top players from around the world. In 2017 six of the top 10 highest paid players in the world were playing in the Chinese Super League.

More than 70% of all foreign takeovers in the top 15 European leagues in 2016 and 2017 involved Chinese investors. Individual entrepreneurs are purchasing clubs or purchasing stakes in clubs in the top leagues around the world. Not only are local West Midlands teams of interest to them but top teams such as Inter Milan, AC Milan and Manchester City. In 2017 a Chinese investor paid in the region of £200 million for an 80% stake in Southampton. The Premier League were keen to point out that they had given permission for the takeover only after a lengthy scrutiny of the source of the new owner's funds. Not easy to do with so much of the wealth in the world being held in tax/secrecy havens. There has been talk at times of Chinese investors being interested in Liverpool and Manchester United.

The Chinese are not just interested in big clubs. Chinese investors have bought a stake in Northampton Town, of the fourth tier. They are also interested in building up a relationship from the grassroots. There has even been a suggestion that a Chinese under 20 years of age team be allowed to compete in the German fourth tier. The two famous clubs from Milan are now Chinese owned, the one with some success, the other badly. AC Milan who were owned by ex-Prime Minister Berlusconi for 31 years, were purchased by a company with Chinese links, with financial support from a US Hedge Fund, one with a bad reputation. The club has big debts, it could face problems.

One example of the dangers that can arise when football becomes involved with geo-politics became apparent in August 2017. The football world was stunned when PSG (Paris Saint-Germain) paid almost £200 million to purchase Neymar from Barcelona. This was more than twice the amount paid in the previous most expensive transfer (£98 million paid by Manchester United for Pogba). Why did PSG pay such a large amount? There are two possible answers to the question. One was that they needed to in order to meet Barcelona's asking price and in order to get the player to move clubs. The second answer is more likely to be correct and more worrying. PSG are owned by Qatar, the richest country in the world. Qatar had already made a name for itself in football, a bad name by using its money to buy votes to ensure that the World Cup in 2022 took place in their country. In 2017 the rulers of Qatar had fallen out with their neighbours, Saudi Arabia, UAE, and Egypt over the alleged support for terrorism by Qatar. The rulers of Qatar were proud and wished to demonstrate their strength and independence. They were willing to spend £200 million on a player just to show that they could do it. An exercise in soft power.

The experienced manager Arsène Wenger pointed to the dangers when countries, or their representatives, owned football clubs. As he said when this happens "everything is possible". With the Neymar transfer there was further criticism regarding the size of the fee paid to his agent, who happened to be his father.

One other new development with a geo-political dimension is the creation of multinational football corporations. Manchester City have established franchise clubs around the world, including one club in New York and one in Melbourne.[2] With the growth of a worldwide fan base the football club has become part of a global entertainment business. It is doubtful if any of the West Midlands clubs will be able to benefit from such developments, although it has been rumoured that Villa were interested in such possibilities. The idea was first promoted by Ferran Soriano when he was a top executive at Barcelona. At that club he did not receive support for his imaginative idea. Barcelona was a club firmly rooted in the city, in the region. The club was partly owned by its fans, with 143,000 having a vote. Soriano was tempted by the club's owners to move to Manchester City who did have global ambitions. They established the City Football Group who own or partly own six clubs.

A number of these multi-club football businesses are being formed. There are at least 12 private owners who have a stake in more than one football club. There are 5 companies and 3 clubs involved in multi-club ownership. A recent example is Atlético Madrid acquiring stakes in the French second division club RC Lens. There are also agents who have an interest at more than one club. The agent problem is discussed below. The danger in all of these multi-club structures is a possible conflict of interest. Players and other assets can be transferred from one club to another.

Inequality

Inequality and globalisation affect the game at all levels. At a national level some countries are now suffering. In Europe attendances are declining not only in countries such as Hungary, Ukraine, Scotland and Romania but also in once top football nations such as Italy, and Holland. It is said that local football fans are staying away from games involving local teams in order to watch games shown on TV from one of the three big European leagues. The local teams lack stars, they lack glamour. The same thing could happen with fans in the UK with fans of teams from the lower divisions. A recent article in *World Soccer* (March 2017) pointed to the dangers.[3] The author concluded that the European game is at a precipice and that change is necessary. There are 55 member countries in UEFA, and they are divided. The smaller countries want (need) more of the income coming from the Europe wide competitions But the big three, England, Spain and Germany dominate the TV audiences for the club competitions as well as for International matches. They are reluctant to give anything away.

Between countries inequality is increasing and within countries the gaps are increasing. In Spain there are only two or three elite clubs and in Germany again two or three elite clubs. In England there is perhaps more competition but there are still only five or six top clubs that can be expected to win the Premier League. The decline in competitive balance in the game does not seem to be harming the overall picture but it does of course harm those who are excluded. Is there a possible tipping point where fans turn away from the game?

Clearly there is not competitive balance in many of the major football competitions but looked at, at a global scale this is not at the present time putting off customers. Those who would like change write and talk about a 'tipping point'. This would occur when all the excesses of the present system such as inequality, greed and corruption lead to the system failing. Those who believe in this idea believe the excesses could reach a point where the followers of football demand reform, where the football fans turn away from the game. At the moment the tipping point seems a long way off. Those in control of the game seem to be able to keep a lid on the scandals, on the excesses. If there were a tipping point it might help the West Midlands clubs.

The gap between the clubs in the top third of the Premier League and those in the bottom third is getting bigger. At the top end Manchester United can afford to spend £89 million on one player, WBA can just about afford to spend £20 million a year on new players. In the second tier are the Blues who are lucky if they can spend net £5 million a year on players. The difference in the levels of annual revenue illustrate the problem. In 2015/16 the revenue for Arsenal was £348 million, for Chelsea £335 million and for Swansea £97 million and the clubs are all in the same league. When Brighton played Manchester City on the first day of the 2017/18 season, the Brighton squad had cost £31.5 million the City squad £388 million.

But the big six clubs, would like an even bigger slice of the cake. When in 2017 the contract over the sale of broadcasting rights to the Chinese was being discussed, the big six made clear that they were not happy with the way the money was being divided equally between the 20 Premier League clubs. The big six wanted a larger share that the others, arguing that, perhaps correctly, the Chinese viewers (in fact all overseas viewers) wanted to watch the matches of the big clubs; not the 'also rans'. They did not win the argument in 2017 but they plan to return to the issue of the division of revenue from the sale of overseas broadcasting rights. They do not believe that the income should be divided equally but believe it should be divided on the basis of popularity. If they do not get their way they could break away or threaten to break away.

There are those at the top clubs who seem to assume they have a right to succeed. In December 2017 Jose Mourinho complained that the amount of money he had spent on transfers since he moved to Manchester United was not enough to turn the club into title contenders. They were second in the League at the time. In the summer 2016, and the January and summer 2017 transfer windows he had spent £229 million. His worry was that his neighbours in Manchester had spent £324 million. Chelsea had spent £86 million and Liverpool £59 million. Mourinho was careful not to blame the owners of United for this difficulty, he said he had the full backing of the owners for his three year plans. His worry was the amount the owners of other clubs were spending. He should look at what life is like for managers at clubs not in the elite few; at the problems these managers face in trying to avoid relegation with relatively poor owners.

For many years there has been talk of a European Super League being formed. The Premier League came into existence in the 1990s when the top 20 clubs broke away from the Football League over the issue of the division of money. The top 6 or so clubs could now break away from the Premier League. The Super League (with or without FIFA's blessing) would consist of the best clubs in Europe. Such a league would attract big money from the sale of the broadcasting rights around the world and from sponsorship from the large multinational companies. None of the clubs in the League would come from the West Midlands or even the Midlands. There would probably be no promotion or relegation. Football fans from the region would be deprived of being able to watch the world's best players – other than on TV. The Super League would take money away from what would be left of the domestic leagues.

Agents

One danger to the game is said to be the agents, in particular the so called super agents. They take a considerable amount of money out of the game. UEFA estimate that more than 3 billion Euros were paid to agents by Europe's top clubs between 2013 and 2016. Agents are also used more and more by foreign owners to advise on the running of clubs, on the managerial appointments and to advise on the purchase of players. Chinese investors have even purchased a stake in one of the top football agencies.

The average agent's fee in England is 13% of the transfer fee. This can result in a significant cost for a club. In the period from Feb 2016 to Jan 2017 Manchester City spent the most of the English clubs on agent's fees, namely £26.2 million, followed by Chelsea with £25 million. There is no typical agent's fee, on smaller value transfers the fee will be higher frequently over 20%. One transfer that hit the headlines was that of Paul Pogba to Manchester United. The transfer fee was £89 million, with his agent Mino Raiola said to have received £41 million. This is big money, much more than the annual revenue of Championship clubs. The problem is that the agents often act as brokers for more than one party. It was said that Raiola was receiving commission from the player, the purchasing club and Juventus, the selling club. The agent can have a big influence over where the player ends up, he will take into account the fees being offered to him.

Agents are a mixed group. There are many of them. The business is competitive with the largest agency only being responsible for 6 of the major transactions in Europe in the summer of 2017. It is not a well-regulated business. In a book entitled *The Deal – inside the World of the Super-Agent* Smith describes meetings with wealthy Ukrainians interested in acquiring Sheffield Wednesday.[4] He believes that much of the money involved in such deals is dirty money and that the investors often have criminal links. Jon Smith makes the point that "People are naïve in the extreme if they think football transactions are only conducted between upstanding businessmen with legitimate funding. It is often a murky world". Strange deals have taken place at a number of clubs including Portsmouth, Leeds and as discussed earlier at Aston Villa. One murky deal was that involving the sale of a player from Leeds to Fulham. It resulted in the Leeds chairman at the time Massimo Cellino being banned by the FA for breaching FA rules. The club were involved in trying to cover up a payment to an unlicensed agent. The club paid £250,000 to a licenced agent for so called scouting services and he then passed the money on to the unlicensed agent – a person who had convictions for fraud and money laundering.

There are of course many different types of agents, most perfectly respectable. The sons of some managers have been involved in some deals. Tony Blair's son has been involved in at least one deal. Agents perform a very valuable role. They have ensured that more and more of the money that has come into the game is received by those who generate the excitement, by those who the fans pay to watch, namely the players. There are only a few real star players, a few real celebrities, and it is agents that have ensured they are paid what they are really worth. The problem is the darker side of the agency work. There are registered agents, but it is not unknown for the registered agent to act as a frontman for an unregistered person. There are also problems with dual representation, with the agent acting for more than one party. Such problems will not undermine the football business, but ethical issues could slow its growth.

The Betting Industry

In 2017 nine Premier League clubs had shirts sponsored by gambling companies. Fourteen of the twenty-four clubs in the

Championship, including Aston Villa were also sponsored by gambling companies. Football is very important for this business and the companies involved are willing to pay to have an opportunity to advertise their "exciting" products to those of all ages who watch football on TV. In 2017 Betway (based in Malta) were paying WHU £10 million a year for shirt sponsorship. SportPesa, from Kenya, were paying Everton £9.6 million for their name to appear on that club's shirts. In 2016 the amount of money bet on football matches was £1.4 billion.

The circle begins with the wish of some people to bet, they spend money with the betting companies, the betting companies spend money in advertising on TV, the TV companies pay the Premier League and the football clubs to be able to show the matches. That money is paid to, amongst others, the players. The glamour surrounding football and the players (possibly) tempts other people to bet. This raises ethical issues. Are some people been encouraged to bet irresponsibly?

It is a fact that the gambling industry helped create the wealth in the Premier League but it is now beginning to cause problems. The players' shirts, the very effective 'moving' advertising hoardings around the pitch giving details of betting sites. The advertising on TV before a match and at half time are very persuasive. The logos of gambling brands have been found to be visible on Match of the Day broadcasts for between 71% and 89% of the time. The dangers of this are known, young people, impressionable people can be influenced by this advertising. This of course is the reason why the betting companies are prepared to spend such large amounts of money advertising their products at football matches. There is occasionally talk about the dangers to young people when their heroes become linked to betting companies. Some clubs have even had gambling companies names displayed on their junior teams shirts.

Those regulating the game, those regulating TV, are reluctant to take steps that would reduce the dangers, because this would reduce revenue. In 2017 the FA did withdraw from a sponsorship deal with Ladbrokes over criticism about a possible conflict of interest. The FA as the regulator were trying to control the betting by players on the outcome of matches whilst themselves receiving sponsorship from betting companies. The deal with Ladbrokes was worth £3 million a year for three years; football was beginning to turn money away. The Labour Party have said that if they were in power they would ban advertising on shirts by betting companies.

One problem is that although it is possible to monitor betting in the UK and most other European countries it is not possible to do so in most of the world. It is possible to see who is betting and to look for unusual betting patterns in regulated countries where bookmakers are controlled but in the huge betting markets in China, India and elsewhere in Asia this is not possible. Betting is officially illegal in these countries so the betting that does take place cannot be monitored.

In contrast to the situation in the UK is the control exercised by those running the richest sports league in the world, namely the National Football League in the United States. To promote the gambling business is not allowed in the NFL. This includes a ban on the advertising of hotels that provide an opportunity to gamble and it does not allow the advertising of tourist resorts that encourage gambling such as Las Vegas. Clearly in the US sport is keen to be seen as socially responsible. It is not the case with football in England.

There is another problem that can arise in football, namely footballers or others connected with the game, betting on the results of games. A ban was introduced by the FA in 2014 on players betting on all worldwide football activity. But the ban has not been totally successful. In 2016/17 the FA took disciplinary action against 30 players for illegal betting. Joey Barton, an interesting and outspoken footballer was given an 18 month match ban (reduced on appeal to 13 months) for betting over 1000 times on the results of matches. His wife had a betting account and Joey gave her money to put in it. He claimed that over half of professional footballers, even some from the Premier League, did gamble on the outcome of matches. It was not being suggested that those involved were betting on the results of matches in which they were taking part, or in competitions in which they were involved, that has been banned for a long time. Many players like a "flutter". The charity "Sporting Chance" support 300 to 400 players with a gambling addiction.

The FA rules ban those involved in the running of clubs from betting on the results of matches or on issues such as transfers. This ban clearly covers directors and executives. It was however decided in a court decision that it did not cover owners. The case arose over an attempt by the FA to charge Maxim Demin, the Russian owner of Bournemouth, for betting on the outcome of matches. The court decided that because the owner was not involved in the day to day running of the club that he was not covered by the FA rules. The decision caused concern because it meant that other owners who were not directors or chairmen were not covered by the ban. A more recent concern in the UK is the increase in the amount of betting on women's football. The betting on the games in the women's top league is now approaching £1 million per match. The women's game is not as well regulated as the men's.

The Regulators

The business side of the sport is not well regulated. One scandal follows another.[5] There are a number of different bodies involved, each with a different role. The rules themselves are not always clear and often they are not enforced properly. It has been known for some time that some of the top regulators have been corrupt.

There are two major problems that the regulators face. First the rules regarding who should own clubs. A number of dubious characters have passed the so called "fit and proper persons" test for club owners. The second major threat to the game arises over the Financial Fair Play rules. The regulators at UEFA, at the Premier League and at the EFL have produced regulations which are intended to improve the competitive balance in the game, to limit the inequality. The rules are based on the principle that no club should be able to spend more than it can afford, no club should be able to operate with big losses. The current regulations are based on a maximum total loss allowed over a three year period. From 2016/17 a club that has been in the Premier League for three years is not allowed to produce losses of more than £105 million over the three year period beginning 2014/15. A club that has been in the Championship for three years is not supposed to produce losses of more than £39 million over the 3 year period. There are detailed regulations concerning what income can be taken into account in the calculations and what expenditure allowed. UEFA has its own rules.

The rules are alright but the bodies enforcing them have appeared to be toothless. One of the numerous clubs investigated over FFP matters was QPR who made losses of £65 million in the 3 years up to 2013. They were supposed to be punished with a £58 million fine. QPR battled with the regulators and in the end settled for a payment of £17 million. Two other clubs that have got into problems relating to FFP are Manchester City and PSG. Both clubs made big losses in the period up to 2014. Both clubs were able to negotiate a modest penalty, what was referred to at the time as a slap on the wrist. The regulators required the clubs to pay relatively small fines, limited their spending and limited their squad registrations. Both Manchester City and PSG are owned by very wealthy investors from Middle East countries. The objectives of the owners is to be a success in football, to promote their countries, they are not concerned with the financial cost.

The big worry in 2017 was how the regulators would interpret the FFP rules following the latest purchases by PSG. The club's latest player acquisition would result in the club making big losses, above the permitted UEFA level. One concern was that they might adopt some creative accounting techniques. They might receive payments from companies and sponsors who are close to the club's owners, what could be called related party transactions. The rules state that any such financial inflow must be at fair market prices, but there had been problems on this issue with PSG in the past.

There was concern in that the regulators seem to treat the top clubs more favourably than the less fashionable clubs. PSG have the wealth of Qatar to support them. Between the time they were taken over in 2011 and the 2017 season they had spent in the region of £600 million to acquire new players. In 2017 they were involved in the biggest deal in football history when they purchased one of the best players in the world Nemar from Barcelona for nearly £200 million. They also had acquired the services of a young French footballer Kylian Mbappe from Monaco for a fee in the region of £160 million. This would be the second most expensive acquisition. The plan was to first acquire the player on loan for one season and then buy him the next season. Mbappe turned out to be one of the stars of the 2018 World Cup.

It was thought that UEFA had instituted rules that would limit the amount clubs could spend on players. When the regulators became aware of what PSG were doing they sent a delegation to Paris to try to obtain more information and to find out how the club planned to satisfy its FFP requirements. Barcelona were not happy with the Neymar transfer, they felt they had been tricked by the player and by PSG. They planned to fight hard to ensure that the FFP rules were strictly enforced.

PSG were given until June 2018 to prove that its books would balance, if they did not sanctions would be imposed. The football industry waited to see how the regulator would act. The Liverpool manager, Jürgen Klopp, was quoted as saying "I thought FFP was made to ensure that situations like this could not happen but it seems it is more of a suggestion than a rule". The football industry waited to hear what the decision of the regulator would be. It was eventually announced that the club had been cleared of breaching the FFP rules but that the club would need to raise £50 million by the end of June 2018 to comply with the regulations. This could mean the club would need to sell players or it could mean more money being put into the club, one way or another, by the owners. The regulator tried to reassure people that the transactions were financially fair; they stated that compliance for the year 2018 would remain under close scrutiny.

Both the Villa and the Blues are currently being held back by FFP rules, by the so called profit and sustainability rules. These rules appear, to many people, to be somewhat of a farce; designed to justify the governing body's existence. But money talks. The reality is that the rules hold back the smaller clubs and make it hard for them to succeed but allow the bigger clubs to become richer and more successful. The name of the rules is somewhat of a misnomer, the fair play relates to the finance, it does not relate to what takes place on the pitch. It certainly does not help bring about competitive balance.

The regulators have not done a very good job in keeping dirty money out of the game. Football clubs, especially in some of the lower leagues and in some of the less high profile countries have for a long time been attractive to money launderers. We know of Carson Yeung. There are tales of gangsters being involved in football in Scotland. It is said that Britain's leading drug trafficker has ownership interests in two or three smaller clubs from the North of England. A Spanish third tier club was said to be controlled by two major Russian crime groups, the President of the club was arrested. There are many other such stories.[6] In some businesses one does not ask where the money comes from![7]

Football in England

What is the future of the Premier League? Andy Burnham, the mayor of Greater Manchester, raised the question following the Brexit vote. It could be that the UK introduces work permits and a control on immigration. This would affect the Premier League. At the moment the owners, managers and players come from around the world. As Michael Cox points out, early in February 2017 the top nine clubs in the Premier League were led by managers from nine different countries. This was not unusual. At the beginning of December 2017 there was only one of the top 9 clubs with an English manager (Burnley). There are those who welcome the overseas takeover of the league. Cox believes "the English top flight takes exotic ingredients from various foreign countries and serves the most diverse exciting and unpredictable football feast in the world".[8]

Could another country take on this "mixer" role? Cox believes not because the other ingredients that make the Premier League what it is are the fans, the climate, the officials and the traditional grounds (those that remain). If because of political changes, of controls on the movement of labour and capital, the leading international league in the world had to leave England, Cox believes it would be a great loss. One reason for this being he believes is that the league is great at promoting Britain (England) around the world, and a second reason is that what would be left for football in England would be rather "bland". Some of the glamour would be missing.

Not all agree with this romanticised view of football in England at the present time. The much respected West Midland based football writer and broadcaster Tom Ross takes a different view. Ross believes that the fans want "our game back".[9] He is particularly concerned about football in the Midlands and his worry is that the game has gone for good. We will return to football in the Midlands shortly but before that what about English football?

The future for football at a national level was very promising. The Premier League is a major success, it attracts the money and the best players from around the world. In the 2018 World Cup the majority of the players in the starting line ups for the teams in the semi-final matches were Premier League players.

It has to be remembered that when the Premier League was formed in 1992 one of the arguments used to support its establishment that it would strengthen the England national team. Up until 2018 it had not done so. The England team had for many years been a disappointment. They had promised so much and delivered little. One of the problems was said to be that the FA had found it difficult to attract a manager who was English with the right abilities. Perhaps this was not surprising when one observes what was happening in the Premier League. The percentage of English players in the starting line-up of Premier League games has been on the decline. In the first year of the League 69% of the players were English, now it is in the region of 33%. On the first day of the 2017/18 season Chelsea had 13 foreign players in their squad, Manchester City and Watford 11.

Young English players have performed very well in under 17, under 19 and under 20 aged International tournaments. The under 17s and under 20s won World Cup competitions. The under 19s winning the European Championship. Unfortunately not many of the young players involved were chosen to play for their club's first team when they returned to domestic competition. Many were sent out on loan to play for clubs in lower divisions. In the 2016/17 season the percentage of minutes played by Englishmen in the Chelsea team was 10.6%, for Manchester City it was 12.6% and, for the Spurs 37%. In only two clubs, Bournemouth (63.7%) and Burnley (52.5%) were English players involved for over half the total minutes played.

For many years the England national team had not performed well in World Cup competitions. This was even the case before the formation of The Premier League. In 2018 the national team performed much better than expected and gave pleasure to many fans and to many with a casual interest in the game. They even found a manager who is English and is respected.

To the surprise of many in the 2018 World Cup England finished fourth. They were a young squad with a good manager. What was not known was whether or not on their return to league football the young players would be given a chance to develop at the highest level. Would they be the first choice of their managers or would some overseas player be the first choice?

What would the success of the young England teams and the senior squad mean for the West Midlands? As already mentioned none of the senior squad played for the local clubs but even worse than that an analysis of the clubs that have recently supplied players to the England under 17s, 19s, 20s, and 21 squads shows that out of 104 players Aston Villa supplied just three, WBA two and the Wolves one. In contrast Chelsea supplied fourteen, Manchester City twelve, Arsenal eleven and Spurs nine. Future talent is only being seen at local clubs when the players are on loan. The Midlands clubs have been bypassed, the top young players wish to play for clubs that are high profile and where they have a chance to win something.

Football in Greater Birmingham

Does football success help a city? Not necessarily. It might bring pride to the city but this does not always result in economic success. Liverpool have a different story to tell. In the 1970s and 1980s Liverpool were one of the most successful clubs in Europe. They were winners of the European Cup in 1977, 1978, 1981 and 1984 (they were also winners in 2005). It did, however, not at the time help in attracting inward investment. It had a reputation as a militant city. It had poor council housing, high unemployment. In 2008 its City Council was labelled the worst performing council in the country. It was one of only two English authorities to receive an inadequate rating. But times have changed. Its economy is now dominated by the service sector and it is attracting more and more visitors. It was awarded the title of the European City of Culture in 2008. The city developed impressive museums and arts facilities. Several areas of the city centre were granted World Heritage Site status by UNESCO in 2004. It is the 6th most visited city in Britain by tourists. It is seen as an exciting city.

It was not that long ago that Villa were the champions of Europe, that Coventry won the FA cup and that the Albion and the Wolves were amongst the most exciting teams in the country. It was not that long ago that two small clubs from the East Midlands, Derby and Nottingham Forest were the champions of Europe. But times have changed.

Like it or not, football clubs are now primarily about making money. The fans do not like this but the owners, the media, the agents and players clearly do. Football clubs are now useful partners who can assist in the selling of products. The success of a club has become dependent on the revenue it can attract or on the money put into the club by the owners. With the new fair play rules commercial income will become of more importance. The Midland clubs are not good vehicles for promoting products either globally or nationally and so have lagged behind in the growth of sponsorship and commercial income. TV income from Premier League games is reasonably well distributed but of course the local clubs have not benefited from the TV income from European games. The local grounds are quite small and they are not often full. For various reasons the clubs have not attracted the 'right' type of wealthy investor. The clubs have not attracted the superstar players; the players who want to play at clubs that give them an opportunity to play in the European competitions.

Those responsible for the 'also ran' status of the local clubs are the owners and executives who have made decisions at the clubs over the last fifty or so years. As demonstrated in earlier chapters the leadership has at sometimes been bad and has at most times been prudent. The owners have let the fans down. Opportunities have been missed especially when English football became global. The local clubs got left behind. The West Midlands clubs did not excite fans from around the world.

What about the future? Money has become the root of a club's success. Do the present owners of the local clubs have enough wealth to be able to build up successful clubs? According to the *Birmingham Post* Wealth List, Guo Guangchang, at the Wolves, is worth £4.2 billion. This is nearly 10 times more than the owners of the Blues. When one compares these figures above with the money behind some of the Premier League clubs then the chance of success in the future for the local clubs seems far away. At the top are the oil rich owners from the Middle East, then the Russian and East Europeans, with Alisher Usmanov worth £12.3 billion and Roman Abramovich worth £8 billion. The Coates family, at Stoke, are said to be worth £5 billion, Joe Lewis at Spurs £4.6 billion and Mike Astley £2.2 billion. The two new shareholders at the Villa are said to be very wealthy. Of course money is not all that matters, some managers can have an impact, but as explained elsewhere in the book for even the few elite managers their impact depends on the owners. They need time, finance, and an owner (or chairman) who understands the game.

The failure of the local clubs does matter, not just to football fans. It is a missed opportunity to promote the city, to help build up the brand name. The new plans to promote Birmingham emphasise the cultural aspects of the city and its heritage. But Liverpool in promoting itself points to "an unbelievable music and sporting heritage". The image of the City of Birmingham could be better. The perception of the city is not good, it has not been helped by the London based media, and by being overlooked in the North-South divide. If the football clubs had been successful there would be more pride in the region, there would be more glamour. Like it or not sporting success would increase the value of the brand name. Birmingham is not associated with success. Unfortunately as far as football is concerned it is now too late. There is no competitive balance in the game.

As explained above there are many problems in the game. There will need to be changes. But there are so many benefiting from the game as it is now, that the changes will not be fundamental. The financial gap is now too great to close. The clubs that are now rich will continue to be able to spend more on wages, more on transfers, than the other clubs. The elite clubs are happy with the status quo. Birmingham will remain a second class city as far as football is concerned. It appears that Birmingham and the region will have to succeed without the support, without the boost that would come from being home to a top football club.

Does this matter, after all football is only a game? Unfortunately it does matter. Football is now so high profile. There are those that even argue that many politicians in power like it this way, that it distracts the populace from the economic and/or political injustices that surround them. It can also be used to demonstrate soft power. It has been used as a means for a country to promote itself, it can be used for a city to promote itself, it can help in being associated with success.

ACKNOWLEDGEMENTS

The feeling one is left with after being a football fan in the West Midlands for over 50 years is one of disappointment. There have been exciting moments, but these are usually linked with a fight against relegation, very few of them are linked with success. Thanks must be given, however, to the many excellent players and to the many not so good but hard working players that have been involved with the local clubs over the last few decades. The lack of success of the clubs has often been more to do with those involved with running the clubs rather than with the players on the field.

Many thanks are also due to the many excellent writers on football. Their books, their articles and reports are often more interesting to read than the material that appears on the front page of newspapers. Football is now a respectable subject for academic research and there are many excellent and revealing scholarly articles on the subject. I acknowledge the contribution of these writers and researchers to this work.

I would like to thank the many people who I have spoken to about football while writing this book, in particular George Applebey. I would also like to thank Cynthia Franklin, Michele Donovan and also my wife Valerie for helping to bring this book into existence. My wife came up with the idea for the cover

Finally I must thank the staff of Brewin Books for taking on the publication of this book. The work began as a study ten years ago into "Whatever Happened to Football in the Midlands". This book attempts to answer the question. I am sure that in ten years' time the same question will still be asked and that some writer, some researcher, will still be wrestling with the problem.

REFERENCES AND NOTES

Introduction

1 Dobson, S and Goddard, J. (2001) *The Economics of Football* Cambridge University Press, p44.

2 Kelly, S.F. (1997) *Bill Shankly; It's Much More Important than That,* Virgin, London.

3 Birmingham Post – Rich List 2017.

4 Anderson, C. and Sally, D. (2013) *The Numbers Game* Penguin, London, p259.
   Szymanski, S. (2015) *Money and Football* Nation Books, New York, p45.
   Hall, S. Szymanski, S. and Zimbalist, A.S. (2002) *Testing Causality between Team Performance and Payroll* Journal of Sports Economics, 3.

5 Kuper, S. and Szymanski, S. (2012) *Soccernomics: Why England Loses* Nation Books, New York.
   Anderson C. and Sally D. op, cit p263.

6 Dawson B, Dobson, SM, and Gerrard B, (2000) *Estimating Coaching Efficiency* Scottish Journal of Political Economy, p47.

7 Szymanski (2015) op cit.

8 Carson, M. (2014) *The Manager* Bloomsbury, London.

9 Green, C. (2002) *The Sack Race* Mainstream, Edinburgh.

10 Calvin, M. (2015) *Living on the edge of a Volcano: The secrets of surviving as a football manager* Century, London.

11 Ferguson, A. (with M. Moritz) (2015) *Leading* Hodder and Stoughton, London.

12 Anderson, C. and Sally, D. op cit p287.

13 Tanner, R. (2016) *5000 – 1, The Leicester City Story*, Icon Books, London.

14 Woolridge, Z. (2016) Director of Sports Science, University of Birmingham, Birmingham Post, 21 Aug.

15 Sports Industry Research Centre (2013) *Analysing the value of football to Greater Manchester* Sheffield University, April.

16 Goldblatt, D. (2014) *Football Nation: A footballing history of Brazil*, Penguin, London.

17 Walker, M. (2014) *"Up There – the North East football, Boom and Bust"* De Coubertin Books.

Chapter 1

1   Sports Industry Research Centre – see reference 15, Introduction. See also – Sport England, *Value of Sport – monitor* 2015. Bell, A. (2015) *Business of Sport Special. A Four Year Review –* Manchester Evening News, 16 January. Ernst and Young (2016) *Leicester City's Premier League Title Boosts Local Economy,* 21 November.

2   Calladine, M. (2015) *The Ugly Game, How Football Lost its Magic* Pitch Publishing.

3   Ernst and Young (2015) *The Economic Impact of the Premier League.*

4   Hill, C.R. (2004) *The politics of the Manchester's Olympic Bid Parliamentary Affairs* Oxford University Press. Cochrane, A., Peck, J. and J. Tickell (1996) *Manchester Plays Games* Urban Studies, October.

5   Beauchampe, S, and Inglis, S. (2006) *Played in Birmingham* English Heritage.

6   Conn, D. (2017) *The Fall of the House of FIFA* Yellow Jersey Press, London.

7   Goldblatt, D. (2018) *The Games: a global history of the Olympics.* Butterfield, M. (2011) *The Olympics: scandals* Franklin Watts. Jennings, A, (2015) *The Dirty Game* Century.

8   Blake, H. and Calvery, J. (2015) *The Ugly Game* Simon and Schuster.

9   Garcia, M. Report (2014) *Corruption in Football; Report to FIFA.*

10 Lee, M. (2006) *The Race for the 2012 Olympics* Virgin, London.

11 Goldblatt, D. (2014) *Futebol Nation: A footballing History of Brazil* Penguin, London.

12 House of Lords Select Committee on Olympic and Paralympic Legacy (2017) *Keeping the Flame Alive* London.
Boykoff, J. (2012) *What is the real price of the London Olympics?* The Guardian, 4 April.

13 UK Govt (2016) *Olympic and Paralympic Legacy* Dept. of Digital, Culture, Media and Sport.

14 Zimbalist, A. (2015) *Circus Maximus: The Economic Gamble Behind Hosting the Olympics and World Cup* Brookings Institute.
Jenkins, S. *Circus Maximus – An Olympic sized Rip Off* The Guardian, 22 May.

15 Government of Scotland Legacy Report (2015), July.

16 Parker, C.B. (2015) *Sports stadiums do not generate significant economic growth* Stanford News, 30 July.
Bergman, B. (2015) *Are Pro sports teams economic winners for cities?* Market Place, 19 March.
Ziegler, M. (2017) *Blame Game begins as Olympic Stadium loses £20 million a year* The Times, 2 Dec.

17 Goldblatt, D. (2014) *The Game of Our Lives* Penguin, London.

18 Bradbury, M. (2013) *Lost Teams of the Midlands* Xlibris.

Chapter 2

1 Cooper, E. (2016) *The Ignominy of Aston Villa* The Wall Street Journal, 23 Feb.

2 Blanchflower, D. (1961) *The Double and Before* London, Four Square Books.

3 Glanville, B. (2008) *The Toughest Job in Football* Headline.

4 Merson, P. and Ridley, I. (1999) *Hero and Villain: A Year in the life of Paul Merson,* Willow.

5 Ellis, D. (2005) *Deadly Doug: Behind the Scenes at Aston Villa* Blake Publishing.
Mourinho, J. (2017) *Interview* The Times, 10 September.

6 Bower, T. (2003) *Broken Dreams* London, Simon and Schuster.

7 Atkinson, R. and Fitton, P. (1999) *Big Ron: A Different Ball Game* Deutsch.

8 Ellis, D. op cit.

9   Glanville op cit.

10 Reade, B. (2011) *An Epic Swindle: the near death of Liverpool FC* Quercus.

11 Kuper, S. (2016) *Why star football managers are overrated* Financial Times, 12 August.
    Bell, A., Brooks, C. and Markham, T. (2013) *The Performance of Football Club Managers Skill or Luck?* Economics and Finance Research Reading.
    Audas R., Robson, S. and Goddard, J. *The Impact of managerial change on team performance* Journal of Economics and Business, 54 (6) 2002.

12 Ferguson, A. *Leading* Hodder and Stoughton, London.

13 Anderson, C. and Sally, D. (2013) *The Numbers Game* Penguin, London.

14 Allardyce, S. (2015) *Big Sam: My Autobiography* London, Headline.

15 Anderson, C. and Sally, D. op cit.

16 Szymanski, S. (2015) *Money and Football: A Soccer Economics Guide* Nation Books p183.

17 Ferguson op cit.

18 Lewis, M. (2003) *Moneyball, The Art of Winning an Unfair Game* W.W. Norton.

19 Swiss Ramble (2016) *Aston Villa – Prophets and losses* March 2012 and *Aston Villa – This house is a circus* 21 March (a blog).

20 Financial Times (2017) *Football's Smartest Spenders* by Ahmed and Murdoch, 3 Feb.

21 Daily Telegraph (2016) *New Chairman to put Villa chiefs in dock* 14 Jan.
    Birmingham Post (2017) *Passionate Leader required for LEP* 17 July.

22 Clover, C., Hornby, L. and B. Blend (2016) *Chinese food additive chief shows appetite for Aston Villa* Financial Times, 20 May.
    Sun TV (2010) *Two Chinese Men* 6 Oct.

23 Ziegler, M. (2016) *New Owner to rename ground Lotus Villa Park* The Times, 21 May.

24 Watts, C. (2016) *Chris Samuelson former Reading FC director involved in Aston Villa takeover* Get Reading, 19 May.

25 Conn, D. (2012) *Reading, Tax Havens, Secrecy and the sale of a homely Football Club* 21 Aug.

26 Connor, N. (2016) *Questions linger over new Chinese owner of Aston Villa* Daily Telegraph, 23 May.

27 Financial Times (2017) *2 Chinese Owners* 10 November.

28 Ward, A. and Griffin, J. (2012) *The Essential History of Aston Villa* Headline, London.
Matthews, T. (2007) *The Legends of Aston Villa* 2012, Breedon Books.
Goodyear, D. and Matthews, T. (1988) *Aston Villa: A Complete Record,* Breedon Books.

29 Morris, P. (1960) *Aston Villa: The History of a Great Football Club 1874-1960.*

30 Whitehead, R. (2001) *Children of the Revolution: Aston Villa in the 1970s* Sports Projects, Smethwick.

31 Whitehead op cit.

32 Ellis, D. op cit.

33 Inglis, S (1988) *League Football and the Men Who Made It* Collins Willow.

34 Denton, G. (2017) *The Odd Man Out: The Fascinating Story of Ron Saunders reign at Aston Villa* Pitch Publishing.

35 Woodward, E. (1980) Aston Villa News, 20 November.

36 Tomas, J. (1996) *Soccer Czars* Mainstream, Edinburgh.

37 Gregory, J. (2001) *John Gregory: The Boss* Andre Deutsch.

38 Private Eye (2002), 15 November.

Chapter 3

The following books and articles between them provide a picture of *The Blues* as a football club over the last 100 or so years.

Ivery, D. and Giles, W. (2014) *Haircuts and League Cups.* UK and Hong Kong. GHI.

Ivery, D – *Almajir* (a blog) and *Often Partisan* (a blog).

Dixon, K. (2017) *Blues Insider* Pitch Publishing, Worthing.

Burrows, S. and Layton, M. (2017) *Keep Right On – A love story of people and football* Bostin Books.

Brady, K. (2012) *Karren Brady – Strong Woman – Ambition, Grit and a great pair of heels* Collins.

Brady, K. (1995) *Brady Plays the Blues: My diary of the season* Pavilion Books.

Gold, D. (2016) *Solid Gold: My Autobiography* Highdown.

Gold, D. and Harris B. (2006) *Pure Gold – My autobiography – The Ultimate rags to riches story*, Highdown.

Allardyce, S. (2015) *Big Sam – My autobiography* Headline.

Macaskill, S. (2010) *David Sullivan threatens to counter-sue Carson Yeung* Telegraph, 5 March.

The Swiss Ramble (2011) *Birmingham City Blues* 14 January, A Blog.

Claridge, S. and Ridley, I. (2000) *Tales from the Boot Camp* Orion.

Claridge, S. (2010) *Beyond the Boot Camps* Orion.

Dixon, K. (2009) *Gill Merrick* Breedon Books.

Smith, J. and Cass, B. (2000) *Jim Smith: The Autobiography* Andre Deutsch.

Fry, B. (2011) *Big Fry: Barry Fry: The Autobiography* Willow.

Redknapp, H. (2017) *It shouldn't happen to a Manager* Ebury Press.

Steinberg, J. (2017) *David Sullivan: I feel I haven't done well enough. Nobody's done well enough* The Guardian, 8 Dec.

Ross, T. and Dixon, K. (2016) *The Games Gone – My Autobiography* DB Publishing.

Matthews, T. (2004) *West Midlands Football* Tempus Publishing.

Matthews, T. (2010) *Birmingham City: the Complete Record* Breedon Books.

Francis, T. and Millar, D. (1982) *World to Play For* Sidgwick and Jackson.

Boyden, M. (2003) *Brums the Word*, The Parrs Wood Press.

Chapter 4

The following books and articles will provide a picture of what has been happening at WBA over the last 100 or so years.

Bowler, D. and Bains, J. (2000) *Samba in the Smethwick End* Mainstream.

McOwan, G. (2012) *The Essential History of West Bromwich Albion*, Headline Books, London.

Wright, S. (2016) *Flight of the Throstle: WBA in the early 1990s*.

Swiss Ramble (2015) *West Bromwich Albion – Like Clockwork* 14 July, A Blog.

Morris, P. (1965) *West Bromwich Albion* Heinemann.

Willmore, G. A. (1979) *West Bromwich Albion: The First Hundred Years* Robert Hale.

Willmore, G. (1997) *West Bromwich Albion FC: The 25 year record 1972-97* Soccer Books Ltd.

Matthews, T. (2012) *WBA; The Complete Record* Breedon Books.

Regis, C. (2011) *Cyrille Regis: My Story* Andre Deutsch.

Rees, P. (2014) *The Three Degrees: The men who changed British football forever* Constable.

The Guardian (2016) *McAuley and Olsson extend West Brom contracts* 15 April.

Sky Sports (2017) *Manchester United Squad tops Premier League for transfer cost per point* Adam Smith.

Chapter 5

Matthews, T. (2012) *Wolverhampton Wanderers: The Complete Record* Breedon Books.

Swiss Ramble (2016) *Wolverhampton Wanderers – After the Gold Rush* 7 June.

BBC Sport (2016) *Wolves Bought by Chinese Conglomerate Fosun International for £45 million* 21 July.

BBC Sport (2017) *Paul Lambert: Wolves head coach's future in doubt over Jorge Mendes involvement* 12 May.

Caulkin, G. (2017) *Chinese Owners, one Super Agent and a team set for the top flight* The Times, 21 October.

Bowler, D. and Bains, J. (2000) *Samba at the Smethwick End*, Mainstream.

Gold, M. (2010) *The boys from the Black Country; A fans history of Wolverhampton Wanderers from way back to just about now* Sports Books.

Samuels, J. (2008) *The Beautiful Game is Over: the globalisation of football* Bookguild.

Giller, N. (2002) *Billy Wright: A hero for all seasons* Robson Books.

Holden, J. (2001) *Stan Cullis: The Iron Manager* Breedon Books.

Chapter 6

Brown, J. (2013) *The Seven Year Itch 2001-2008* Desert Island Football.

Brown, J. (1998) *Coventry City: The Elite Era. A Complete Record* Desert Island Football History.

Dean, R. (1991) *Coventry City: A Complete Record* Breedon Books.

Smith, G. and Hadsley, N. (2006) *Sky Blue Heaven Volume II. An Encyclopedia of Coventry City FC* Juma.

Brown, J. (2016) *Coventry City at Highfield Road 1899-2005* Desert Island Football Histories.

Hill, J. (1998) *The Jimmy Hill Story: My Autobiography* Hodder and Stoughton.

Geroski, R. (1998) *Staying Up: A Fan Behind the Scenes in the Premiership* Little Brown, London.

Matthews, T. (1999) *The Saddlers: The complete record of Walsall Football Club* Breedon Books.

Jackson, C. (2017) *We want our Walsall Back* Express and Star, 13 Jan.

Chapter 7

1 Chinn, C. and Dick, M. (Editors) (2016) *Birmingham, the Workshop of the World* Liverpool University Press.
   Hopkins, E. *The Rise of the Manufacturing Town* (1998) Revised edition, Sutton Publishing, Stroud.

2 Upton, C. (1993) *History of Birmingham* Chichester, Phillimore.

3. Jacobs, J. (1968) *The Economy of Cities* Random House.

4 Beauchampe, S and S. Inglis (2006) *Played in Birmingham* English Heritage.

5 Kerslake, B. (2014) *The Way Forward. An Independent Review of the Governance and Organisational capabilities of Birmingham City Council* London, Department of Communities and Local Government.

6 Thorne, S. (2003) *Birmingham English: A Sociolinguistic Study PhD thesis* – University of Birmingham.
   The Times (2008) *Pig ignorant About the Brummie Accent* 4 April.

7 Bryson, B. (2016) *The Road to Little Dribbling* Black Swan.

8 BBC *Inside Out – North West* 09.02.2007.

9 BBC *Mind the Gap London v the Rest* 07.03.2014.

10 Swerling, G. (2017) *Birmingham Has Most People on Benefits* The Times, 14 April.
   Morris, N. (2017) *Blighted City* The 'I', 17 April.
   O'Neill, S. (2017) *Booming Birmingham Struggling* The Times, 24 Feb.

Bradley, M. (2013) *A Tale of Two Cities as the BBC Overlooks Us* Birmingham Post, 7 Nov.

11 The Economist (2012) *Second City, Second Class*, 10 Nov.

12 Griffiths, K. (2016) *Birmingham? You Couldn't Pay Me to Go There* The Times, 10 September.

13 Nelson, F. (2013) *Our Second City is Third Rate* Daily Telegraph, 15 Nov.

14 Bryson, B. (1999) *Notes From a Small Island* Transworld, London.

15 Rough Guide to 2015 *Top 10 Cities*.
Johnson, I. (2013) *First Place Goes to...* The Independent, 1 Nov.

16 Earle-Levine, J. (2013) *Birmingham instead of London* New Yorker Magazine, 25 Oct.

17 Bailey, D. and Berkeley, N. (2014) *Regional Responses to Recession: A Case Study of the West Midlands Regional Studies* 48 (11).
Brown, G. (2015) *Birmingham named Start-ups hub as Entrepreneurs taking city seriously* Birmingham Post, 6 Jan.
PWG + Uli (Urban Land Institute) (2015) *Emerging Trends in Real Estate* Jan.
Frank, Knight (2016) *Global Cities, The 2016 Report.*

18 House of Commons – *Business, Energy and Industrial Strategy Committee Report*, Feb 2018.

19 Chinn, C. and Dick, M. (2016) op cit.

Chapter 8

1 Kidd, A. (2006) *Manchester: A History* Carnegie Publishers.
Hylton, S. (2003) *A History of Manchester* Phillimore & Co.
Jenkins, S.L. (2015) *The secret negotiations to restore Manchester to greatness* The Guardian, 12 Feb.

2 Bell, R. (2016) *Manchester beats other UK Cities in Commercial Property Development* B Daily, 1 Aug.

3 PWC/ULI Op. cit Chapter 7 Reference 17.

4 Mercer (2015) *European Cities Dominate the Top of the List for Highest Quality of Living.*
Global City Report (2015) *The City Prosperity Initiative.*

5 Barclays Bank (2016) *UK Prosperity Map.*

6 Osborne, H. (2015) *Manchester Offers Best Quality of Life for Young Graduates* The Guardian, 7 July.

7   Conn, D. (2013) *Richer than God: Manchester City, Modern Football and Growing up* Quercus, London.
    Johnson, A. (1994) *The Battle for Manchester City* Mainstream.
    James, G. (1997) *Manchester the Greatest City: Complete History of Manchester City Football Club* Polar Print.
    James, G. (2012) *Manchester – The City Years: Tracing the story of Manchester City from the 1860s to the modern day* James Ward.
8   Bose, M. (1999) *Manchester Unlimited: The Rise and Rise of the World's Premier Football Club* Orion Business, London.
    Bose, M. (2000) *Manchester Unlimited: The Money, Egos and Infighting behind the world's Richest Soccer Club.*
    White, J. (2008) *Manchester United: The Biography, the Complete Story of the World's Greatest Football Club* Sphere.
9   Edwards, M. (2017) *Red Glory, Manchester United and Me* Michael O'Mara Books.
10 Ferguson, A. (2013) *My Autobiography* Hodder and Stoughton.

Chapter 9

1   The Economist (2016) *A Country of Two Halves* 13 Aug.
2   Hill, J. and Williams, J. (Editors) (1996) *Sport and Identity in the North of England* Keele University Press.
    Morley, P. (2013) *The North and Almost Everything in it* Bloomsbury.
3   Bowler, D. and Bains, J. (2000) *Samba in the Smethwick End* Mainstream.
4   Bennett, R. (2015) *Brummie Accents Rated Least Intelligent* The Times, June 16 See also, Chapter 7 reference 6.
5   Centre for Cities (2014) *Economic Gap Between Cities.*
6   Hatherley, O. (2012) *A New Kind of Bleak: Journeys through Urban Britain* Verso.
7   Powell, T. (2017) *Manchester Attack. Mayor Andy Burnham says Spirit of City will Prevail After Evil Act* Evening Standard, 23 May.
8   See Goldblatt, D. (2015) *The Game of our lives* Penguin, London.
9   Kelly, S.F. (1997) *It's Much More Important Than That: Bill Shankly, The Biography* Virgin, London.
10 Syed, M. (2017) *Oligarchs and Sheikhs come and go but fans ensure the Game will live for ever* The Times, 22 May.

11 Clarke, G. and McAllister, G. (1995) *Captains Log: The Gary McAllister Story.*

Chapter 10

1 Ivery, D. and Giles, W. (2014) *Haircuts and League Cups.*

2 Foar, R. (2005) *How Soccer Explains the World: An unlikely theory of globalisation* First Harper.
Giulianotti, R. (Ed) (2007) *Globalisation and Sport* Wiley, Blackwell.
Goldblatt, D. (2006) *The Ball is Round: A Global History of Football* Viking.
Samuels, J. (2008) *The Beautiful Game is Over, The Globalisation of Football* Brighton Book Guild.

3 Conn, D. (1997) *The Football Business: Fair Game in the '90s?* Mainstream, Edinburgh.
Conn, D. (2004) *The Beautiful Game? Searching for the Soul of Football* Yellow Jersey, London.

4 Shiller, R. J. (2003) *The New Financial Order, Risk in the 21st Century* Princeton Press.

5 Stiglitz, J. (2002) *Globalisation and its Discontents* London, Allan Lane.
Stiglitz, J. (2013) *The Price of Inequality* Penguin, London.

6 Milanovic, B. (2016) *Global Inequality: A New Approach for the Age of Globalisation* The Belknap/Harvard Press.

7 Kay, O. (2013) *Incompetent Owners Have Poisoned Great Clubs* The Times, 6 May.

8 Deloitte Sports Business Group *Annual Review of Football Finance* Deloitte, London.

9 Pawlowski, T. (2013) *The Fans View on Competitive Balance in Football League* UEFA Direct.

10 Zimbalist, A.S. (2002) *Competitive Balance in Sports Leagues: An Introduction* Journal of Sports Economics.
Szymanski, S. (2001) *Income Inequality, Competitive Balance and the Attractiveness of Team Sports* Economic Journal 111.
Szymanski, S. (2003) *Economic Design of Sporting Contests* Journal of Economic Literature, pp.1137-1187.
Szymanski S and T. Kuypers (2000) *Winners and Losers* Penguin, London.

11 Michie, J. and Oughton, C. (2004) *Competitive Balance in Football: Trends and Effects* Football Governance Research Centre, Birkbeck.

Chapter 11

1 KPMG (2017) *Football Clubs Valuation: The European Elite 2017* May.
2 G. Tremlett (2017) *Manchester City's Plan for World Domination* The Guardian, 16 Dec.
3 Menary, S. (2017) *Mind the Gap* World Soccer March.
4 Smith, J. (2016) *The Deal: Inside the World of the Super Agent* Little Brown Book.
5 Jennings, A. (2006) *Foul the Secret World of FIFA: Bribes, vote rigging and tax scandals* Harper Collins.
   Conn, D. (2017) *The Fall of the House of FIFA* Yellow Jersey.
6 Private Eye, No 1458 (2017) *Organised Crime on Planet Football* Dec.
7 Buschmann, R. and Wulzinger M. (2018) *Football Leaks* Faber.
8 Cox, M. (2017) *The Mixer* Harper Collins, London.
   Montague, J. (2017) *The Billionaires Club: The Unstoppable Rise of Football's Super Rich Owners* Bloomsbury.
   Wallace, S. (2011) *Chinese Cash Could Change Landscape of English Game* Daily Telegraph, 8 Sep.
9 Ross, T. (2016) *The Game's Gone* DB Publishing.
   Cloake, M. (2015) *Taking Our Ball Back: English Football's Culture Wars* Martin Cloake.
   Bowyer, T. (2003) *Broken Dreams: Vanity, Greed and the Souring of British Football* Simon and Schuster.
   Samuels, J.M. (2008) *The Beautiful Game is Over; the globalisation of football* Brighton, Book Guild.
   Kuper, S. (2017) *A Bigger World Cup will be A Duller One* Financial Times, 10 Jan.

INDEX